W9-CFE-490

ACES WILD

ACES WILD

THE RACE FOR MACH 1

AL BLACKBURN

A Scholarly Resources Inc. Imprint
Wilmington, Delaware

Scholarly Resources Inc.
104 Greenhill Avenue
Wilmington, DE 19805-1897

Library of Congress Cataloging-in-Publication Data

Blackburn, Al, 1923–
   Aces wild : the race for mach 1 / Al Blackburn.
      p.   cm.
   Includes bibliographical references and index.
   ISBN 0-8420-2732-7 (alk. paper)
   1. High-speed aeronautics—History. 2. Supersonic planes—
Research—United States—History. I. Title.
TL551.5.B58   1998
629.132'305—dc21
                                     98-22438
                                        CIP

To Donna

Acknowledgments

*With deep appreciation for invaluable assistance
from the great team at
North American Aviation
especially
Ed Horkey
who contributed so much of his time and his data bank
and for the friendly guidance from
Walt Williams of NACA
and
Dick Frost of Bell Aircraft*

Contents

Introduction

Initially this book was going to be about flight testing in the early era of jet fighters, with a chapter dedicated to the long-hidden story of the first supersonic flights. But as more interesting testimony and supporting data came to light during the writing of the book, its primary focus shifted to those initial Mach-busting events during the fall of 1947 at what is now Edwards Air Force Flight Test Center in the Mojave Desert of southern California.

When we look back at the supersonic challenge and taking in a perspective that now extends over more than half a century, it appears that the world has chosen to pay little attention to the modest blessings of manned supersonic flight. That singular achievement of October 1947 seems to evoke the feeling "supersonic—so what?" Such a response should not be surprising in view of the fact that the relevancy of supersonics to the military lies almost exclusively in the domain of unmanned vehicles, missiles, and spacecraft. And in the world of commercial air transport, the environmentally unacceptable sonic boom and the economically prohibitive drag associated with sonically induced shock waves have relegated the supersonic *Concorde*, with its now thirty-year-old technology, to money-losing operations carried on purely for the sake of national prestige. Of course, the manned space shuttles do reach supersonic speeds as they exit our atmosphere, and when their landing is at Edwards they quite assertively rattle the skyline of Los Angeles with sonic booms on their return to earth. However, these occur with such a random infrequency that they rouse little organized ire among the good citizens of LA.

Ever since the dawn of the industrial age in the early nineteenth century, man's progress has been measured by the increasing tempo of the transport available to move people and goods over great distances. Beginning with the early steamships and chugging locomotives and then quickly moving forward with the development of swift ocean liners and bullet trains, the world arrived some forty years ago at the age of jet air transport, for passengers and freight alike. Thus, after meeting the challenge of creating ever-faster forms of transport for more than a century and a half, technology successfully nosed through the so-called sonic wall at last . . . and then backed off. For the past forty years the world has been saying that six hundred miles per hour is quite fast enough, and the steadfast march up the ever-steepening speed slope came to an abrupt halt on a high subsonic plateau. For four decades the problems of dealing with sonic booms and the high cost of dragging along fuel-gobbling shock waves have stymied those daring to operate beyond the sound barrier.

Some scientists believe that the challenges are manageable and that the world of commerce would reap great benefits from supersonic transportation, but the rather large investment required for such development is not yet in hand. With huge back orders for all sizes of subsonic jet transports still filling their in-baskets, the large aircraft companies have little incentive to muddy the waters. Perhaps an impatient China will take another great leap. The Cold War wasn't all bad; it did take us to the moon.

The purpose of this book is to penetrate the mists of hazy memories, to blow away the smoke of overinflated egos, and to lift the fog of political cover in order that the light of truth may illuminate the events that occurred in the cloudless skies above a sun-baked Mojave in October 1947. If there is a hero in this story, it is North American Aviation, an aggregation of the ablest and most dedicated managers and artisans I have been privileged to know. During the 1940s they produced, among other outstanding warplanes, the finest fighter aircraft of World War II, the *Mustang*, and then proceeded to create the margin of superiority in the air war over Korea, the *Sabre*. With no technical assistance whatsoever from the X-1 research rocketship program, the *Sabre* made the first supersonic flight for a manned aircraft operating on its own, without benefit of a mother ship to carry it aloft. This occurred far earlier than the "official" date of April 26, 1948, the date approved by the U.S. Air Force. Indeed, we know for certain that North American test pilot George Welch took the *Sabre* supersonic prior to November 13, 1947. Whether this occurred before the X-1's historic flight of October 14, readers of this narrative may decide for themselves. Many North American alumni, long bound to silence, are convinced that their *Sabre*, with the inimitable "Wheaties" at the controls, deserves the laurels for the first manned supersonic flight.

A.W.B.

Prologue

It was a duel of classic proportions, but the results remain cloaked in official secrets, corporate ambitions, and competitive animosities. Present perceptions have been shaped, most of all, by the ascendant power of the self-appointed mythmakers. Decades after the events of October 1947, an unusually gifted author selected one of the protagonists and anointed him with walk-on-water attributes of a magnitude for which politicians, or others who make their way through life on carefully orchestrated public adulation, would sell their souls.

The other contestant, equally worthy but less heralded, has long been dead. In 1954, almost seven years to the day after he may well have won that first contest, he lost his life in one of those ultimate moments of truth that only a handful in his profession are called upon to meet—demonstrating the "upper right-hand corner" or the point on the chart of aircraft speed versus structural loads at which maximum forces of the wind encountered at ultimate speed meet the peak maneuvering stress the aircraft is designed to withstand. The high-risk privileges, such as proving the upper right-hand corner, are traditionally the domain of the civilian experimental pilots relied upon by their employers to test the integrity of new aircraft before they can be delivered to combat forces or commercial users.

Although his death went virtually unnoticed much beyond the Mojave, the less celebrated pilot lost his life opening pathways that future aviators might safely follow, led by his quiet courage. He died pressing on into the unknown, beyond the accumulated technological wisdom of his day. Due to sacrifices such as his—and to the dramatic growth in computer power, speed, and agility—test pilots today can fly flight corridors clouded by far less uncertainty.

Two top teams of aviation achievers—each with its own creative designers, builders, and testers—were heavily engaged on separate projects in 1947, as summer turned to fall in California's Mojave Desert. There was absolutely no connection between the two, except that the manifestation of their leading-edge ventures into the unknown would meet at the same historic milestone: the attainment of supersonic speed by a manned aircraft. The locus of both operations was the Muroc Air Force Base, which only a month before had been a U.S. Army Air Corps base and which in a few short years would be renamed Edwards Air Force Base. Muroc was a relatively quiet base that fall, which means that despite the heavy cloak of national security, each team had a clear picture of the pace of activity in the other camp.

One of these projects featured a stubby, one-of-a-kind, rocket-powered research aircraft that would lead (as would become typical of similarly successful research efforts of that era) to yet another, even more advanced probe into the unknown. Its purpose was to prove that a manned aircraft can go supersonic and make an uneventful landing. Typically, it was carried aloft clinging to the belly of a specially configured B-29 mother ship and launched from an altitude of some 20,000 to 25,000 feet. It was called the

Bell X-1. Its shape was derived from the nose of the supersonic 50-caliber machine-gun projectile. (The little research aircraft was initially named the XS-1, for "experimental supersonic, number one." When it became apparent that there would be a number of X designs to follow, the S was dropped. However, the craft was officially the XS-1 for the first several years of its history. The simpler X-1 designation is used throughout this book.)

The No. 1 Bell X-1 is lined up alongside the No. 2 aircraft, which is just ahead of the loading ramp for attaching the research rocketships to the B-29 mother ship in the background. The principal difference between the two is that the No. 1 aircraft had a thinner wing. *Courtesy of Archives II, College Park, Maryland*

The other project was the flight test of a new jet fighter, the first in the United States with a dramatically swept-wing design fashioned to reduce the great drag increase caused by sonic shock waves. Its purpose was to provide our Air Force with the most advanced air superiority weapon that technology could create. It operated quite independently, without benefit of a mother ship, and some three years later it was to make the difference in the air war over Korea, with a better than eight-to-one advantage in kill ratio against enemy MiGs. Some say the ratio was closer to ten-to-one—it depends how you keep score. Developed by the same splendid team of creative designers and fabricators that had brought forth World War II's top fighter, the *Mustang*, thousands of this new best-of-the-breed would be produced, both in the United States and under license by friends and allies abroad. The first proto-types—three were built—were called XP-86s. Then, as the Army Air Corps became the U.S. Air Force and "P" for pursuit became "F" for fighter, there followed the large family of F-86 *Sabres*—the "A," the "D," the "E," the "F," the "H," the "K," and the "L"; and one should not forget its worthy Canadian cousins, the *Sabres* Mark 5 and 6, or the CA-27 *Sabre* built "down under" for the Australian fighter forces. For those who flew it, that first, simpler *Sabre* of the early postwar era, before computers started intruding between the pilot and his aircraft's control surfaces—the *Sabre*, the pure, unvarnished *Sabre*—was the finest-handling fighter ever built. It was also the most photogenic. Over the years, followers of the aviation arts have learned that pretty airplanes are nice to fly.

It is appropriate to pause briefly to identify more clearly the heritage of the *Sabre*—North American Aviation. A Los Angeles-based corporation led by its chairman, the dynamic Dutch Kindelberger, and president, the cerebral Lee Atwood, North Ameri-can was the aeronautical dynamo of World War II. Besides the top fighter of that conflict, the P-51 *Mustang*, the company also devel-oped and produced in prodigious numbers the foremost medium bomber, the B-25 *Mitchell*, and the AT-6/SNJ *Texan*, the most effec-tive trainer for both Air Corps and Navy and most of our allies. The intellectual and highly creative momentum of that experience car-ried the company well through the 1960s as it led the effort to land American astronauts on the moon. As a testament to the durability of its products, whenever there is a gathering of World War II war birds, the tarmac is dominated by *Mustangs, Mitchells*, and *Texans*, smartly revving up for a race or a memorial flyby.

Following the *Sabre*, from the same North American team there would come the *Super Sabre*, with so many changes that it was dubbed a new airplane with a new number, the first of the Century Series fighters—the F-100. It was the first operational fighter in the world capable of supersonic speed in level flight, a feat demonstrated shortly after takeoff on its very first flight in the able hands of the same experimental pilot who had made the inaugural flight of the XP-86. On October 1, 1947, or very soon thereafter, the first of the three *Sabre* prototypes had flown faster than the speed of sound, laying down solid sonic booms on the Air Force base at Rogers Dry Lake. The second of those prototypes was used, a few months thereafter and flying from the same airfield, as the vehicle for the first supersonic flight made by a British pilot.

Although the stubby little X-1 rocket plane had been created and funded by the federal government to provide advanced technological information regarding transonic aerodynamics for the U.S. aviation industry, none of the knowledge that was gathered from the rocket project was passed on to the developers of the new North American fighter prior to completion of Phase I and II flying for the XP-86. This was true even though actual flight tests for the two aircraft were being conducted simultaneously from the same Air Force base, in the high desert of the Antelope Valley, some sixty-five miles north of Los Angeles. Indeed, the detailed design of the XP-86, as well as its fabrication and initial probe into the realm of manned supersonic flight, had all been completed before the first preliminary information on X-1 design and test results was provided to U.S. industry at a highly classified briefing on January 9, 1948. No matter—in that early era of supersonic flight, such information was of little interest to serious designers of advanced high-performance fighter aircraft. North American Aviation relied on captured German technology unearthed by U.S. technologists out of Wright Field and passed along to the technical leadership in America's aviation industry—men such as George Shairer at Boeing and Ed Horkey at North American. Shairer immediately used the knowledge he received to create the swept-wing B-47 bomber.

Horkey had convinced his boss, North American chief engineer Ray Rice, that they should send their people back to the drawing boards just as the final design for a straight-wing XP-86 was being readied for release to the shop floor. Detailed analyses by the likes of Horkey and Harrison Storms, wind tunnel tests conducted by aerodynamicists Dale Myers and Larry Greene, and performance studies by Jack Daniels all created a groundswell of confident excitement. Based on the findings of this truly creative team, Lee Atwood and Dutch Kindelberger convinced the Air Corps technical leadership that North American should make the bold move of changing from a straight wing to a swept-wing configuration. The approval was received in the summer of 1945, and there followed some highly concentrated work to make that change and still meet the schedule. It was the same kind of pressure-cooker environment that earlier, as World War II turned up the heat, had yielded the P-51 *Mustang*. Perhaps decisions come easier and designs happen more gracefully when there is not time to take a vote on the location of each rivet. The incredibly talented North American team of the forties and fifties seemed to perform best under such conditions. Besides, computer-based management systems had yet to be invented. Whatever the cause, in the world of fighter aircraft development the *Mustang* and the *Sabre* came close to being the ultimate manifestations of grace under pressure.

It is of more than passing interest that not a single supersonic fighter emulating the X-1's straight-wing plan remained long in U.S. operational forces. Lockheed's Mach-2 F-104 *Starfighter* did have a straight wing, but after a brief tour in the Air Defense Command it was almost exclusively sold to our allies. In the newly emerging Luftwaffe, the death rate among *Starfighter* pilots became a national scandal in West Germany. Clearly, it was the swept-wing F-86 (née XP-86) that led the United States—and the world—into the era of supersonic flight. And these early *Sabres* taught much of what needed to be learned about high Mach numbers at low altitude, where air pressures are immense and quite capable of twisting tough, high-strength alloys into catastrophic failure, and where the divergent flutter of wings, or empennage, is an ever-present threat. Flutter characteristically occurs at a particular true airspeed, and when that airspeed is flown at lower altitudes, where the air is much denser, huge forces are created that in a fraction of a second can rip asunder stout skins and heavy spars as though they were toothpicks and tissue paper. In the thinner atmosphere at high altitude, the effect is much more benign.

Two vastly different technologies were being demonstrated almost simultaneously, and each passed the same milestone in man's reach for the stars at virtually the same instant in history. Their takeoffs were from the same dry lake bed in the Mojave Desert—the X-1 safely tucked in the tummy of its four-engine mother ship, while the wholly independent XP-86 blasted across the desert floor and lifted into the blue, powered solely by its single air-breathing turbojet engine. The X-1, the experimental rocketship and its later rocket-powered stablemates, conducted its research almost exclusively in the outer reaches of the atmosphere and beyond, giving the United States the technological base for taking the lead in space, where Mach number is an irrelevancy. It rocketed through Mach one in a climb, paving the way for Neil Armstrong's landing on the moon, where he arrived ahead of the Soviets—so far ahead that they gave up the race. The XP-86 took its pilot in a supersonic dive, exploring forces down low where the air is dense, pressures are immense, and battles are won. It led the way for freedom's forces, enabling them to gain and retain air superiority over the aggressive seekers of world enslavement, the

The No. 1 Bell X-1 fires its rocket engine after being released from its B-29 mother ship above the Mojave Desert. *Courtesy of Archives II, College Park, Maryland*

dictatorial socialist regimes. Once stopped by U.S. *Sabres* in the air over Korea, those malignant forces never regained momentum and in time collapsed.

Which of these aircraft carried a man at supersonic speed for the first time? The separation in time may have been a matter of but a week, two at the most, or perhaps less than a day. For people trained in the aerodynamic arts and sciences, there were few mysteries—just surely soluble challenges and active inquiring minds. To the cognoscenti, terms such as "sound barrier" or "sonic wall" were symptomatic of a Luddite mentality, better left to the sensationalist world of media hype, where they proved great for burnishing egos and providing fillers on slow news days. David Lean's forgettable film *Breaking the Sound Barrier* premiered with great fanfare in New York in 1952, with the Air Force chief of staff, General Hoyt Vandenberg, making a generous introduction. Technically informed viewers left the theater with unmistakable discomfort.

In a later television skit, comedian Sid Caesar's not very subtle parody of the film's more gripping episodes, "Sneaking through the Sound Barrier," helped to provide a bit of balance.

1 Foresight

Before the First Real Ba-Boom

From the Cockpit

During my service with the Marine Corps, I was privileged to fly the Chance Vought *Corsair* fighter. After leaving active duty in June 1950, I continued to fly this bent-wing beauty with the Marine Reserve squadron at Squantum Naval Air Station near Boston while seeking a graduate degree in aeronautics at MIT. One year ahead of me was a truly dedicated student named Charles Richbourg. Charlie was headed for a career as an experimental test pilot. We used to talk about that, especially about how to translate classroom savvy into useful experience that could turn well-informed flight observations into design enhancements—higher performance, better handling, improved mission capabilities. And we talked about flight test techniques—how to test for stability and control, obtain good stick-force gradients, and nail the upper right-hand corner.

Charlie eventually followed his star to Convair in San Diego, where he became project pilot on the XF2Y-1 *Sea Dart*, a delta-winged jet fighter for the Navy. The *Sea Dart* operated off the water on hydroskis. In August 1954, Charlie took this unique twin jet supersonic in a dive, the first such event for a seaplane. The following month he lost his life when the aircraft went divergent in pitch and came apart over San Diego Harbor during a low-altitude, high-speed pass at a public relations show for visiting admirals. It was much the same set of circumstances—high transonic speed and low altitude in a highly swept-wing fighter with no horizontal tail—that eight years earlier had claimed the life of famed British test pilot Geoffrey de Havilland.

On weekends in Boston, some years before Charlie's death, I compared theory to practice in the already well-proven *Corsair*. One Sunday I explored techniques for demonstrating the upper right-hand corner. That would be 7.3 g's at Mach 0.76, which equated to 350 knots indicated air speed at 20,000 feet altitude. The trick was to dive from 30,000 feet at full power, then, when the speed reached 0.76 Mach number to pull quickly back on the stick. If it were done too slowly, the speed would drop below the target speed and not pass muster as a valid demonstration point. On the other hand, too swift a motion on the stick and you might overshoot, exceeding the maneuver limit of the aircraft. That shouldn't have been serious because there was a 50 percent safety factor designed into the aircraft. Thus, it should have been able to go to nearly 11.0 g's before any primary structure might come unglued. In between, a rivet or two could pop or some wing skins might wrinkle, but the old bird should still bring you home safely.

So there I was over Boston Harbor, practicing dives and shooting for the upper right-hand corner. It was long before the jet age in commercial aviation, and traffic wasn't a problem. I had completed several preliminary runs and the next one was for the money. With the airspeed indicator needle perfectly lined up with the barber-pole Mach indicator hand beneath it, I was diving at exactly 0.76 Mach number. My indicated airspeed was approaching 350 knots as altitude closed on 20,000 feet. When all the gauges lined up on the target values, I moved the stick back smartly and then sharply forward as the "g" meter left its telltale needle right at the desired 7.3 g's and dropped quickly back past the normal gravity figure of 1.0 and overshot to -1.0. But before I could grab my flight chart, which had floated up to the top of the canopy, there was a sharp *POW* like the sound of a concussion grenade going off just outside the cockpit. I immediately retarded the throttle and pulled the nose above the horizon. Gingerly I checked the controls and scanned the cockpit instruments. All appeared to be normal. Back on the ramp at the Squantum Naval Air Station, there was no evidence of any damage anywhere on the aircraft. What had caused that bang?

The next day I had an aerodynamics class under the tutelage of Professor Robert Halfman, one of the truly great unravelers of the mysteries associated with how airplanes (and baby albatrosses) make their way through the atmosphere. I related my experience to him and asked about the crazy *C-Cr-RACK*. All he could say was that noise is associated with changes in air pressure—the more abrupt the change, the sharper the sound. It would be nearly forty years before I got an answer that really explained what I had heard that day over Boston Harbor.

Not long ago, while doing research for this book, I talked to Dick Frost, who had once been a test pilot for Bell Aircraft and had served as flight test manager for Bell at Muroc for the company's X-series aircraft. In discussing that tour of duty, he related the tale of a sonic bang heard by his flight test crew at the edge of the dry lake bed. The bang emanated from the number two Bell X-1 aircraft, which was being flown by Bell test pilot Slick Goodlin as he performed the requisite structural demonstration for the Army Air Corps. It occurred on February 5, 1947, as Goodlin was diving the research aircraft directly at the Bell group. On reaching a speed of 0.79 Mach number, he pulled up sharply to 8.7 g's—he was shooting for 8.0 but overshot—then pushed over sharply to zero g. This maneuver was accompanied by a sharp crack heard distinctly by the Bell people on the ground. Frost immediately contacted Goodlin on the radio, told him of the sharp bang, and asked if there were anything amiss. Slick responded that he had not heard it and that everything seemed all right. Frost advised an expeditious, minimum-stress return to the runway. The landing was uneventful, and no signs of damage could be found.

What happened? Note that this was the number two X-1 and that it had the thicker wing—10 percent of the chord as opposed to 8 percent for the number one model, which had been modified with a thinner wing at the factory. It's a well-established fact that as an aircraft's speed in level flight advances above 0.75 Mach or thereabouts (depending on how thick the wing is), the air passing over the top of the wing must accelerate to Mach 1.0, at which point a shock wave is formed. The air atop the wing must go faster than that underneath because it has farther to go. Once the shock wave exists, air piles up ahead of it, becoming denser, while the air behind slows down and becomes thinner. We have passed from the world of subsonic aerodynamics, where it is safely assumed that air is an incompressible fluid, to the transonic, where compressibility effects must be accommodated.

It's easy enough in steady-state circumstances, with the aircraft stabilized in level flight at, say, 0.79 Mach number, to create a standing shock wave at the maximum thickness point on the wing. With the sun at just the right angle, the pilot can witness this quite natural event from the cockpit. If there is a lot of moisture in the air, there will be condensation at the shock wave, and ground observers can get a good look at what is happening. There are a number of photos of this in the aeronautical archives.

Now let's climb into the cockpit of the X-1 (or even of my ancient *Corsair*). We're in a shallow dive at 0.79 (or 0.76) Mach number, pointed straight at our friends on the ground. Abruptly, the stick is pulled back so that the wing generates seven to eight times the lift that is needed for level flight. Then with equal swiftness, the stick is shoved forward to eliminate the lift altogether—to a zero g pushover. That shock wave standing on the wing is going to be super compressed and, almost instantaneously, it's being told to dissipate. An explosive expansion of the air on top of the wing must accompany the rapid disappearance of the shock wave—yes, nature does abhor a vacuum. It's like those natural sonic booms that occur when air rushes in to fill the voids created by sudden superheating and ionization accompanying lightning bolts. It's called thunder. It may also be likened to the earliest of manmade supersonic noises, the cracking of a whip. Goodlin in his X-1 and I in my *Corsair* were simply playing "crack-the-whip."

Although only I, and perhaps some fish in Boston Harbor, heard the *C-Cr-RACK* emanating from the *Corsair*, Dick Frost and his teammates, standing on the dry lake bed at Muroc, directly in the line of fire, heard the sharp report from Goodlin's X-1. It was a real bang all right, but not the booming explosion that Cal Tech's renowned aerodynamicist Dr. Theodore von Karman had predicted, or that Wernher von Braun's V-2 missiles had recorded many times at Peenemünde. For Muroc, that was still a few months away.

From the Laboratory

One of his close wartime companions wrote about Major Fred Borsodi: "For Fred, a little of the best is better than a lot of the commonplace. He was the finest guy, in every way, that I have known in the Air Corps." In mid-1944, Dutch Kindelberger, chairman of North American Aviation, sought from General "Hap" Arnold, commanding general of the U.S. Army Air Forces, the name of a seasoned fighter pilot who might bring combat smarts to the challenge of developing ever improved fighter planes at North American Aviation. Hap offered two candidates. One was Fred Borsodi.

The story of the event-filled and all-too-brief life of Fred Borsodi is a complete volume in itself. The Tiger Woods of the amateur golf circuit in the mid-1930s, he graduated from Yale with an engineering degree in 1939, won his Navy Wings of Gold in May 1940, and then was mustered out of the Navy five months later for breaking the rule that newly commissioned officers were not to marry for two years. (Nowadays, military pilots may get kicked out for not marrying the girl.) Fortunately, Fred found he did not have to give up the addictive habit of flying high-performance aircraft. He was hired by Pratt & Whitney, the foremost builder of large-piston engines for the U.S. military, as an experimental test pilot. Concurrently, he joined the Army Air Corps Reserves in Connecticut, where he was commissioned as a second lieutenant. Three days after Pearl Harbor he requested active duty. He soon found himself in the North African campaign with the 86th Fighter Squadron. For the most part the 86th's P-40s were fully occupied with supporting General Bernard Montgomery's drive across North Africa, in the course of which Borsodi rose to the rank of major and was made squadron commander. He shot down three German aircraft and damaged a fourth. After 130 missions he was ordered home, embellishing the journey by making it in a captured Ju 88 twin-engine Luftwaffe bomber that Wright Field wanted for evaluation purposes. His earlier test flying experience at Pratt & Whitney made him a natural for the developmental test work being done by the Army Air Corps' Flight Laboratory at Wright Field, where he joined (and was later made chief of) the Fighter Flight Test Section.

In July 1944, Major Borsodi made a number of full power vertical dives from 40,000 feet in a North American P-51D to assess the compressibility effects on the aircraft's handling. He achieved a maximum Mach number of 0.86, at which point severe buffeting of the empennage was noted. A more interesting observation was Fred's report of a visible shock wave extending from wing root to tip at the point of maximum wing thickness. When his boss hinted that maybe he had been working too hard, Fred had a camera mounted in the cockpit and repeated the test with full movie coverage. At least one of his fellow test pilots was able to replicate the visual shock wave to his satisfaction: It was a matter of putting the sun's rays at just the right angle.

A number of engineers and scientists from both industry and university laboratories sought out Fred Borsodi at Wright Field to view his films with him. Among them were Ed Horkey of North American Aviation and his respected mentor from the California Institute of Technology, Dr. Theodore von Karman. The films brought tears to von Karman's eyes. He explained that a vertical shock wave in the shape of the Greek letter *lambda* was precisely what he had predicted in his mathematical projections. With this confirmation of his theory, von Karman went on to broaden his creative grasp of supersonic aerodynamics, which he summarized in his Wright Brothers Lecture for the Institute of Aeronautical Sciences, prepared in the spring of 1947.

As for Fred Borsodi, he turned down North American's offer of a position as experimental test pilot. He was wholly wrapped up in the flight test work he was doing at Wright Field, which included development tests of the Lockheed YP-80. Named the *Shooting Star*, it would become the first operational jet fighter in the United States. Much of this testing was done at Muroc Air Base, later to become Edwards Air Force Base. The job turned down by Borsodi was readily accepted by triple ace Major George Welch, of Pearl Harbor fame, who commenced flying for North American out of Los Angeles in late July 1944.

During frequent visits to aviation enterprises on the West Coast, Borsodi delighted in showing his Mach wave film from the P-51 dive tests. Welch, who had immediately become involved in testing advanced models of the *Mustang* upon his arrival at North American, took a great deal of interest in the shock waves associated with supersonic flows. In the spring of 1944, the company had embarked on design of jet fighters for both the Air Corps and the Navy. Looking beyond development of the *Mustang* into the coming jet age, Welch confided to his good friend, aerodynamicist and chief technical engineer Ed Horkey, that the supersonic mythology didn't seem to be all that big a threat. Publicly shrugging off big media hype was a typical personality trait of George Welch. So was his habit of quietly boring in on newly evolving technology through his own fast-scan total-absorption reading skills and unobtrusive chats with engineering leaders such as Ed Horkey, whose talents he had learned to respect.

Borsodi pressed on with the P-80 tests and was selected to go with Major Marcus Cooper to England to demonstrate the new jet to the RAF. The war was nearing its climax, and the appearance of Nazi jets, especially the Me 262s, was somewhat demoralizing. Marc Cooper, who would later become the commanding general at the Edwards Flight Test Center, made the first flight out of Burtonwood AAF near Liverpool. The British were impressed. The following day, Fred made an equally impressive display of the new jet's prowess until, during a final high-speed pass at minimum altitude, a fuel system failure caused raw kerosene to be pumped into the tail section, blowing it off and scattering the *Shooting Star* in a fiery trail along the runway. The Army Air Corps had lost one of its most skilled and experienced flight test researchers. It was Sunday, January 28, 1945. Major Fred Borsodi had been twenty-eight years old.

His close friends and colleagues at Wright Field said that without question Borsodi would have been involved in the race for supersonic laurels. Had he still been around, they said, he would have insisted on a place in the X-1 tests. It was his kind of program. One of those colleagues, Gus Lundquist, did indeed fly the X-1; another, Wally Lien, became an experimental test pilot for

North American shortly after the war. It was a close-knit band of brothers there at Wright Field who were privileged to help usher in the era of jet propulsion and supersonic aircraft. Lost in that highly successful and typically American adventure were some of the most dedicated and capable young men in our nation's history.

From the Drawing Board

Clarence Gilbert Taylor overcame a crippling bout with polio in infancy to become an aviation legend. One of his more creative contributions to the art of aircraft design is little noted, however—indeed, it is given no more than a dismissive shrug by his loyal league of supporters. C. G., as the early pioneer was known, devised a simple method for giving pilots smooth, precise, and effortless pitch control throughout the attainable speed range of their aircraft. It was an adjustable stabilizer to enhance the handling qualities of a small, light aircraft, and it was featured on his own B-2 *Chummy*. It may be less than surprising that the introduction did not make much of a splash, considering that it came on the scene in the fall of 1929, in the wake of the century's most disastrous financial crash.

The Taylor B-2 evolved through several models to the J-2 and then the J-3, otherwise known as the Taylor *Cub*, which later became the Piper *Cub* and eventually the *Supercub*, which is still in production. Any and all of them can quite easily swoop and chandelle through Mach 0.1, and in a terminal dive they are known to double that speed. All are graced with a small hand crank mounted on the left cockpit wall beneath the throttle that allows the pilot to adjust the incidence angle of the horizontal stabilizer. By so doing, the force on the stick required to maintain level flight may quite precisely be reduced to zero. As a demonstration for fledgling pilots of the redundancy of the *Cub*'s flight controls, a flight instructor may take his hands off the stick and land the aircraft using only the stabilizer trim for pitch attitude, the rudders for keeping the wings level, and power variations for controlling the rate of descent—but don't try this on a gusty day.

The point is that nearly two decades before man's first supersonic flight, aircraft designers provided a trim crank in the cockpit for moving the leading edge of the horizontal stabilizer up or down as may be needed to achieve pitch control with minimum effort. I regularly tow gliders with Piper *Supercubs* and adjust the stabilizer from the cockpit to minimize stick forces and maximize elevator effectiveness. The Piper *Pawnee* ag-planes use many *Supercub* parts, including the wing and the horizontal stabilizer. The earlier *Pawnee* models retain the pitch trim device from the *Supercub*, and it works just fine. Why it was later abandoned for a variable tension spring in the elevator control loop, I have no idea. Perhaps the spring is less expensive to manufacture. Other aircraft from that earlier era employed the adjustable stabilizer method—some of the old Waco biplanes, for example.

In the Army Air Force's *Preliminary Pilot's Handbook for Model XP-86 Aircraft*, a "Restricted" publication dated September 19, 1947, the text reads:

> Adjustable Horizontal Stabilizer
> The angle of incidence of the horizontal stabilizer can be varied between plus 1 and minus 10 degrees. Stabilizer position, electrically controlled by rotation of a knurled wheel on the control stick grip, is shown on an indicator at the upper left hand corner of the instrument panel. Adjustment of the stabilizer is extremely critical and is limited with increase in airspeed.

North American designers anticipated the large predicted pitch changes when their new fighter would be called upon to accelerate through the transonic regime, and they turned to the simple method employed by C. G. Taylor in the late 1920s. Long before the hidden mysteries of the X-1 stabilizer design were revealed to the world, or even hinted at in aviation's rumor mills, North American engineers had arrived at the Taylorcraft solution and had employed it in their initial design of the XP-86 *Sabre* and all of the F-86A's that followed. The trimmable stabilizer mechanism installed on the X-1 was viewed by its designers as a ground adjustment device, not to be employed in flight. It was not until Chuck Yeager was prepared to abandon his supersonic attempt because he ran out of elevator effectiveness at 0.94 Mach number that the creative engineer Jack Ridley proved to Yeager's satisfaction that the device for trimming the stabilizer on the ground would be quite satisfactory as an auxiliary and essential pitch control mechanism that could be used in flight for moving into the realm of the supersonic. Yeager's cool confidence in Ridley's technical skills was unbounded and wholly justified.

Meanwhile, across the Atlantic, Geoffrey de Havilland, eldest son and namesake of the de Havilland Aircraft Company founder, was convinced that the swept-wing DH.108 *Swallow* was a record breaker. On September 7, 1946, RAF Group Captain Teddy Donaldson had set a world record at 615.78 miles per hour in a Gloster *Meteor* IV. In those days speed records had to be attempted in level flight without exceeding an altitude of 1,100 feet, and thus his speed equated to a Mach number of 0.81. On September 5, de Havilland had taken the *Swallow* to nearly 0.9 Mach number at 34,000 feet. It was the aircraft's fourth outing. On September 26 he had seen 0.82 Mach in level flight at 9,000 feet. Of course, he knew that at 34,000 feet the air is less than a third the density he would encounter in his sea level runs, but at 9,000 feet the thickness of the air is nearly three-fourths as great. The company's chief test pilot was confident that the world's absolute speed record was his for the taking.

When Geoffrey de Havilland took off late in the afternoon of September 27, it was his intent to put the *Swallow* in a shallow dive from 10,000 feet so as to reach 0.87 Mach, or a lesser speed in the event he encountered excessive pitch sensitivity, which the engineers anticipated only if the aircraft exceeded the 0.87 mark.

He would then level the flight path down low over the waters of the Thames Estuary in simulation of the actual record attempt, to make sure there would be no awkward control problems in his high-speed pass in that thickest segment of the atmosphere near sea level. Some media miscreants suggest that Geoffrey was really trying to break the sound barrier. That is nonsense. He knew there was difficulty for the *Swallow* lurking down low as he approached 0.87 Mach. Had he been seeking the supersonic, he would have started at a much higher altitude, as indeed was done by John Derry a couple of years later when the *Swallow* became the first British aircraft to exceed Mach one, at roughly 30,000 feet from a dive commenced at 45,000.

It was a clear afternoon with no turbulence even at the lower altitudes as the *Swallow* dipped toward the sea, anticipating the flight path required for the record run. Yet something went terribly wrong. Careful analysis of the flight data recorded in the course of the flight and recovered from what remained of the stricken *Swallow* shows that, shortly after his shallow dive, a speed of Mach 0.88 was attained at about 8,000 feet. At that point a violent pitch oscillation was encountered at a frequency far too high for even a skilled test pilot to damp out. His trained reaction to the threat only exacerbated the fundamental instability. As he sought to tame the Mach-wave-induced forces, they alternated first behind and then ahead of the center of gravity of the tailless *Swallow* as it pushed into a regime of much too heavy air. This was a maneuver that should have been methodically explored in the thinner air at a higher altitude, where aerodynamic forces build up much more slowly and peak at lower values, and where man's limited reaction times stand a better chance of taming that bucking bronco.

Observers saw the nose of the aircraft pitch sharply down, then swiftly up. The wings broke and folded above the cockpit as if in prayer, and the pieces fell near the shore of the estuary. Geoffrey received fatal injuries, and his body, apparently thrown clear as the *Swallow* disintegrated, was not found until ten days after the crash. Ironically, shortly before the fatal flight, a hydraulic pitch-control augmentation device was demonstrated to Geoffrey de Havilland on a full-scale flight control system test rig. He was given the option of having it installed for his further tests, including the record run. As was the case with so many pilots of that era, however, myself included, he had an innate distrust of mechanisms that intruded between the control column in the cockpit and the control surface at the tail. He decided to stay with the fully manual control. The device was installed on the two remaining *Swallows*, and it did improve matters somewhat. The indomitable British Navy test pilot Winkle Brown replicated de Havilland's last flight in a *Swallow* with the improved pitch control; he encountered very nearly the same wild pitching maneuver and he survived, but just barely.

One of Geoffrey's successors at de Havilland, the quietly talented John Derry, who favored the hydraulic-powered pitch control, nursed the *Swallow* through an out-of-control dive from 45,000 feet that nonetheless took him supersonic. It is doubtful he would have survived the wild gyrations without the boosted control system. That was on September 6, 1948, nearly a year after the Americans had laid down their marker in a much more repeatable and far less ostentatious manner. Still, the *Swallow* was the first British design to fly supersonic. Others nibbled around the edges, but Derry's wild flight was the only time the *Swallow* exceeded Mach 1.0. (British test pilot Roland "Bee" Beamont had already taken the North American *Sabre* prototype supersonic over Muroc Dry Lake on May 21, 1948, to become the first British pilot to experience supersonic flight—albeit in a much more prosaic manner than that of John Derry in the errant *Swallow*.)

By a strange twist of fate, John Derry would become best known for a catastrophic crowd-killer of a flight in a later, and certainly supersonic, DH.110 night fighter—it later became the

Royal Navy's *Sea Vixen*. It happened before a large crowd at the Society of British Aircraft Constructors' Farnborough Air Show. Pulling up in a tight turn after a high-speed, low-altitude fly-by, the big twin-engine fighter lost its tail and came completely unglued. Both engines lost the airframe. One fell harmlessly on the runway, but the other went into the crowd. Derry, his observer, and twenty-eight people on the ground were killed. Sixty others were injured. It was exactly four years after Derry's first Mach marker for a British aircraft. He was thirty-one years old at the time. Like Geoffrey de Havilland he would be sorely missed, especially in the fraternity of experimental test pilots.

From the Pentagon to the Executive Suite

They called it "mahogany row," but it was the same set of offices Dutch Kindelberger and Lee Atwood, along with other senior executives, had occupied throughout the war. Some dark paneling had replaced the ubiquitous light green that covered walls and ceilings elsewhere in the plant. It was rumored that Dutch had gotten one hell of a deal on several railcar loads of that particular paint. Even with the paneling, the executive offices were unpretentious.

On a morning in late September 1947, Lee, Mr. Inside, was in Dutch's office. Dutch, Mr. Outside, was the more gregarious of the pair. He was also a gifted engineer. Before the war, he did some truly creative work on high-rate production tooling. It was a major factor in making North American the leading mass producer of top-quality military aircraft in the world. As the war wore on, Dutch spent more and more time with the customers, mostly U.S. Army Air Corps leaders. Someone had to ensure that enough orders came in to keep the lines humming, cranking out trainers, bombers, and fighters—P-51 *Mustang* fighters, best of the show in World War II. Dutch truly loved the give and take with his Air Corps customers. Lee spent much of his time with his engineering managers, seeking to ensure that what rolled off the line was of the highest quality that available know-how could provide. More often he would be leaning over the drawing boards, making sure that the technology being created at North American stayed well ahead of the competition. Dutch Kindelberger and Lee Atwood were an unbeatable team.

In 1947, North American was transitioning to the jet age. The company's new entry in the fighter sweepstakes was being prepared for its first flight at Muroc Dry Lake in the Mojave Desert. Perhaps Lee was in Dutch's office to discuss the tragedy that had occurred when, during an engine run-up of the prototype XP-86, a member of the flight test crew had been sucked into the inlet duct and killed. In those days one did not have to contend with the fast-buck tort lawyers that now crowd the U.S. jurisprudence system. Still, the matter had to be dealt with, and a genuinely warm concern for all members of the North American team had always marked the Kindelberger-Atwood leadership style.

According to Atwood, their discussion was interrupted by the intercom buzzer. Dutch picked up the phone.

"Who? Oh, but of course, put him on. . . . Hello, Stu. Congratulations on the new job. . . . No, we haven't flown the new fighter yet. Looks like sometime next week. It's a real beauty. Come out and have a look for yourself. . . . Yes, we're sure it'll be faster than anything flying now. . . . No, we'll creep up on the top speed quite carefully. . . . Don't think there's much danger of that. . . . It's the kind of problem we'd like to have. . . . OK, OK, I understand. I'll pass it along. Anything else? . . . Hope to see you in the Pentagon in a couple of weeks. . . . Bye."

Dutch hung up the telephone and chuckled in his inimitable manner. Lee furrowed his brow. The quiet quizzical expression said he was waiting to hear all about it.

"That was Stu Symington. He was asking about the P-86. Doesn't want to hear anything about the airplane going faster than point nine three Mach number. Good God, he's just taken on the job as the first secretary of our brand new Air Force and already he's telling us how to do our flight test work. What's it all about?"

Lee smiled. "It's about Larry Bell, who can walk into Harry Truman's office anytime he so wishes, and about two guys from Missouri—Truman and Symington—along with some feisty Langley engineers and the National Advisory Commission for Aeronautics rocket research aircraft that's getting ready for an assault on Mach one. To make sure the Air Corps . . . uh, Air Force . . . is on board, Bell has pulled its company test pilot off the project. Some Air Force captain will be flying it. The perception is that whoever is in the cockpit for the first flight past Mach one will be a big hero, perhaps even an aviation immortal."

"Damn," said the Dutchman. "When I was at Wright Field last week, I told Bill Craigie that our designers believe the P-86 will go supersonic. Now that's leaked to Bell and old Larry is not about to be one-upped."

Lee shrugged, raising his hands palms up in full anticipation of his colleague's response. He was not disappointed. While making more and better aircraft than any other firm to help fight and end the war, they had worked through too many really tough challenges to be stumped by this bit of ego massage. The creases on Kindelberger's face were half conspiratorial, half genuine amusement. He loved the business of making the world's best aircraft and had no intention of surrendering that position to anyone—not if he could help it. And certainly not to some one-of-a-kind rocket ship of limited utility.

"When will we be ready to fly?"

"Some time early next week."

"Welch?"

Lee nodded.

"Hell, no one told him to get airborne at Pearl Harbor, and how many Nips did he shoot down?"

"At least four. Maybe more. Then a dozen or better in New Guinea."

"I don't guess anyone needs to paint the big picture for George. How about the rocket ship?"

"Bell's bringing the Air Force guy up to speed now. They're creeping up on it pretty carefully. Al Boyd's trying to keep a lid on it. Rumor has it this captain they've put in the cockpit is straining at the leash. Every one at Muroc has had a look at the P-86. They know it's a contender."

"Is it? Will it go supersonic?"

"Not in level flight, but take it to 30,000, maybe 40,000 feet and put it in a dive . . . yes, almost certainly."

"How good is our intelligence? How do we keep current with what's happening up at Muroc?"

"Oddly enough, our best source seems to be through Pancho's girls. The pilots and crews spend a lot of time at her place. The food's good, it's handy, and Pancho didn't hire any of those girls by mail."

"And?"

"Well, there are some who are betting on the rocket ship. They see it as an Air Force show. Really, it's an NACA operation, but the Air Force is in control. Still, I believe we have a stronger cadre of grass-roots support. The idea of a fighter built for the new Air Force taking the supersonic laurels, that's hard to resist. . . . And after all, George Welch is a real Air Force hero, even though it was the Army Air Corps at the time."

Lee hesitated for a moment, then continued. "The whole X-1 show is like a three-way taffy pull. You've got Bell, but they've been pushed out of the picture—only they know more about the airplane than anyone, and the program really can't get along without them. Then you've got the brand new Air Force, all hot to do something spectacular, only they really don't have the kind of smarts and in-depth technical skills to match the active egos at work. Finally there are the folks at NACA, who believe they are in charge. Between John Stack, at Langley, and Walt Williams, at Muroc, you couldn't find better technical and operational leadership; but everyone's looking over his shoulder, budgets are tight, and too much is falling between the cracks. Because of the split management and tight postwar budgets, they've already made a number of goofs. Still, nobody knows as much about liquid fuel rocket engines as they should, nor about the handling of liquid oxygen at temperatures near absolute zero."

Dutch leaned back in his chair with hands clasped behind his head. He was weighing the relative risks to the company that he and Lee had put together. And he was reviewing all those long evenings in hotel suites in Dayton and Washington where mutual respect between the company and its principal customer had been carefully shaped, often around a bottle of good whiskey, sometimes swapping stories from the shop floor for tales of air warfare. But mostly the talk would be about how to build better combat aircraft and how to get them to fly farther and faster.

Mr. Outside swung forward in his chair, elbows on the desk, right hand in the air, two fingers extended. "Look, Lee, there are two Air Forces. There's the Air Force that's dominated by politicians and the political generals. And then there's the Air Force that won the war. I don't give a damn about the clout that Larry Bell has with Harry Truman and Stu Symington. I care about the guys who can make the tough decisions. Like the time we agreed with Mark Bradley to put extra fuel in the *Mustang* fuselage and in a few weeks we were escorting our bombers to Berlin. That's when Göring knew his war was over. And all it took was a handshake. I tell you, Lee, the real Air Force wants to see our new fighter . . . hell, it's their new fighter . . . be out front on this one."

Atwood could only smile. Dutch's instincts in such matters were rarely wrong. The infectious grin uncovered all of Kindelberger's teeth. "Besides," he added, "there's nothing in our contract that says the new Air Force secretary can tell us how to run our flight test program." There were to be no memos from the head shed, no verbal orders to hold back on the opening of the high-speed end of the envelope. Later, Atwood would tacitly approve a flight test agenda that called for retracting the landing gear on the very first flight of the new XP-86, a most unconservative procedure. Generally, companies in the business of developing new aircraft viewed the primary goal of any first flight as an uneventful landing. Consequently, the accepted practice was to leave the wheels extended. The XP-86 would be an exception. A handful of people, mostly those directly involved with the flight test efforts at Muroc, knew that there was a race in progress, but no one was going to talk about it, much less circulate a memo to that effect.

In reviewing this chapter, Lee Atwood, as alert a nonagenarian as one might expect to find in a world of increasingly alert senior citizens, confirms that this is pretty much the way it went in Dutch's office some fifty years ago. He's still writing technical articles on why the *Mustang* was the best of its breed, and quietly but effectively upholding North American's honor in the matter of the tragic *Apollo* fire.

From the Launch Pad

From the launch control facility at the Peenemünde missile test facility overlooking the Baltic Sea, Dr. Wernher von Braun contemplated the secret rocket test site that for ten years had been the focal point of his prodigious energies. Six hundred feet to the west, standing on its tail and pointing straight up, was his A-4 missile. Looking like a smaller-scale version of the old *Graf Zeppelin* but aimed at the stars, the A-4 stretched 46 feet skyward and was painted in a black-and-white test pattern that gave it the look of a killer whale. The date was October 3, 1942, and the success of this fourth shot was critical to the future of the entire rocket program. The failures of the first three had shaken the Führer's confidence.

One rocket had not even left the launch pad. Painstaking analyses of those fiery malfunctions and careful remedial redesign had greatly enhanced the self-assurance of the burly rocket scientist—this fourth try would be a winner. He was certain of it.

As the rocket ignited, lifting smoothly off the launch pad, von Braun punched his stopwatch. The missile rapidly accelerated, straight up at first, then arced smoothly to the northeast until a 40 degree angle of climb was attained. Soon only the smoke from the rocket blast could be seen; then that too disappeared from view. Wernher smiled—it was twenty-four seconds from liftoff. The A-4 would at that instant be going supersonic. The down-range telephone rang and was picked up at once by the space scientist.

"Ja. Ja. Ba-boom. Jawohl! Danke schön."

The observer stationed some 5 kilometers along the flight path had clearly heard the sonic boom as the A-4 accelerated through supersonic velocity on its way to Mach four or five. Von Braun curled his large hands into fists and raised them above his head, then slowly lowered his arms and quietly ground the right fist into his left palm. It was all the emotion the young Prussian would permit himself. Prandtl, von Karman, Buseman—the great European leaders in the world of aeronautical science—they had been correct. Supersonic flight, at least in its early manifestations, meant a shock wave that would make a cracking sound just like the one made by an artillery shell going faster than sound. It was all as predicted. He was confident that the remainder of the flight would follow the planned trajectory. But much work, hard work, still lay ahead.

The difference now was that the program could build on this first real success. Although failures on the launch pad and down range continued to plague the program, achieved altitude, range, and maximum speed inexorably increased. In its final production configuration, the A-4, later known as the V-2 (for vengeance weapon number two), typically exceeded a Mach number of five and an altitude of 250,000 feet. A winged version, called the A-4b, which it was hoped would more than double the A-4's range of 200 miles, had one partially successful flight. The aerodynamic controls on the trailing edges of the tail fins were made much larger than those on the standard A-4. This was necessary to force the tail of the missile down, and consequently the leading edge of the wings up, causing them to generate the lift needed to get the desired range. The wings were swept 45 degrees and had a span of nineteen feet. A manned version with more conventional flight controls was on the drawing board when the war ended.

During a 200-day period—from September 5, 1944, to March 27, 1945—the basic A-4/V-2 vehicle had some 3,165 successful operational flights, dumping as many tons of high explosives on Great Britain and the Lowlands. All firings exceeded Mach one less than thirty seconds after launch and returned to earth at supersonic speeds. These numbers do not include the many test flights, successful and otherwise. Control by deflection of the rocket exhaust gases was augmented by aerodynamic control surfaces on the trailing edges of the four fins at the rear of the big spacecraft.

If there was any concern because the A-4 would be traveling at supersonic speeds under aerodynamic control, such concern is not evident in the literature covering these development programs. That the German rocketeers were cognizant of supersonic aerodynamics is shown in their swept-wing design for the A-4b. Their failure to provide for the excessive heat associated with high Mach numbers is probably the cause of the failure of the one A-4b that made a successful launch out of the atmosphere, only to have its wings break off upon re-entry—probably because of extensive structural heating. Such heat problems were, of course, not a problem at Mach numbers of less than two.

A comparison of the A-4/V-2 and the Bell X-1 is interesting. For one thing, the German rocket did not require a mother ship. It could take off on its own. On the other hand, its landings were not of a kind that would endear them to anyone riding along—

supersonic, straight into the ground. Still, there was a design concept for a manned version that might have proved quite manageable and most assuredly supersonic. And remember, this capability was being demonstrated out of Peenemünde at up to five times the speed of sound some five years before the X-1 managed to "smash through the sonic wall," but just barely. These A-4 launches were occurring at an average of more than fifteen times a day over that 200-day period. The A-4 was substantially larger than the little rocket research ship. The missile was over 43 feet long, while the X-1 had a length of but 31 feet. The diameter of the A-4 fuselage was 65 inches; that of the X-1 but 55. The maximum weight of the A-4 was 28,380 pounds, compared with 13,034 pounds for the X-1. And the lifting surfaces of the A-4b had wing loadings at launch and after burnout very nearly identical to those of the X-1 under the same circumstances.

Two and a half years before the X-1 made its historic penetration of the "sound barrier," an A-4 missile completed the 3,165th operational flight for the series, its last. Substantially larger than the X-1 and more than twice its weight, each of those unmanned rockets experienced a speed in excess of Mach four. Were the scientists at Peenemünde distressed that their rocket ships might disintegrate as they struck the "sonic wall"? No one has been able to detect any signs of such concern. Besides, they had substantial wind tunnel data to validate their designs. Whereas, like the Americans, the Germans had had trouble getting conventional wind tunnels (wherein air is circulated in a closed race track pattern by powerful electric blowers) to operate satisfactorily in the transonic regime between Mach 0.85 and 1.2, they did have a number of blowdown tunnels in which air raced at supersonic velocities through the test section en route to large, evacuated steel spheres. Models were suspended in test sections as large as 16 by 16 inches through which air passed into spheres 40 feet in diameter. With these huge chambers almost totally devoid of air, a large valve was opened upstream from the test section, and outside air at normal atmospheric pressure came in at very high speed, whistling into those spheres past the models being tested. The air striking the models in the test throat reached speeds as great as 4.4 Mach number. This technology and much of the associated hardware, along with the engineers and scientists who had created them, were shipped to the United States shortly after the war.

Did the scientists and engineers of NACA and the U.S. Army Air Corps know of these German rocket exploits and of high-Mach tunnel testing? Of course they did. Even before the end of the war, von Braun and key members of his team had been hustled off to New Mexico. By April 1946 the first V-2 missile, of the more than seventy shipped from Germany, was launched from the Army's White Sands Missile Test Range. Sixty-six more would follow over the next six and a half years, each generating its typical sonic *ba-boom* as it transitioned to the supersonic less than thirty seconds after launch. The technological leaders of that era were a responsible aggregation of people who were quick to explore all available research, both foreign and domestic. They also have always had the challenge of ensuring that Congress and the public be ever enthusiastic about appropriating sufficient funds for the research essential to maintain America's lead in aeronautics. Thus, a bit of media hype—hey, a lot of media hype—however out of touch with reality, was not always challenged. If some of the star players had appealing personalities and only a vague sense of the technical truths, well, that was perfectly all right. Show business is show business on whatever stage is handy.

From the Mythmakers

Prior to the December 22, 1947, issue of *Aviation Week*, which broke the highly classified fact of the X-1's venture beyond Mach one with Yeager at the controls, the aviation press and popular science publications had hyped the terrors of the supersonic. Chuck Yeager managed to mock these doomsayers even as he rocketed into history. After noting in his transmission to Jack Ridley that he had seen a strange jump in the Mach meter, he still sought to preserve some sense of confidentiality—after all, it was a highly classified project. So when Ridley suggested that Yeager was imagining things, Chuck replied, "Must be. I'm still wearing my ears, and nothing else fell off neither." In fact, the data would show that he had reached a Mach number of 1.06. Official policy kept his lips sealed. Good thing—there wasn't anything very exciting about it. In his book he admits to a letdown. Not even a bump in the road to let him know he had "just punched a nice clean hole through that sonic barrier." His sealed lips let him seem to be professing frustration that he could not relate to the hungry reporters how really hairy it was, how he had barely escaped. Creative gap-fillers among the press could and would furnish wild speculation to slake the public's thirst for postwar heroes and harrowing, death-defying feats at the outer limits of man's endurance. Actually, it had been a pretty smooth slide. Sometimes being a good ole country boy, honor bound to protect the dramatic secrets of the nation, made life tolerable. When the Brits had a really tough go, they could usually offer a brave smile and assure those within earshot that it had all been a "piece of cake." But what if it really had been a piece of cake? Better the sealed lips. The press was sure he was hiding a harrowing adventure. The diffident shrug and "twarn't nuthin' " smile were worthy of an Academy Award.

Before and after that historic event of October 1947, many World War II pilots remained firmly convinced that they had taken their propeller-driven fighters supersonic in steep dives, often as local shock waves rattled their craft and caused the angle of those dives to become uncontrollably steeper. More often than not the center of lift moved aft on their wings, and Mach-induced turbulence blanketed the normal control surfaces on the tail. For the lucky ones, the descent into denser air slowed the airplane, while the higher temperatures at lower altitude meant that the Mach number for a given true airspeed was lower. Consequently, local shock waves tended to disappear. A normal recovery, as from any steep dive, could usually be effected. It is interesting that the Luftwaffe pilots of their early jet and rocket fighters—the Me 262 and Me 163—made no such claims. Perhaps they were too busy trying to ward off Allied bombers. Or did their scientists advise them that it just wasn't in the cards for those particular designs? Either the wings were too thick or the sweep angle was too small, or both. And after all, the Me 163 rocket ship was fabricated mostly of wood. In fact, the German flight research laboratory conducted dive tests on these two aircraft and found the Me 163 uncontrollable above 0.82 Mach number and the Me 262 unmanageable above 0.85. The prop-driven Me 109 was quite manageable up to 0.79 Mach, but a number of German fighter pilots pushed it beyond into such severe buffet that they were convinced that they must have penetrated the sonic wall and reported, indeed, that they had done so. They may have reached 0.81 Mach number. But the press loved to speculate and would note, "*Oberleutnant* So-*und*-so may just have exceeded the speed of sound." This kind of misinformed speculation would continue long after the war was over.

An old acquaintance of mine who flew F6F *Hellcats* for the Navy is to this day convinced that, because he was able to coax his *Hellcat* to 44,000 feet, nearly 10,000 feet above its proven service ceiling, and cunningly roll it into a vertical dive, he had assuredly blasted through the sound barrier—even though his fighter disintegrated about him as he struck denser air during his descent. No matter that the later *Spitfires*, with a demonstrated ceiling of 45,000 feet, a much thinner wing of elliptical planform, and a lower profile liquid-cooled engine, could never register a maximum speed greater than 0.9 Mach number. That is the highest recorded speed, by a substantial margin, of any propeller-driven fighter. Oh yes, in the course of one such dive, on entering the denser air around

20,000 feet, the *Spitfire*'s propeller and much of the engine cowling parted company with the rest of the aircraft. Getting to 0.90 Mach number wasn't easy, yet it remained a long way from the other side of Mach one.

Before the first unequivocal ventures by man into the realm of the supersonic, there were many recorded tales of not-even-close encounters with the real thing whose purveyors insisted on being granted entry into the hallowed hall of the immortals. Clear demonstration of the true nature of the challenge does not deter those intrepid pseudoMach-busters. For now, let's explore what actually happened more than fifty years ago in October 1947.

2/ The Challenge

High: Thin and Cool—Low: Thick and Hot

A basic problem in sorting out all the factors associated with manned supersonic flight is the question, Supersonic where? "Supersonic" has the connotation of "fast." But supersonic is faster in some places than in others. Supersonic means faster than the speed of sound, but the speed of sound in the earth's atmosphere is substantially greater at sea level than it is at, say, 40,000 feet. The speed of sound varies with altitude? Well—yes, but only because the temperature of the air varies with altitude. The colder the air, the slower the speed of sound, regardless of the altitude. In what is called the standard atmosphere, the seasonally adjusted average of the physical characteristics of the atmosphere as measured around the globe, the speed of sound at sea level and at 59° Fahrenheit is 761 miles per hour. At an altitude of 40,000 feet, where our standard atmosphere charts tell us that the temperature is –67° Fahrenheit, sound travels at 662 miles per hour. Go down to the

Imperial Valley in southern California, or the Libyan Desert, or Saudi Arabia where sea-level temperatures frequently reach 120 degrees, and we find, when the mercury is high, that the speed of sound is more than 805 miles per hour. Indeed, even at the 2,300-foot elevation of Muroc Dry Lake, temperatures of 120 degrees (and thus a speed of sound of 805 miles per hour) are not uncommon. Thus, fighter aircraft traveling at 0.92 Mach number at low altitude over a hot desert floor were actually going more than 60 miles per hour faster than the rocket-powered X-1 on its first supersonic flight when, on October 14, 1947, it reached Mach 1.06 at an altitude of 43,000 feet.

Only since World War II have aviators concerned themselves with speed as measured in Mach number, and even then, for the most part, only at the higher altitudes. In the earlier days, "indicated airspeed" was used to tell the pilot how well he was progressing through the air. At sea level, in that standard atmosphere noted above, indicated and true airspeed are essentially the same. If there is no wind, ground speed, which is the speed relative to the ground as opposed to speed relative to the air mass, is also the same. Knowing ground speed is nice because it informs the pilot how long it will take him to go from point A to point B and other good things, such as whether or not he has enough gas to get there. But indicated airspeed is also important, since the aircraft's stall speed is directly related to indicated airspeed. Entering a stall, which occurs when the indicated airspeed is allowed to fall below the stall speed—at which point airplanes tend to fall out of the sky—can be quite demonstrably unhealthy, especially if it happens when flying close to the ground.

Indicated airspeed provides another bit of information important to the pilot. It's really a measure of dynamic pressure, which is also known as "q" in the technical vernacular. It measures the force exerted on each square foot of surface thrust into its path. This "q" is proportional to the density of the air—five times greater at sea level than at an altitude of 45,000 feet—multiplied by the square of the true airspeed. The "q" when traveling at Mach one at 45,000 feet above the earth's surface is only one-seventh that encountered at a sea-level Mach one. Normally the pilot is separated from these high and potentially hostile winds by his cockpit and its windscreen and canopy, in pressurized and air-conditioned comfort.

Let's leave airplanes for a moment and go for a spin in an automobile. Put an arm out the window, with the palm outstretched and the thumb pointing skyward. Drive at a speed of 15 miles per hour. There is a small force exerted on the hand, but only a few ounces. Accelerate to 30 miles per hour and the force rises to perhaps half a pound or more. Actually, it is four times the force felt at half the speed. As predicted in the equation for dynamic pressure, or "q," the force rises as the square of the speed. Now, watch your mirror and go to 60 miles per hour. The force on your hand has again quadrupled to two to three pounds—four or more if you have a big hand.

Just imagine that you could go 600 miles per hour. The force on your hand would be one hundred times that experienced at 60, some several hundred pounds. The foregoing all assumes a drive along the coast at sea level. If we do a ridge run at a height of some 22,000 feet in Nepal, the forces at the same speeds would be halved because the density of the air at that altitude is but half as great. Again, at 40,000 feet above sea level, where we've quite run out of highways, the air density is but a quarter of the sea level value, and the forces for a given speed are found to be reduced proportionately.

To put the differences into a context of particular interest to denizens of the cockpit, suppose a pilot must leave his aircraft at sonic speed. At the higher altitudes, such as 45,000 feet, he might experience a force of some 650 pounds as he exits in his ejection seat. This would give him an acceleration of 2 to 3 g's—nothing compared with the 7 to 9 g's a fighter pilot might routinely encounter during combat maneuvers, snug in the semireclined comfort of his F-16 *Falcon*. But in a sonic ejection at sea level, the forces on the departing pilot and his seat would reach 3,500 pounds and the acceleration loads will be 12 to 18 g's. Moreover, the swirling vortices will tear at his face and limbs with six times the strength of the swiftest hurricane, seeking to dismember flailing extremities and separate head from torso.

North American test pilot George Smith could testify to the wholly unpleasant nature of such devastating forces. On February 26, 1955, he made the first supersonic ejection on record. It was from an F-100 *Super Sabre* at an altitude of only six thousand feet. A failure in the flight control system put his craft into an unrecoverable vertical dive while on a routine acceptance test flight over the Pacific Ocean near the southern California coast. Had he not been over the water, his abnormally high rate of descent as a result of the several panels ripped from his parachute with the violence of its opening would have been fatal. The proximity of a pleasure boat to his point of splashdown made possible early aid and rapid transport to intensive care. But months of rehabilitative surgery and years of therapy never restored him completely. High-speed, unprotected encounters with our atmosphere at low altitude can be brutal.

Forces on the aircraft also vary dramatically with altitude. Down low, where the fighter pilot must often go to seek and destroy his targets, tornadolike forces will shake, rattle, and rip at his graceful craft. Up high, where the rocket ship thrives, often seeking to exit the atmosphere altogether, air pressures are relatively benign. At a Mach number of 1.06 at 43,000 feet, the "q" forces are but slightly greater than those encountered by Jimmy Doolittle at the maximum speed he needed to win the Schneider Cup race back in 1925, flying just a few feet above the Chesapeake Bay near Baltimore in an open-cockpit Curtiss R3C-2 biplane with floats.

The forces encountered by the X-1 in its first supersonic flight were slightly less than the ones impacting the Supermarine floatplane flown by Flight Officer Waghorn of the RAF when he won that same Schneider Cup race near Cowes, England, in October 1929—almost exactly eighteen years before the first manned, rocket-powered supersonic flight.

Out of My Own Logbook

To illustrate the contrast in cockpit sensations and aircraft behavior when one seeks to fly very fast in dense, hot air down low, as opposed to reaching for maximum speed in the thin, cold air up high, there follows a description of what it was like to fly a North American *Sabre* during engineering tests in three distinctly different environments. One of these flights was just below, the other two clearly beyond, the speed of sound: The first involved a climb to maximum altitude—above 50,000 feet—in a *Sabre*. An instant's inattention at the start of the descent resulted in supersonic speed. The only clue might have been the needle on the Machmeter—an instrument that the prototype *Sabre* didn't have. The second was a structural demonstration to prove for the U.S. Air Force that the aircraft was capable of sustaining maximum design maneuvering loads at maximum indicated airspeed (also known as maximum "q," or dynamic pressure). The third was a demonstration flight to prove that the F-86H would not experience flutter at maximum attainable Mach number. This test was held in relatively dense air in a full-power vertical dive from an altitude of more than 50,000 feet.

SLIPPING THROUGH THE SONIC WALL, JULY 22, 1955

After taking off from the Palmdale Airport at the west end of the Mojave Desert, I pointed the nose of the *Sabre* southward in the general direction of Los Angeles and looked back over my left shoulder. Some twenty miles to the northeast the light beige expanse of

Rogers Dry Lake marked the site of Edwards Air Force Base. Not too long before it had been known as Muroc. A little more than a year had passed since that day in June 1954 when I had joined North American Aviation as an engineering test pilot. The company's experimental flight test operations were then being conducted out of North Base. North Base—that was a euphemism for a rusty, dusty collection of overgrown Quonset huts set on the northwest corner of Rogers Dry Lake where builders of new military aircraft once tested their latest, often exotic, designs. At least they were exotic then, more than a little bit. There were one or two that might be better classified as weird. And some of the things we were occasionally asked to do in them could turn a comfortable wage into an aggravated insult.

Soon after I started work at North American, flight test operations were shifted from North Base to a brand new facility on the Palmdale Airport. It was called Air Force Plant 42. Lockheed, Northrop, and General Dynamics also had constructed new buildings at Palmdale for their flight test work. The expanse of Edwards Dry Lake was still available for special tests when the comfort of more extensive takeoff or landing space seemed advisable.

In the cockpit of my southward winging F-86H, the Mach meter needle settled at 0.75—three-fourths the speed of sound—and the rate of climb indicator told me I was climbing at better than 10,000 feet per minute. The Coast Range that separated the Mojave Desert from the Los Angeles Basin unfolded beneath me.

"Nine-eight-four, this is Gordy." My *Sabre* was number 984. Gordy was Gordon Helgeson, the flight test engineer monitoring my flight from the Palmdale tower.

"Yeah, Gordy."

"Blackie, J. Ray just got airborne in five-nine-eight and needs a target. Five-seven-nine isn't ready yet. Can you help him out?"

J. Ray was J. Ray Donahue, another of the company's engineering test pilots, and 598 was an F-86D interceptor sporting an improved radar that J. Ray had been testing. Five-seven-nine was an earlier F-86E that we used for test support. It was just past ten in the morning. I was taking the "H" to the Los Angeles plant for installation of some new flight test instrumentation. It would be laid up for several weeks, so an hour's delay in its arrival wouldn't upset any timetables. I was scheduled for a test flight in an F-86D with an improved afterburner out of LA, but that wasn't supposed to be ready until midafternoon.

"No sweat, Gordy. Where do I meet him?"

J. Ray broke in: "Thirty thousand, heading east over Tehachapi."

Swinging the nose of my *Sabre* in a wide arc to a northerly heading, I continued my climb. Tehachapi Pass separates the low-lying Tehachapi Range bounding the western edge of the Mojave Desert and the High Sierras rising in rugged magnificence to the north. Through the pass, thirty-five miles to the northwest, lies Bakersfield in the San Joaquin Valley, one of the richest agricultural areas in the world. Bakersfield was also big in oil. The wells of the prodigious Elk Hills field polkadot the valley southwest of town. The little community directly to its north was named Oildale.

I leveled out at 30,000 feet and picked up a heading of east. Throttling back to seven-tenths Mach number (about 475 miles per hour), I observed J. Ray closing from the south on a course perpendicular to my own. Instead of the old pursuit curve used by the fighter pilots of World War II, during which the attacker put the pipper of his gunsight the right number of mils ahead of the target and followed a continuously curving flight path that almost invariably ended in a tail chase, the latest all-weather fighters of the midfifties featured what was dubbed a collision-course guidance system. The fighter's radar and its associated computer sought to position the interceptor on a course roughly perpendicular to that of the target at approximately the same altitude. The pilot then flew wings level toward the target. When the computer calculated that the target angle and range combined with the speed of the attacker's rockets were such that the rockets would quite precisely collide with the target, the pod in the fighter's belly was extended and the rockets fired automatically. These rockets were purely ballistic—that is, once fired, they traveled in the direction they were pointed as gravity inevitably sucked them earthward. Already under development were rockets that had minds of their own. Incorporating sensors in the nose, they would guide themselves to the target after having been launched by the interceptor.

However, these tests were being conducted for the radar and computer only. No rockets were loaded. At least there weren't supposed to be any. If there were, it would be J. Ray's ass; we weren't over the range where hot firings were permitted. It had already been proven rather dramatically that the rockets worked. In an earlier test over the Gulf of Mexico near Florida's Eglin Air Force Base, the target had been an unmanned, radio-controlled B-17. Nearby was another B-17 carrying a lot of Air Force brass to observe the demonstration. The interceptor pilot of the F-86D, an Air Force colonel, had locked his radar on the wrong B-17. There were no survivors. That was the kind of weapons effectiveness testing the Air Force could well do without. J. Ray completed his first run and continued on toward Mount Whitney for a pass in the opposite direction. The North Base at Edwards was disappearing under my right wing.

In the late 1940s, North American had quickly put together the AJ-1 *Savage* in response to the Navy's determination to give its aircraft carriers an atomic weapons delivery capability. In addition to the two piston-powered, 2,000-horsepower Pratt & Whitney R2800's up front, the *Savage* mounted an Allison jet engine in the aft fuselage behind the bomb bay. It was a rapidly executed and workable solution, but not without losses: North American test pilots Jim Brown and Al Conover at Los Angeles and Navy test pilot Mac Moise at Patuxent River—all three "bought the farm" in the *Savage*. The Navy had since decided to go to all jets for their carrier-based strike forces. Already, Douglas was delivering its A3D *Skywarriors* to the fleet.

My excursion in time was rudely terminated by a sharp explosion directly overhead. It was J. Ray lighting his afterburner as his tailpipe cleared my canopy by maybe thirty feet. He pulled up into a lazy barrel roll.

"Wake up, Blackie. You can go home now. Thanks, old buddy."

I resisted the urge to rat race with J. Ray. His "D" was really no match for the "H" I was flying, which got more thrust from its J73 engine without any afterburner and was lighter in weight. Besides, J. Ray was carrying drop tanks. Directly below me was Soda Lake, a white expanse of dry alkaline salt that looks like a large inverted map of the South American continent. From deposits such as these, twenty-mule teams had hauled the lakebed minerals westward to the little town of Boron, which lay just a few miles northeast of Rogers Dry Lake. There the wagon loads had been processed into borax and other commercial chemicals. Swinging the nose on my *Sabre* around to pick up a southwest heading, I advanced the throttle to give me 96 percent rpm on the engine tachometer and depressed the mike switch on top of the go handle.

"Roger, J. Ray. See you at Patmar's."

The Machmeter climbed to 0.85. Nearly 600 miles per hour, ten miles in one minute. Although I was more than halfway to Las Vegas when I turned, I would be at Los Angeles International Airport in twenty minutes; in less than five, I covered what would have been a full day's trip for the twenty-mule teams.

The Los Angeles basin was unusually clear for a midsummer morning. Already in the mid-1950s, smog was a growing problem. The prevailing westerlies coming over the ocean would keep the air fairly clear, except for the mountains ringing the city from Malibu on the northwest all the way around to the Laguna Hills above Newport Beach to the southeast. The eastward flow of air is trapped by the mountains and stagnates over the center of the city. One perhaps not-so-mad scientist proposed putting huge fans in the mountain passes to suck the fetid air from the city and blow it out into the deserts beyond. The stinky, ozone-laden haze will probably lace the atmosphere of the basin, more often than not, as long as I have any interest in the matter. Historians tell us that before the white man came, Indians called what was to become Los Angeles "valley of the smokes."

Passing over Lake Arrowhead and Old Baldy, I throttled back and started my letdown. By the time I had reached the Hughes Aircraft installation at Culver City, I was down to 10,000 feet. The wide macadam strip at the Hughes plant was as long as I was high. Reportedly, it was the longest private strip in the world. And beside it, equally long and at least four times as wide, was a beautifully manicured sod strip. Howard, it was said, preferred landing on grass.

The coastline was just ahead, leading south to the Palos Verdes peninsula. Off to the right lay Catalina Island. As the LA airport passed under my left wing, I pressed the mike button.

"LA tower, *Sabre* 984, 5,000 feet over the coast off the end of two five heading south. Landing LA."

"Roger 984. Call base for two five left."

Forty years ago, life had sure been a lot simpler. No flight plan, no approach control when the weather was clear. Just let the tower know where you were and what you wanted. Civil transponders to help FAA radars find you in the murk were still in the future. Even in bad weather, we could come in from the desert on top of the clouds without prior clearance and get sequenced into the traffic for an approach on instruments as a "pop-up." If the traffic were heavy, we might have to circle above the overcast for five or ten minutes. The commercial jets that brought explosive expansion to the world of air commerce would not start operations until the latter part of 1958.

And there was no speed limit. Some years later, all aircraft below an altitude of 10,000 feet would be permitted to fly no faster than 250 knots (or 288 miles per hour) as indicated on the airspeed dial. In the airport control area, maximum speed is now 200 knots for jets. Before the new rules, we would routinely enter the traffic over the tower at the Palmdale Airport at 400 knots. That extra push once saved me some embarrassment and maybe my life when my engine quit just as I broke at 400 knots and 1,000 feet above the tower. The extra speed gave me the excess energy I needed to reach the runway with a flamed-out engine—but just barely. I left the landing gear retracted until the last moment and squeaked onto the numbers just as the wheels locked down.

As I continued my descent while turning onto the downwind leg of the traffic pattern south of the LA airport, my *Sabre* was indicating 400 knots. Throttling back, I leveled off and extended the air brakes. As the speed dropped below 200, I lowered the landing gear and closed the air brakes. Directly below was Patmar's. I checked the parking lot. Dan Darnell was just driving up in his new Corvette. It looked like Silky Morris was with him. Silky didn't miss many chow calls. Breakfast had been a long time ago. I figured I'd have time to join them.

"Nine-eight-four left base. Gear down. Three green."

Always I litanized the gear, even when there was no tower to hear, even if I were flying a fixed-gear bird, and especially after a go-around. The practiced instinct as the words were uttered was to glance quickly at the gear handle and check the bright glow of the green lights that indicated all three wheels were extended and locked in the landing position. Conventional aviation lore held that there were pilots who had made wheels-up landings and those who were going to. I was still concentrating to keep that experience ahead of me.

"Nine-eight-four follow the American DC-6 on a straight-in, just passing Hollywood Park."

"Nine-eight-four roger."

Full flaps were extended as I slowed to 140. The downwind leg was extended to give the airliner plenty of room. As I turned onto final approach, the DC-6 was just clearing the runway.

"Nine-eight-four clear to land."

"Nine-eight-four roger."

I slowed to 120 and added a little power to keep out of the approach lights. Over the fence, power back to idle and air brakes out, I put the *Sabre* onto the runway right at the numbers. Very little braking was required to make the midfield turnoff leading directly to North American's flight test hangar on the south side of the airport. As I shut down the engine, I noticed a brand new F-86D on the ramp. It was a later version of the all-weather inter-ceptor *Sabre*—the "Dog"—that J. Ray had been flying over the Mojave. The starter cart was hooked up, canopy open, and the cock-pit access ladder was in place. So much for lunch at Patmar's. I grabbed a plain hot dog and a carton of milk from the mobile lunch wagon that toured the plant parking lots at midday. After all, it was Friday.

Going over the test card with the flight test engineer, I noted that it was a simple climb schedule check: a maximum afterburner power ascent to service ceiling, then land back at LA. "Service ceil-ing"—you knew you were there when the airplane wouldn't climb better than 100 feet per minute. The engineer explained that the designers, working with the engine people at General Electric, had provided a better flow of cooling air around the afterburner in the tail of the aircraft. This permitted higher fuel flow and consequently more thrust without exceeding the temperature limits of the struc-ture around the tail. The only instrumentation was some thermal-sensitive paint applied in small patches to the critical areas of the afterburner nozzle. The color of these paint swatches after I re-turned would tell the engineers the peak temperature reached by each of the painted pieces during the course of the flight.

Otherwise the airplane was a standard F-86D, one of the latest off the production line. In the cockpit, the instrumentation was also standard. I was cautioned to pay special attention to the tailpipe temperature gauge to ensure that it did not go over redline. Unlike other *Sabres,* the "Dog" featured a fully electronic fuel control that was supposed to keep the tailpipe temperature precisely at redline when the throttle was full forward. Still, with this new afterburner fuel schedule, one couldn't be too careful.

I observed that the airplane was clean—no drop tanks. Service ceiling would be somewhat better than 50,000 feet, and I wouldn't have much fuel when I got there. More and more the flight surgeons had been warning that for flights above 45,000, pressure suits should be worn. But this flight was up and down. It was not as though I'd be spending a long time in the more hostile upper regions. Besides, I hated the clumsy paraphernalia called a pressure suit. It had expandable tubes, called capstans, running down both sides to the ankles and from shoulders to wrists. The worst part was the helmet, anchored by cables to chest and back, which restricted head motion. Then there was the face plate that, even were it clear, would block good peripheral vision. But it was not clear. It was embedded with wires that in the best of circumstances distorted the vision. The wires were there to provide heat to evaporate the frost that formed in the event of sudden decompression. Finally, there was the simple fact of the hot discomfort of this attire on a mid-July afternoon on the airport tarmac.

But suppose a pilot really did experience loss of cabin pressure while suited up at very high altitude. Then the capstans all inflated, and you were for all the world like the creature in the Michelin tire ad, barely able to bend elbows or knees and with a helmet that wanted to blast free through the canopy, held only by the cables attached to the inflated suit. Twisting your head to look to either side would be virtually impossible. The idea was that by putting mechanical pressure on as much of your epidermis as possible, in order to replace the lost cabin pressurization, your blood would be kept from boiling, as would otherwise be its wont in that very low pressure situation. Well, it would be discouraged from vaporizing at least long enough for a safe return to lower altitude and higher pressure. All of this assumed you were able to manipulate the controls from inside the rigid cocoon in which you found yourself.

My suit was at Palmdale. No one raised the issue, and I couldn't have been more pleased. Unburdened by a clumsy pressure suit, I settled quickly into the cockpit, adjusted the seat belt and shoulder harness, plugged in the oxygen mask, mike, and headset, signaled the crew chief for a start, and flipped the switches. I watched the engine rpm climb, brought the throttle into the idle position, and observed fuel flow and tailpipe temperature gauges. Everything normal. I gave a thumbs-up for "OK," then a thumbs-out to remove the chocks.

"LA ground, *Sabre* zero-five-five at the North American ramp—taxi, takeoff, local test flight."

"*Sabre* zero-five-five, taxi runway two-five left. Winds out of two-seven at ten. Contact tower one-twenty-two-five for takeoff. That was a quick turnaround, Blackie."

"No need to get caught in the Friday night traffic."

Life was pretty relaxed at the Los Angeles airport in those days. We got to know most of the tower personnel by their voices and were always grateful for their help. The respect was mutual. Taxiing to the head of the runway, I closed the canopy and ran through the checklist, then switched to the tower.

"Zero-five-five, ready for takeoff, two-five left."

"Roger zero-five-five. I've got a PanAm three miles out. Can you take it rolling?"

"Zero-five-five rolling."

Turning quickly onto the runway, I advanced the throttle all the way forward for full military power—that's as much as the engine would produce without lighting the afterburner. A scan of the engine gauges told me all was OK. I snapped the throttle outboard to ignite the afterburner. The acceleration of the *Sabre* down the runway paused as the eyelid on the engine nozzle opened. Then suddenly the afterburner lit and an extra ton of thrust made things happen much faster. More than half the runway was still before me as the lightly loaded interceptor leapt into the air and climbed steeply into the cloudless sky. With gear up and flaps retracted when I cleared the end of the airport, I was already above 1,000 feet. Holding runway heading through 5,000 feet, then arcing to the south in the general direction of Catalina Island, I switched to the company frequency and checked in with the flight test engineer covering the flight. The aircraft accelerated to its optimum climb speed and for a while I was going up at 15,000 feet per minute.

Some days everything seemed to come together just right. A beautiful, clear sky, a sleek, brand new jet still redolent of its newplane smell, not unlike that of a new car, and a slicing climb that seemed as though it would continue into orbit. There were wings on my heels reminiscent of the wild passion of an early spring, and in my mind's eye I was singing and dancing in a bravura performance that might have evoked the envy of Gene Kelly. Below, the dust and grime, the drudgery and daily cares in dull earth tones had turned to greens and blues and pleasant prospects, viewed from a vantage point higher than the vanishing condor's. In those days before the introduction of commercial jetliners, more often than not we fortunate few had sole possession of the upper reaches of the earth's atmosphere.

Surely I must be one of the most privileged of mortals; and for this, God's smile, there must be a balancing out, a debt, a payback, a broader responsibility. But what, when, how much, and to whom? Perhaps I would have time to think about it after I rejoined my earthbound fellow travelers. For the moment, enjoy. Passing through 35,000 feet, I noted Catalina Island sliding by under my left wing. Swinging back around toward the Palos Verdes penin-sula, I continued the climb on a northerly heading. Everything was going smoothly. The tailpipe temperature needle hung just below the redline. The Machmeter read eight-tenths the speed of sound.

"Zero-five-five climbing through 35,000."

"Roger, Blackie."

At 40,000 feet, the rate of climb had slowed to 3,000 feet per minute. I eased the stick forward to let the Mach number build to 0.82. Above 45,000 feet, the air was really thin. Indicated airspeed was just over 200 knots. But I was still climbing at better than 1,000 feet per minute. I held the airspeed at 200 and the Mach num-ber climbed toward 0.85. I apparently had moved into a colder air mass, because the climb held steady for a couple of thousand feet. Forty-eight, forty-nine, and yes, it looked as though fifty was well in hand. Indeed, the altimeter read 51,200 feet before the climb rate flattened to essentially zero. I had nearly 2,000 pounds of fuel remaining.

"Zero-five-five at fifty-one two. That's about it. I'm coming home."

"Roger, zero-five-five."

I was just east of the Los Angeles airport. From nearly ten miles high, I could see the floor of the high desert beyond the San Bernardino and San Gabriel mountains ringing the Los Angeles basin. The dry lake beds at Rosamond, Muroc, and El Mirage stood out clearly. From this height and distance, the High Sierras seemed almost dwarfed. Past Santa Barbara on the left, the coast stretched to Point Conception, then bent abruptly north, but no, San Fran-cisco was out of range. To the right was Palm Springs, a shimmer-ing Salton Sea, and, farther south, the deep, deep green of a lush Imperial Valley.

Coming out of afterburner, I retarded the throttle slightly and swung the nose to the right while simultaneously pushing over for my return to reality. I couldn't quite make out San Diego, but surely there along the beach to the south was Oceanside and Camp Pendleton, whence as a second lieutenant rifle platoon leader I had embarked for the last major campaign of World War II on Okinawa.

Damn, damn, damn! Dumb, dumb, dumb!

Pay attention, old buddy. You might be up there all by yourself, but you could still get into a peck of trouble. Taken up with sightseeing and a general sense of euphoria, I had not been minding the store. I'd let the nose get too steep; from that altitude, a 15- to 20-degree dive would do it. My Machmeter read 1.02. I was supersonic and the nose of the *Sabre* was pointing directly at downtown Long Beach.

In one swiftly synchronized movement I retarded the throttle to idle, opened the speed brake, hauled back on the stick, and depressed the mike button.

"Zero-five-five, five north of Palmdale, headed home."

"Roger, Blackie."

The flight test engineer was supposed to record all transmissions and their time. I just hoped he had an accurate watch. I waited awhile as I winged northward toward the Santa Monica mountains, then:

"Zero-five-five, over Burbank. Going to tower."

"Roger, zero-five-five."

All right, dummy, maybe the atmospherics had been such that the boom had never reached the ground, and from that altitude it had probably been too weak for anybody to notice. Yeah, maybe, but when Welch had demonstrated the F-100's supersonic capabilities to the press a couple of years prior, he had nearly demolished the small frame operations shack at the Palmdale Airport.

On the ground, everyone was pleased. There was no evidence of overheating around the tailpipe, so it looked as though the designers had been right. It was not yet two o'clock of a Friday afternoon. Plenty of time to finish up my flight test reports, and there was nothing to hold anyone late, no special problems to take home for the weekend, at least not for the engineers.

Saturday morning—I was up early at my cottage in Manhattan Beach. I quickly gathered in the *Los Angeles Times* from my doorstep. There it was—front-page story, albeit lower-right corner: "Mysterious Blast Cracks Plate Glass Windows in Downtown Long Beach." The culprit was unknown—no blasting in the vicinity—no aircraft capable of supersonic flight in the area at the time. Whew! Something to be said for the simpler era when radar coverage of all flights was viewed as just another nutty way to spend money. But in the *Sabre*, going supersonic, even inadvertently, was so easy, especially from that altitude. Less than a decade earlier, there had been some who had thought it might be more of a challenge.

THE UPPER RIGHT-HAND CORNER, FEBRUARY 7, 1956

To demonstrate to the people paying the bills that an aircraft does everything the contract specifications say it can do, the company must send its experimental pilots aloft to fly the aircraft to all four corners of the V-n diagram. ("V" stands for speed and "n" stands for normal acceleration, usually measured in gravitational, or g, units.) With speed measured horizontally and normal acceleration measured along the vertical axis of the V-n diagram, the curve starts at zero g and zero airspeed, curving upward and to the right, passing through the stall speed at 1 g and continuing along this path until it reaches the maximum maneuvering load factor at the minimum speed for which this load factor is attainable. For the F-86 this peak design load was 7.3 g's. At that point the diagram proceeds horizontally to the right until it encounters the maximum speed of which the aircraft is capable, as measured in indicated airspeed—or, put another way, the highest dynamic pressure, "q," the aircraft is expected to encounter, typically in a dive at full power. This is the "upper right-hand corner," where the peak structural stresses on the aircraft in combination with the greatest aerodynamic loads come together. If anything is going to come unglued, it is most likely to occur at that juxtaposition of max "q" and max g—in layman's terms, the strongest winds and the largest bending forces.

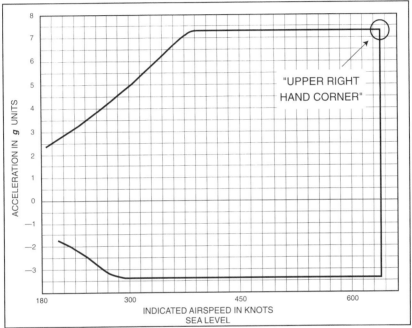

Operating Flight Strength Diagram
Typical USAF Jet Fighter of Late 1940s

The test airplane was an F-86F-40, the first off the production line of that last model in the F-86F series. A total of 280 "dash 40s" were built. The earlier F-86Fs featured a wing leading edge that had been extended—six inches at the fuselage and three inches at the tip—but without the leading edge aerodynamic slats of the previous *Sabres*. For the dash 40, improved aerodynamically actuated slats had been fitted into the leading edge extensions, thus enhancing high-altitude maneuverability and reducing landing speeds. It was a truly delightful fighter to fly. There was only one little problem—wing roll.

The wing roll characteristics of the F-86 were noted very early in its development. The cause of this anomaly was believed to be small differences in the way the wings were fabricated. The result was that when the pilot applied aileron control to roll the aircraft to the left, for example, the aerodynamic forces exerted by the aileron out on the tip of the swept-back wing would twist the structure and cause the aircraft to roll in the opposite direction. This would occur only at high transonic Mach numbers, 0.93 to 0.95, and only in the denser air below 20,000 feet. But it was random and varied from one aircraft to another. Sometimes the direction of the unwanted rolling motion could be reversed by applying aileron with the unwanted roll instead of the normal reaction to apply aileron against the roll. At very high speed, the aileron could act as a servo tab and actually twist the entire wing in a way to roll the aircraft in the direction the pilot really wanted. This technique wouldn't work down low in the densest air, however, and in any case it wasn't something the company wanted to put in the pilot's handbook. The solution was actually quite simple—slow down by either extending the speedbrakes or pulling the nose up. This is just fine if the wing roll occurs during a training exercise, but with a MiG on your tail just south of the Yalu, it was another matter.

This wing roll was a source of considerable frustration, both to North American Aviation and the Air Force. To the best of my recollection, although it was alleviated, this one quirk in an otherwise truly splendid fighter was never cured. It was certainly still present in the F-86F-40 that I was flying from the company flight test facility at Palmdale to the Marine Corps Air Station, El Centro, one bright February day in 1956. That model *Sabre* was just about the last in a line that had been turning out F-86s for nearly a decade.

We went to El Centro to do the upper right-hand corner demonstrations for two reasons. First, on almost any day of the year, it can be counted on to be the hottest place in the United States. Even in February, average peak temperature is 72 degrees, while the mercury can be expected to climb to 96 degrees on the warmest day of that month. Second, located at the south end of the Imperial Valley near the Mexican border, it is only twenty miles from the Salton Sea, the surface of which lies at 235 feet below sea level. High temperature and low elevation gave me the best chance of getting to the required demonstration point of 7.3 g's at 635 knots indicated airspeed. Down low and hot, unwanted Mach effects like wing roll occur at higher numbers on the airspeed indicator.

Flying the chase plane would be Bud Poage. Bud had been a pilot in World War II. Before he'd had to bail out of his burning fighter over enemy territory, he had destroyed six German aircraft on the ground. He spent the rest of the war in a prison camp.

The 200-mile run from the North American flight test facility at Palmdale down to El Centro took only twenty-five minutes. It was not yet noon when we landed, but the temperature on the ground was already up to 78 degrees. We topped our fuel tanks, took off, and headed for the Salton Sea, just north of the air station. Bud was chasing in an earlier model F-86E. From 10,000 feet, I entered a shallow dive and watched the airspeed build up to 600 knots, then slowly rise to 620 as altitude went below 1,000 feet. I turned the instrumentation on to start the data recorders and pushed forward on the stick to steepen the dive. The airplane started to roll to the left. Even with full right stick the left roll continued. As the bank angle approached 90 degrees, the speed was stuck at 625 knots. I had to pull up before the wings got vertical—besides, I was running out of altitude. I pulled back on the stick to 7.3 g's, and, with the attendant deceleration, the wings rolled level.

"Did you get it?" That from Bud in the chase plane.

"Nope."

"Looked hairy. Wing roll?"

"Yep."

I turned off the instrumentation and climbed in the crystal blue sky for a second try. The instrumentation was an oscillograph that recorded airspeed, altitude, g's, roll, pitch and yaw attitude and the rate of change of those attitudes, along with the position of all the flight controls. I started again from 12,000 feet and made the dive a little steeper. I got almost to 630 knots before the wing roll stood the airplane on its left wing and I had to terminate the dive with a sharp pull up.

"Get it?"

"Not quite. One more time."

I needed to get it on the third try or go back to El Centro and refuel. The point had to be made with at least 80 percent of full internal fuel. For the final run from 12,000 feet I angled the dive still steeper. As I passed through an altitude of 500 feet, I put the aircraft into a right turn just before wing roll started, and pushed over to zero g's. Again I had 630 knots, and the surface of the lake 235 feet below sea level was coming up at me fast. Despite full right stick, I was rolling left. As the bank angle approached 45 degrees, left wing down, I pulled back again to 7.3 g's, but the airspeed was still hung up at 630 knots.

"Let's go get some gas."

From the resignation in my voice, Bud knew we'd have to come back for another try. "How about lunch?"

"Sounds like a good idea." The desert sun burning through the clear Plexiglas canopy felt good. It was almost at its apex in the southern sky. Once more we landed our *Sabres* at El Centro and taxied back to the operations line for fuel. There was a snack counter in the operations building and a weather man. I learned that the temperature had risen to 82 degrees and was headed for 85 degrees. We each grabbed a sandwich and a carton of milk and walked back to the airplanes. Our instrumentation technician had flown down from Palmdale in a *Navion*. "I've replaced the paper in the oscillograph," he said. "There was probably enough for another flight, but why take a chance?"

"Thanks. I haven't lost anything down here. This time I'll bring back a roll we can sell to the Air Force. See you in Palmdale."

Turning to Bud, I said, "It's about five degrees warmer now. I think I'll get it on the first try. Nothing like a little practice. . . . How far was I above the lake on the last run?"

"Three to four hundred feet."

That meant I had five to six hundred. Bud was always conservative. He'd had the clanks for a long time, maybe ever since he came out of the stalag. In pilot jargon, "the clanks" is a nervous apprehension that impairs one's ability to perform hazardous tasks. Starving in the stalag must have been a grim experience. Legendary stunt pilot Bob Hoover, then a North American test pilot, had put in time in the stalag, too; and in the shower, even now, they both looked like Holocaust survivors on the day after release. It was certainly not because they'd been on short rations recently. At Patmar's, our favorite watering hole near the LA plant, Bud, rarely commenting on anything, would quietly inhale three or four martinis and then stagger off to curl up in Mona's arms and worry about tomorrow. Mona had been one of Pancho's girls and theirs was a true love match. Hoover would lead the conversation with arm-waving descriptions of the day's flights, keeping pace with the crowd drink for drink, then go to the men's room before departing, put a finger down his throat, and throw up, lest the booze interfere with the later challenges of the evening. Bud would transfer to the transport division to fly the *Navions* and the DC-2 used for moving people and equipment between LA and the Mojave. Hoover abandoned test flying for exhibition flying and has become world renowned. Although he has busted beyond repair some forty-odd aircraft, he's still putting on air shows at age seventy-seven. If he ever had the clanks, nobody knows of it. Bud Poage, not yet forty-five, died quietly in 1965 of a coronary.

Back in the warmer desert air above El Centro, our two *Sabres* climbed quickly back to 12,000 feet. Diving toward the surface of the shimmering Salton Sea, I observed the air speed creeping up beyond 600 knots . . . 610 . . . 620. I rolled into a right turn. My altimeter showed 700 feet above the desert lake, but there was lag in that reading. Back to the airspeed: 625 . . . 630 . . . 632. I was at 0.93 Mach number and here came the wing roll. I pushed over for an instant to zero g as the wings rolled into a 45-degree left bank despite full right stick—but there was 635 knots! I pulled back to 7.3 g. The graceful swept-wing craft decelerated quickly and the wing roll vanished. I pointed the nose of the *Sabre* skyward and did a slow roll, then keyed the mike.

"Nailed it."

"Good show, Blackie, but you didn't leave much room for the sea gulls to fly beneath you."

Several days later, I was in the flight test office in LA with Roy Ferren, chief flight test engineer, going over the oscillograph record of the flight.

"Hey, Blackie, this wasn't supposed to be a rolling pullout. For God's sake, you've got in full right stick."

"Right, Roy, now tell me the direction of roll."

"Wing roll?"

"You guessed it."

"Yeah, but Blackie, that's not all."

"Oh?"

"It's the first upper right-hand corner we ever recorded at 150 feet below sea level."

"Don't tell the Air Force. They're not big on submarines."

Down low and fast the much denser air was treacherous for a *Sabre* at high subsonic Mach numbers. At 20,000 feet the wing roll was there, occurring at the same Mach number, but it was easily corrected with aileron. Above 35,000 feet, it was barely perceptible to nonexistent. At 45,000 to 50,000 feet, as noted before, there were times when a little high-Mach warning could keep a guy out of trouble.

SUPERSONIC FLUTTER, MARCH 23, 1956

Danny Darnell's got the clanks. It was being whispered knowingly among the close coterie of experimental pilots at North American, both in Los Angeles and at Columbus, the Ohio extension of North American that developed and produced Navy aircraft. It wasn't something that you let outside of the tight fraternity; it was a matter for the individual to deal with in his own way. If it was just a passing chillout, it would vanish and no one need make a big fuss about it. Meanwhile, he would undertake only the most routine of flight testing. If the clanks did not go away, it was usually a propitious time for seeking a different occupation.

Now, Danny had good reason to have the clanks. He'd been a test pilot for eight years and had experienced his share of close encounters. His good buddy Joe Lynch had been killed attempting a roll on takeoff in the two-seat F-86 just two years earlier. It had happened at Nellis Air Force Base near Las Vegas as Lynch sought to demonstrate to Air Force pilots what a nice handling aircraft the two-seater was. Then, six months later, his old friend George Welch was killed trying to get the final point in the structural demonstration of the F-100. Danny could have been picked to complete that demonstration once the engineers figured they had corrected the problem that caused the *Super Sabre* to come unglued.

Danny would have done a good and thoroughly professional job on that demanding probe into uncharted territory based on the engineering rethink of the problem that had brought about Welch's demise. Danny wasn't an engineer. He believed pilots should do the flying and engineers should do the design work. And he had a way of putting down pilots who sought to demonstrate their technical sophistication. At a meeting to discuss the F-100 fixes, one of the company's pilots with an engineering degree volunteered,

"Obviously, there's not enough C-N-Beta." A senior Air Force officer standing next to Danny whispered, "What the hell is he talking about?" Danny chuckled and responded, "He means he doesn't like the color of the paint."

Still, he had an uncanny knack for seeking out engineers who put their theories in simple terms that the uninitiated could clearly grasp. Ed Horkey, chief technical engineer in the early *Sabre* era, remained an especially close friend even after leaving North American in 1953. Larry Greene, head of aerodynamics at North American, had put together a great team, and one of that team's most talented members was Rose Lunn. Rose had agonized over the breakup of the F-100 and knew that it was an aerodynamic problem, not a structural one. Rose spent many long nights rethinking the original analyses that had been used to describe for the structural designers the kinds of aerodynamic surfaces required to permit the F-100 to do all the crazy things that fighter pilots demanded—such as pulling 7.3 g's at 1.55 Mach number, down low. The equations that link the various maneuvers are extremely complex and, in 1954, the computers were crude to nonexistent.

Ideally, six equations are used to describe the aerodynamic forces on an aircraft in flight, and there is linkage between them all. In the era of limited computer tools, if one of these equations could be shown to have weak linkage to the rest, with trivial impact in terms of forces, that equation almost surely would be dropped from the analysis—with a dramatic reduction in the time required to complete the calculations. That had been done in the initial assessment of the *Super Sabre*'s flight characteristics. The equation dropped was the one that linked yaw with roll. After the accident, Rose suspected that this had been a mistake. The burning of much midnight oil proved her right. The solution was simple: Add more vertical tail. Ironically, the first two prototype YF-100s had had taller fins. For the production aircraft, the performance people thought they could reduce drag with a shorter tail without

any loss of handling qualities. The drag reduction had been mi-
nuscule, the consequences tragic.

Danny spent a lot of time with Rose. He knew she did her
homework. More important, she took the time to translate the results into an easy-to-understand cockpit vernacular. So Danny was
satisfied that he could have completed the structural demonstration of the F-100 *Super Sabre* without further incident. It carried a
bonus of $10,000 (about $65,000 in 1995 dollars). But he turned it
down. He'd already made up his mind to move to a different kind of
work. He would complete the demonstration on the F-86H and hang
up his 'chute. J. O. Roberts, a former "top gun" with the Air Force,
would take over the F-100 structural demonstration and finish it
in a wholly professional manner and no more busted airplanes.
Zeke Hopkins, recently resigned as an Air Force captain stationed
at Edwards, a West Pointer with a master's degree in aerodynamics from Princeton, completed the spin tests. This was after Bob
Hoover, originally assigned to do the spins, prematurely embarked
on a bit of freelance investigation in an uninstrumented F-100 without spin chute in the tail or spin recovery rockets in the wings. Bob
bailed out from an unrecoverable flat spin much to the embarrassment of the company, but it provided one more point to his reverse
ace score that put him well ahead of Gabby Gabreski's record on
the plus side.

I drop these names assuming that everyone is my age or older
and everybody remembers Gabby—Colonel Francis S. Gabreski. He
was a leading ace in Europe with thirty-one victories in the air
plus two and a half on the ground. It was on a ground strafing run
that his propeller struck a mound of earth, bending it useless. He
had to ditch in a field and ended up joining Hoover, who'd been
shot down earlier, in a stalag for the balance of the war. Gabby had
actually started the war at Pearl Harbor on December 7 but never
got airborne during the attack. He rounded out his combat career
in Korea where he became a jet ace, adding six and a half MiGs to

his air-to-air total and bringing his lifetime figure up to forty if
you count a couple destroyed on the ground.

From the outset, Hoover's instincts for survival seemed to
beggar the escape skills of Houdini and are the despair of actuar-
ies who run out of zeros trying to figure the probability of actually
surviving such a run of thoroughly demolished aircraft. Not long
after the F-100 spin event, Bob gave up the challenge of flight testing for the much more lucrative air show business. Now, more than
forty years later, he's still at it. There was a brief hiatus. Because of
an obscene and truly mean-spirited action by some FAA pipsqueak
inspectors, whose bosses' kneejerk support is yet another scream
for less intrusive government, Hoover had his medical permit canceled. For a while he could perform his incredible aerobatic demonstrations only outside the United States. In places like Australia,
more objective flight surgeons and privatized (meaning less bureaucratic) civil aviation administrations issue him pilot licenses
and find that he passes muster physically—and psychologically.
They find the FAA's indecipherable psychobabble concerning
Hoover's ability to fly a truly weird abuse of governmental authority. Of some interest to those supporting less government control
is the fact that civil aviation is managed by a corporate entity in
Australia, as it is in most other advanced and civilized societies.
Even though his appeal was refused a hearing from the Supreme
Court, the head of the FAA in a demonstration of bureaucratic courage and good sense gave Hoover his license back. If he can keep up
with the late Steve Wittman, he has close to twenty years left on
the circuit.

But back to the clanks: After passing up the F-100 demonstration, Danny returned to his primary project, the F-86H. There
remained the structural demonstration and the maximum Mach
number dive, the latter for ensuring the absence of flutter. These
tests dragged on and the wrinkles on Danny's physiognomy grew

deeper. He has always displayed a wonderfully tuned sense of humor, so one might say the wrinkles came from self-induced laughter. But he had an equally imaginative penchant for introspection and worry. For a guy in his midthirties, his face bore the imprints of more careful survivors of twice those years. But wrinkles, said Racine, are the imprints of exploits, and exploits he had known. Soon after he joined North American as an experimental pilot, Danny and Bud Poage barely escaped from a burning and disintegrating AJ-1. Now, there were the recent losses of close friends. We all knew that Danny was going to hang it up, and he damn sure wasn't going to do something stupid so he'd get carried out in a pine box.

That's how I had found myself contemplating the flight schedule board at the Palmdale facility that March morning in 1956. My flight had been postponed until the afternoon. By Danny's name was an F-86H flight listed for stability and control evaluation. The airplane was number 380, which I recollected as the one instrumented for the structural demonstration. I recalled flying chase for Danny a couple of weeks earlier as he wrapped up the demonstration program in that airplane. But earlier on this particular morning he hadn't been on the DC-2 that routinely flew us up from Los Angeles to Palmdale, and nobody seemed to know where he was.

"Q. C." Harvey, flight test engineer for the F-86H program, asked me if I'd make the flight. I protested that it was Danny's program, but Q. C. said all the main points had been done, that this flight was just to test directional stability at maximum Mach number.

"For real, maximum Mach number?"

"For real," Q. C. responded.

He knew exactly what I meant. Some months ago, I'd been told to land the F-86H and immediately apply maximum force on the brake pedals. I argued that such a procedure would blow both tires and grind the wheels down to the axles. A check was made with the engineers in Los Angeles. Yes, they meant "maximum force on the brake pedals."

"For real?" I had asked.

"For real," was the response.

I was right about the tires, but the wheels were ground down only halfway to the axles. An alert fire crew limited the damage to the wheels.

Now it was "for real, maximum Mach number." I protested again that it was Danny's program and that he ought to do it. Q. C. argued that it was no big deal, Danny was not to be found, and it was Friday. This was the last point on the demonstration and the company would like to wrap it up. They were already behind schedule.

I shrugged an OK and ran through the maneuver in my mind. Full power climb to 50,000 feet. Turn on the data recorder. Split-S to a vertical dive with throttle still two-blocked. Should reach maximum Mach number at about 20,000 feet. Pulse the rudder, level out, and return to Palmdale. Seemed simple enough. But if so, why wasn't Darnell here?

"What Mach do you expect?"

"About 1.14, maybe 1.16."

The climb to altitude was uneventful. At 51,000 feet I did a half roll to inverted flight, then pulled the nose through until I was pointing straight down with the engine at full power. A lot of elevator trim was required to maintain the 90 degree angle as the *Sabre* hurtled earthward. Almost immediately, I was supersonic. No wing roll up there. As I passed 30,000, the Machmeter read 1.14 and was still inching higher. At 27,000 it was at 1.16, and at 25,000, 1.18! It wasn't supposed to go that fast.

I started to pulse the rudder when the aircraft did it on its own. Several sharp quick pulses beat on the soles of my boots as my feet lay against the rudders, followed by a strange whistle from the tail of the aircraft. Just a *blltt*, then a whistle, but clearly some-thing was seriously awry.

Steady, old boy, don't do anything rash. The technique in such circumstances was to pull back on the power and get the nose headed up rather than down, but to do so gently to avoid exacer-bating any structural damage that might have occurred. And let somebody know you might have a problem. I already had the throttle back to idle and was easing back on the stick. As the nose slowly lifted above the horizon, I extended the speed brakes and keyed the mike.

"Q. C."

"Yeah, Blackie."

"I think I got some flutter." I described what had happened and noted that there was virtually no rudder movement, even un-der hard pressure on the pedals.

"Where are you, Blackie?" That was Danny Darnell. Where in hell had he come from?

"Over Rosamond, 25,000 feet, 250 knots, heading for Palmdale."

"I'll be there in a couple of minutes. How does it feel?"

"OK, but the rudder's locked up."

Danny slid in underneath me and took a position on my right wing. He was in our F-86E chase plane.

"Your rudder's bent. Looks like the center hinge failed. I don't see anything else wrong. Think you can land it?"

"Let me slow it down and see how things work with the gear and flaps down."

Fortunately, single-engine jets didn't need much rudder. With the landing gear extended and full flaps, it felt fine down to 120 knots. I could bleed the rest off over the runway.

"Feels OK, Danny. I'm switching to Palmdale tower. . . . Palmdale tower, *Sabre* three-eight-zero, ten miles northeast, what are your winds?"

"Three-eight-zero, winds are 270 at 10 knots."

"Roger, Palmdale. I'd like a long, straight-in approach to two-five."

"You got some kind of problem, three-eight-zero?"

Before I could respond, Danny broke in: "Structural damage to the aircraft. This is five-seven-nine. I'm on his wing."

"Roger. Three-eight-zero, you're cleared. No other traffic. Call five miles out."

The approach and landing were unremarkable. The North American facility was at the northwest end of the runway near the completion of my rollout. With differential braking I was able to arc onto the company ramp, where I stopped and shut the engine down without trying to maneuver into our normal parking area.

Walking out to greet me along with Q. C. was Neil Scott, senior flight test engineer, who was in charge of flight testing the F-86H. He and Q. C. made a good team.

"Thanks for bringing it back in one piece, Blackie." Neil extended his hand. "What happened?"

"Classic flutter is my guess. Four to six cycles and it was gone."

"How fast were you going?"

"I was right at one-point-one-eight when it happened."

"That's the fastest it's been. One-point-one-six is the highest I'm aware of for any of the previous flights."

"Well, Q. C. said 'for real' maximum Mach number. Maybe the air's cold up there today."

Neil was already up on a test stand having a closer look at the rudder. Its fast but brief wild flailings had broken the center hinge and the control surface was bent, jamming the leading edge into the recess at the trailing edge of the vertical fin. Fortunately, the rudder was still pretty much aligned with the fin; otherwise, the aircraft would have flown in a skid and I would have had to use Edwards Dry Lake for my landing.

Danny strolled over wearing his inimitable, slightly sardonic grin. "I see you've still got that horseshoe stuck up your ass, Blackie.

Neil says you've been doing all your max Mach dives with the speed brakes out. You trying to grow up like Stan Holtoner?" Holtoner was the Air Force general who flew an evaluation of the new F-100 with the speed brakes extended and complained that even in full afterburner he couldn't get the airplane to go any faster than 0.8 Mach number.

Why Danny hadn't been on hand for his flight earlier in the day and how he had gotten airborne so quickly once I'd had a problem was never a subject of discussion. I didn't ask. He didn't tell. It just wasn't necessary. From his look of resignation it seemed his mind was going over a shift in plans. His program that was all but wrapped up now had some new problems. He would have to delay his switch to another line of work. He was a professional. He wasn't going to walk away and dump it all on someone else. Funny thing about Danny. I think he really liked being a test pilot, liked the challenge of flight testing, but he really wasn't all that hooked on flying. He was just the opposite of Hoover.

The Clanks

It was noted earlier, perhaps gratuitously, that Danny had the clanks. The term addresses a state of mind that can occur in any line of work but is found especially in those viewed as hazardous. In my experience the term is used only by aviators. Some clinical psychologist or research psychiatrist may have defined it, but probably not under that imprimatur. Onset of the clanks is not easily predicted, nor are there any ready cures. Often it will be found when youthful enthusiasm, exploratory zeal, and a sense of immortality are abruptly transformed by mature introspection and a strong desire for sharing a future with grandchildren. More often than not it will afflict those who seem most quiet, cool, and wholly unflappable. And there are those who stay in the game long past the time that keenness of vision, hearing acuity, and rapidity of response would seem to dictate a less challenging arena. Once you've made it to Carnegie Hall, steady practice and good sense can keep you performing well past normal retirement mileposts. Lots of practice and an overdose of common sense will keep the clanks at bay.

Symptoms of the clanks are an inability to think rationally and act decisively in what the uninitiated might view as pressure cooker circumstances. In some cases, it occurs when individuals are thrust into demanding situations that they either do not understand or for which they have simply not prepared themselves physically, intellectually, or psychologically. There are times when an event or series of events, quite catastrophic in nature, triggers protective mechanisms in a close observer who but for the grace of God might have been the victim of those events. My first close encounter with a fellow pilot afflicted with the clanks occurred in January and February 1949. Our squadron of F4U-4 *Corsairs* was flying from the aircraft carrier *Midway* during a deployment to the Mediterranean. From the start, a series of unrelated tragedies marred the exercise. First, a member of the flight deck crew was sliced in half by the mid-deck elevator. Then, a squadron aviation machinist's mate walked into a spinning propeller on the flight deck—neither trauma was survivable.

As flight operations commenced after a stormy Atlantic crossing, the big Pratt & Whitney R-2800 engines on our *Corsairs* were well salted and responded crankily to demands for full power as launches began from the old hydraulic catapults on the carrier's bow. For the first day of flight operations, I was assigned as a spare to be ready for launch in case any of the scheduled aircraft had a maintenance problem. As such, I was in the cockpit of my *Corsair* near the deck-edge elevator with engine idling on the hangar deck. I could hear the disciplined ballet that is the hallmark of flight operations on a U.S. Navy aircraft carrier: the roar as engines are asked for full power, the slam of the catapult, the launch officer on the loudspeaker, the air boss on the radio. Then, ominously, there was a pause, and a sheet of flame passed along the port side of the *Midway* by the deck-edge elevator. After another moment of silence, I heard on my radio, "All right, bring up the spare."

A flight deck crewman maneuvered me onto the elevator. Beyond, there was only the blue Atlantic. In addition to the continuous rolling and pitching of the big carrier, there was a 30-knot wind roiling off the deck in a turbulent vortex that buffeted the bent-wing *Corsair*. The handling from the cockpit was all the more awkward because the wings were still folded above the fuselage as if in prayerful supplication to whatever gods might be listening as the flight deck *danse macabre* continued. Once raised to flight deck level, I was given the signal to spread and lock my wings, then maneuvered onto the flight deck and lined up for takeoff. I quickly checked the mags and gave a thumbs-up to the flight deck control officer. Then the air boss up on the bridge ordered, "Hold that spare. Bring the helicopter aboard." In less than a minute, a helicopter landed on the flight deck just ahead of me. Some medics rushed over and loaded a body onto their stretcher; covered with a blanket, it was carried beneath my left wing. The helicopter took off and resumed its station just aft and to the starboard of the carrier.

"OK, launch that spare."

This was the original *Midway* with the straight deck. If you didn't catch an arresting wire, you got to plow into the cable barrier erected between landings for just such a goof—otherwise, your prop would chew up a bunch of perfectly good aircraft that had landed ahead of you. That early *Midway* still had hydraulic catapults. Many a carrier pilot suffered neck troubles from the rude slams of acceleration imparted by that primitive mechanism. And the carrier had real, live landing signal officers in those days. Each one had a personality of his own, and the squadron swore by ours. He also acted as father confessor to the pilots, especially those with less experience or the ones who seemed a bit rusty. It would be more than a dozen years before the *Midway* would go into a three-year overhaul to be modified with those wonderful Limey inventions—the angled deck, the steam catapult, and the mirror landing system.

"That spare" was me. Since all the other squadron aircraft scheduled for flight that morning had departed, the deck ahead was clear. I would not need the catapult. I again gave the flight deck officer a thumbs-up. He in turn rotated his left hand, meaning that I should go to full throttle. A quick check indicated the engine was turning up maximum power. I nodded and the ballet master dropped his left hand to his knee and, in an exaggerated arc of his right hand, which held a checkered flag, pointed down the flight deck. I released the brakes and started slowly toward the bow into that 30-knot wind. The engine seemed to be popping and giving less than its best. I must have been bending the throttle with the force I was applying to make sure it was fully forward. I was at the deck edge and barely had flying speed.

Once clear of the carrier, I eased the nose over and retracted the landing gear. A few more sputters and the hesitating engine cleared its throat and gave me full power. Holding about ten feet above the wavetops, I watched the airspeed grow to 90 knots and then started looking for the rest of the squadron. Observers on the signal bridge later told me I kicked up spray with my prop for a mile or so ahead of the ship before I finally picked up climbing speed. I also learned that the pilot who had made the big fireball as I waited on the hangar deck—his engine had quit as he cleared the catapult—had emerged from his *Corsair*'s cockpit none the worse for wear, only to see the bow of the *Midway* heading for him at 30 knots. The big ship parted his legs and struck his seatpack parachute and life raft head on; then the bow wave rolled him off sharply to the starboard, clear of the ship and its churning propellers. The plane guard helicopter was over him before he had a chance to inflate his life raft. The injuries were painful sprains and bruises,

not life threatening but sufficient to put an end to further partici-
pation in the squadron's Mediterranean cruise exercises. Evacuated back to the States, he quickly recovered, and the Marine Corps
in its wisdom sent him to school to learn how to become a landing
signal officer (LSO), the guy who stands back on the carrier's fan-
tail with the beribboned paddles in his hands and guides his squadron mates to a safe arrested landing on the flight deck. Of course,
the mirror landing system has long since replaced those guys, but
remember that this was back in 1949, and the big war was still
more than a distant memory.

Three lousy bouts of bad luck, you'd think that would be
enough for one cruise, but there was more to come, at least one
more big one. It happened the next day. I was not scheduled to fly,
so I was up on the signal deck overlooking flight operations from
just aft of the bridge as the twelve *Corsairs* of the other Marine
squadron of F4U-4's, VMF 461, came back aboard. There was a lot
of competition between squadrons. One of the most closely watched
measures of performance was landing interval. The challenge was
to bring the squadron of twelve aircraft aboard the carrier as
quickly as possible. There is a sound tactical reason for minimizing the time for recovering aircraft. To get all its aircraft back on
board, the carrier must hold a steady heading into the wind—no
maneuvering. The heading may take it into harm's way, and a constant course is just what enemy submarines prefer to ensure the
accuracy of their torpedoes.

Paralleling the carrier's course, the three divisions in a column of four-finger vees passed on the starboard side of the ship at
a height of about 500 feet above the water. They started their break
just past the bow and set up their downwind leg on the port side of
the ship. The landing gear and tail hook were dropped before starting the final turn, and wing flaps were extended as speed was reduced to about 10 knots above the stall. Timing the turn for the
final approach is critical to meeting the goal of being in the groove

and ready for a "cut" from the landing signal officer, the guy with the paddles, who is telling you if you are high or low, fast or slow, by the position and movement of his paddles. The real pros in this challenging aerial ballet will require not the first flicker of the paddles as they keep their mounts steady in the groove for the entire approach, at the end of which the LSO brings his right (outboard) paddle abruptly across his chest, telling the pilot to cut his throttle, let the nose drop slightly, then back stick to squeak it onto the deck in a three-point attitude. Catch an early wire and the deceleration was quite smooth. If you skipped to the last wire, beyond which you would go into the barrier, the arresting action would be quite abrupt.

In either case you were safely down, but there was no time to dally. As the arresting wire pulled your aircraft back slightly, you had to hold your position with the brakes as you retracted the tail hook, then you had to taxi smartly forward beyond the barrier, which was being lowered to let you join your mates who had just come aboard ahead of you and to clear the deck for the wing man, who should be within a few seconds of being positioned to take his cut behind you. If he were too close, he had to be given a wave-off and would come around for another try. If he were too far behind, he would be wasting everybody's time and would hear about it from the rest of the flight and the LSO.

The first ten *Corsairs* did very well indeed. The interval was close to fifty seconds. If maintained, it would mean bringing the twelve aircraft aboard in less than ten minutes. But number eleven was in trouble. His approach was much too fast and he was given a wave-off by the LSO. His wing man stayed with him to give such assistance as might be needed. The pilot in trouble was Captain Frank Collen; his wing man, First Lieutenant George Dodenhoff. It seemed that Frank could not reduce power from near full throttle without the engine quitting. He tried a second approach and a third, still too fast. George was running low on fuel and, after Frank's third pass, came aboard with no problems and taxied past the barrier. Frank too was getting low on fuel, and the LSO told him he would give an early cut so some of the excess speed could be bled off before he reached the deck.

Frank was coming in low and fast. Not low enough and much too fast. The LSO gave the cut, but despite the loss of power the ailing *Corsair* climbed up to deck level and beyond. Frank spiked it onto the deck with the tail high in the air. The tail hook missed all the wires. The compressed energy in the landing gear oleos thrust the *Corsair* back into the air—up above the barrier, up till I was eyeball to eyeball with a really busy Frank. His right wingtip was scraping the quarter-inch steel fence bounding the signal bridge two levels above the flight deck. If he'd been two feet higher, I'd have been headless.

I looked forward and there was George, standing up on the seat of his *Corsair*, getting ready to dismount. He was absolutely frozen in place, his eyes bulging, less in fear than in disbelief, as Frank, his aircraft now past the barriers, again spiked it onto the deck right behind his wingman's tail. As if in slow motion, the huge four-bladed, fourteen-foot propeller started chewing up Dodenhoff's blue bent-wing fighter, grinding it to bits of fabric and aluminum. First the rudder and the elevator, then the fin and horizontal stabilizer—inexorably the voracious scythe chewed up the rear fuselage, gobbling up the antenna less than halfway to the cockpit. George, still motionless, had shrunk against the forward canopy bow, his arms instinctively raised to cover his face. There was a spray of glass as the retracted canopy was shattered and then . . . all was quiet. The big blades had halted their death march, their hunger slaked, their energy depleted. Only the armor plate on the rear of the seat, devised to protect the pilot from enemy machine guns, remained between them and the wholly unarmored and unamused Dodenhoff. The rest of the badly abused *Corsair* settled onto the deck, its propeller pointing up at an abnormally steep angle as if to say, "Time to get the hell out of here!"

I turned to descend to the flight deck and almost bowled over the tall, taciturn Gil. His jaw muscles were alternately tensing and relaxing, his gaze focused on some distant spot beyond the mess on the flight deck. He made no comment, just shook his head and turned to walk slowly down the ladder. He did not stop at the flight deck but continued below toward the wardroom. Gil was one of the abler and more senior pilots in the squadron. He had served with Pappy Boyington's Black Sheep Squadron during the war and had a distinguished combat record.

Gil didn't show up in the wardroom that evening for dinner. He was out on the flight deck, at the bow as the *Midway* plowed its way eastward. He stood in the stiff breeze looking toward the horizon for some time. It was early January and even in the Gulf Stream it was cold in the North Atlantic. After a few minutes, he turned and strode to one of the *Corsairs* tied down on the forward flight deck. The lanky aviator opened the canopy and climbed into the cockpit. For a half hour, he sat there looking at the familiar instruments, touching each of the controls, closing his eyes as he checked his memory for all the various levers and switches. It was dark when he climbed out and went below to his cabin.

It was two days before we flew again. Gil kept pretty much to himself. His name was not on the schedule, nor was he listed for the escort flights the following day as we cleared the Gibraltar Straits into the Mediterranean. During launch operations, he could be found aft on the fan tail or one deck below in the spud locker watching the roiling wake of the big ship as it churned ever eastward. When it came time to recover the flights, he could be found up forward around the gun tubs alongside the flight deck. Nobody made much of it, but in time it began to leak out. Gil had the clanks. The skipper, Major Charlie Kunz, an ace in the recent fracas and one great natural leader, never said anything; still, he did what was necessary to keep Gil off the schedule. He knew that if or when Gil wanted to fly again, he would put himself on the flight board. Some of us—mostly the new boys—were happy to fill in. We couldn't get enough. It wasn't just the carrier operations, which have to be the most magnificent example of tight team cooperation since Marine General Pedro del Valle devised time-on-target coordination of ship-based guns and field artillery. It was also the opportunity to fly in a different environment, to tangle with the British *Spitfires* out of Malta, to break away from the home base, to travel 5,000 miles away and believe, really believe, that if push came to shove we could get the job done.

Gil had been in the southwest Pacific, and he had proved to himself and those who flew with him that he could get the job done. When he had tangled with those *Zeros* and *Kates* and *Vals*, it wasn't just some rat race. It was a live ammo exercise in the highest-stakes game around. He learned that the longer you were able to hang in there, the better your chances of surviving another week, another month. It was like the chances of a replacement platoon leader versus those of the veteran with several months of intense combat on the line.

Aviation brings an extra dimension of threat to longevity. Gil knew that even in the combat theater he lost more friends to operational misadventures than to enemy guns—a lot more. That recollection, coupled with the multiple mishaps early in the cruise, drove him to an irrational inability to cope with the highly complex challenge of flying *Corsairs* off the *Midway*—an exercise he had long before reduced to a commonplace. No denying it, Gil had the clanks. He'd seen it before and had had little patience with the afflicted. Now it was his turn, and he was glad Charlie Kunz was his skipper.

Trapped aboard the carrier, it was hard to hide the simple fact that Gil just wasn't on the flight schedule anymore. Ashore, it would have been a simple matter to arrange for a transfer to the group staff or get assigned to one of the many educational options the Marine Corps offered. After the cruise, I lost track of Gil. I left the corps that summer and went back to school. I suspect he may have done the same thing. Like most people who get the clanks, he had a sharp and creative mind. Bud Poage and Dan Darnell certainly met those criteria—so did George Welch. Bud and Dan eased themselves out of their test flying jobs on their own terms. Welch did not. He could not frame a life elsewhere and there was no evidence that his cockpit performance suffered. Still, the stress was etched in his face. Perhaps he should have moved to a nonflying job, but no one could envision what that job might entail. For him, as for so many warriors, the peacetime world is more than difficult, it's deadly dull. Test flying offered an acceptable alternative, the ultimate peacetime high. Careful pacing can run the string out to retirement and beyond, but increasingly, good judgment must supplant inexorably growing demands. It may not be enough to keep the mortality scales in balance. Uppers and downers with martini-laced evenings made it all too easy for the ever quicker, more agile, more complex fighters to gain the upper hand.

Did George have the clanks? Most probably not. He knew he had a huge challenge on his last flight. He bet he could stay on top of it and bring the aircraft home in one piece. In his own unique style he prepared for a confrontation with wholly unexplored aerodynamic behavior well beyond the sonic wall. His recently acquired friend guarded his rest through the night before that flight, but she would not be with him at the end. Two fellow experimental pilots would cradle his head and staunch his wounds till the stout heart succumbed. She would grieve later and alone.

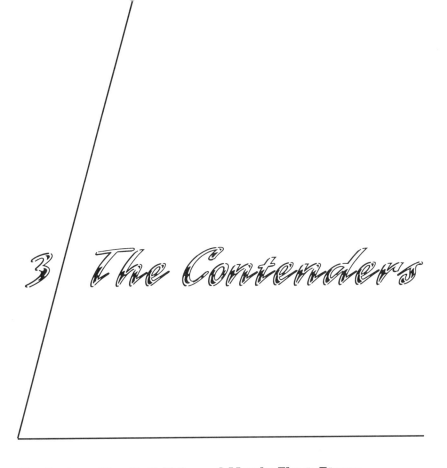

3 / *The Contenders*

Rocketry, the Bell X-1, and Man's First Steps toward the Moon

Even in those seemingly uncomplicated days between World Wars I and II, any youngster seriously enthralled by the exploits of Lindbergh, Doolittle, and Roscoe Turner knew that for truly out-of-this-world journeys, rocket power was the only way to go. The exploits of "Flash Gordon in the Twenty-First Century" were carefully portrayed in daily comic strips followed by a full page in glowing color on Sunday. For sophisticates, there were the more scholarly tomes of Jules Verne and H. G. Wells. The message from both was the same: For voyages beyond the earth's atmosphere, only reaction motors would do. For all practical purposes—and a lot of impractical ones, for that matter—this meant rockets.

While employed at Republic Aviation on Long Island, New York, in the early 1960s, I had a colleague who was working on ion propulsion. In theory, it should have been an efficient reaction device for use in outer space. He managed to spend millions of the tax-payers' dollars, but the maximum thrust he was ever able to develop was measured in fractions of a mouse fart. Rockets are different. The Chinese were firing rockets as far back as the twelfth century. Even so, it was not until the 1930s that dreams of space ventures were translated into rudimentary hardware with clear genetic tracks to exoatmospheric voyages. Robert Goddard's liquid-propellant rocket engines terrified his neighbors in Massachusetts, where aberrational perversities of almost any genre usually have little trouble gaining broad popular acceptance, if not appeal. Undeterred, Goddard moved his experiments to the desert of New Mexico. There, in 1935, one of his rockets climbed to 7,500 feet.

The Germans were also busy with rocket power. Autos propelled by rockets sped across frozen lakes at speeds greater than 200 miles per hour, and as early as 1928 they launched a manned glider using a liquid-fueled rocket engine—probably the first manned rocket flight on record. Continued research, accelerated by the war, brought a first glide flight of the Messerschmitt 163 *Komet* in the summer of 1941, and on its fourth powered flight, October 2, 1941, test pilot Heini Dittmar unofficially broke the world speed record when he reached 622.6 miles per hour. In both the A and B models, this fighter, the fastest of its time, featured wing spars of laminated wood and plywood skins. Armament was two 30-millimeter guns in the wing stubs with sixty rounds each. Although it could climb to 30,000 feet in two and a half minutes, it had but two to three minutes of fuel remaining when it got there. Its takeoff wheels, mounted on a detachable dolly, were jettisoned at liftoff. Landing was made at some 140 miles per hour on a skid. And having burned up all of the fuel on board, the pilots of these first (and only) operational rocket fighters had to get the landing right the first time. There was no go-around for a second try. That is why the first test pilots for the *Komet*, Heini Dittmar and Rudi

Opitz, came from the German glider tradition. For the glider pilot, every landing is a "dead-stick" landing.

What's really nice about rocket-powered aircraft, at least from the designer's point of view, is that they don't have to suck in any air. Conventional jets use the oxygen in the atmosphere for burning their fuel. This means they must provide a passage for air to flow to the engine, where it can be compressed, mixed with the kerosenelike liquid, burned, passed through nozzles and turbine blades, and then ejected at high velocity out the tailpipe. We're talking about moving a lot of air, and getting the right inlet for all that air is a tricky configuration challenge, especially as an aircraft approaches sonic speeds—more a black art than a science.

While I was a graduate student in aerodynamics at MIT, Tony Ferri, a professor at Brooklyn Polytechnic Institute, came to give a guest lecture on inlet design. It was a subject on which he was one of the world's leading authorities. I'll always remember his opening remarks: "There is no good place for an inlet on a turbojet aircraft. The task is to find that location which is least bad."

Because rocket planes carry both fuel and oxidizer, their aerodynamic shapes are unembarrassed by awkward little details such as where to bring the air in and how to minimize the drag associated with that function. This is why the X-1 was formed in the shape of a 50-caliber projectile. There was no need to interrupt those smooth ogival lines to provide an inlet for an air-breathing engine. Such bullets were known to spin quite smoothly and, with proven stability, exit the gun muzzle at better than twice the speed of sound.

Another interesting aspect of rockets is that for the same propellant flow, thrust increases with altitude and reaches its maximum beyond the atmosphere. As a consequence, rocket-powered research craft are almost without exception launched from converted-bomber mother ships so they do not have to waste a lot of fuel breaking through the heavy air down low where most of us work and breathe but where the rocket performs poorly. The jet engine, on the other hand, produces maximum thrust at sea level, losing power as it climbs because the thinner air has less oxygen for its burner cans. Thus, rockets are principally for moving things about out of this world, beyond its atmosphere. They have little utility operating within it.

X-1 pilot Chuck Yeager explains to Smithsonian aviation's patron saint, Paul Garber, the business end of the four-cylinder rocket engine that powered the X-1 research aircraft to its date with destiny. *Courtesy of Archives II, College Park, Maryland*

The Bell X-1 (née XS-1) was an admission by NACA that there were limitations to the high-speed capabilities of their wind tunnels. Pressed by the irrepressible Langley aerodynamicist John Stack, NACA selected the Bell Aircraft Company to build the first of the X series aircraft. This meant a move to the great wind tunnel in the sky, and the location would be over the Mojave Desert oper-ating out of the Muroc Army Air Base on Rogers Dry Lake. Earlier, Muroc had been used for initial tests of the first U.S. jet fighter, the Bell P-59, followed rather quickly by the more promising Lock-heed P-80.

From the start the X-1 was designed for one purpose—ex-ploring the realm of transonic flight by a manned aircraft, includ-ing just beyond Mach one. It had no other function. Walt Williams, who was assigned by the director of the Langley Research Center in Virginia to head up the National Advisory Committee for Aero-nautics (NACA) operations at the Muroc Air Base in 1946, tells of a visit by a Marine general to the X-1 operations in 1947. He doesn't recall the general's name, only that he wore wings and more than one star. The general circled the little research craft several times, inspecting it more carefully with each circuit. Finally, he stopped and inquired half rhetorically, "But where are the guns?"—then shrugged and walked away with much the same frustration as that of the sailor who, having boated a beautiful mermaid, returned her to the sea after a brief, albeit perceptive, assessment as to the possibility of any truly meaningful relationship.

The X-1 was not designed to operate like a normal aircraft. It did have landing gear, but only for setting down on the dry lake after its weight had been reduced by some 5,000 pounds of rocket propellants, or more than 40 percent of its launch weight. Except for one abortive attempt to prove otherwise near the end of its useful life, in order to accomplish its research tasks the X-1 had to be carried aloft in the tummy of its B-29 mother ship to a launch altitude of 20,000 feet or greater.

The North American XP-86: Victory Margin in an Unforeseen War

By any measure one might care to choose, the North American *Mus-tang* was the finest fighter of World War II. Key members of the team that created the P-51, by some happy confluence of leadership and enthusiastic confidence in their destiny, stayed together to go for similar laurels in the newly emerging world of jet fighters. And once again it all came together for them.

But let me diverge for a moment. I have just ensconced the *Mustang* at the apex of the great ziggurat for fighter aircraft of the last (and only) really big air war. How can I say that? Although I saw out that war as a Marine platoon leader, it was an experience that greatly enhanced an early romance with aviation. At the end of the fracas, as quickly as possible I pushed my way into flight training. My World War II vintage fighter became the Chance Vought *Corsair*—that beautifully long-nosed powerhouse with the inverted gull wing.

Earlier, in June 1944, I recall watching these blue beauties roar over the officers' club at the Naval Air Station, Jacksonville, Florida, barely clearing the trees as they clawed for altitude, props in fine pitch conveying their special message to a bevy of stunningly fair maidens sunning around the pool to not waste too much time with the black-shoe sailors and mud Marines—your flyboy will be back before sundown. We were fresh-caught Navy ensigns and Marine brass-bar cadets just released from the boat school at Annapolis and sent to Jacksonville for two weeks of aviation indoctrination before entering the fray. We had been graduated one day after D-Day, the 6th of June. The quickly devised introduction to the rudiments of air operations was a measure of how swiftly the steep learning curve of combat had forced the replacement of battleship admirals with those who had acquired some savvy about airplanes

Bent-wing widow-makers they called the *Corsairs* then. It was an apt sobriquet. The big fighters with their inverted gull wings seemed so full of grace as they arced skyward, but from the cockpit they were a handful—and a footful. Advance the throttle too briskly for takeoff and you'd better be standing on that right rudder. Otherwise, the torque from 2,000 horses revving a 14-foot prop at 2,800 turns per minute is going to pull you and your bent-wing off into the marshy weeds and cattails on the left side of the runway. Absent a fire, you could probably walk away from that and have a chance to explain it all to the Accident Board. And maybe even get to try it again.

Once safely airborne, you're not home free. Control force changes with variations in speed, and adjustments to power are high. The *Corsair* pilot is forever resetting rudder and elevator trim to minimize maneuvering forces and optimize his ability to exact that ultimate in agility an aptly flown *Corsair* can display. And suppose you're practicing combat maneuvering—rat racing, some call it. Your opponent is on your tail. Pull up into a sharp left turn, apply full power, and wind it up close to the stall. Close but not into it. Get real close and maybe you can do a quick reverse and gain the advantage. Wind up on his tail. Overdo it, stall that wing, and *whammo*, the left wing drops out from under you and you've snapped into an inverted spin. In which case, there better be several thousand feet between you and terra firma or you are about to join your ancestors.

There were also challenges in the landing pattern, and in taxiing behind that fourteen feet of fuselage and engine cowling stretching to the front and upward from the windscreen. I'm a pretty short fellow, barely making the minimum standards of that era for admission to the Naval Academy. (It's not clear they have such standards anymore.) If I got long in the groove coming aboard the aircraft carrier, I'd have to fly the final portion of the pattern in a right skid to keep the landing signal officer in sight.

Yes, occupying the *Corsair* cockpit was quite an experience. Learning to handle it effectively was kind of like breaking a wild mustang. Once mastered, it was one of the very best. On the other hand, the real *Mustang*, North American species, was tamed early by its designers. For decades I have watched stunt pilot Bob Hoover do crazy things down low in his P-51 at air shows and speculated on his insurance rates. And then, as recently as August 1994, I finally got my first ride in a *Mustang* and learned up close what a truly splendid product those Inglewood engineers had wrought—and in a dramatically short time, 160 days from first sketches to first flight. Today, with the magic of computer-aided design and modern management techniques plus a barnful of owlish bureaucrats, the gestation period for a new fighter is more like ten years, with abortion and stillbirth constant threats along the way.

The particular *Mustang* I was privileged to fly never came off the assembly line, so it really had no serial number. Its owner put it together from various components lying around in history's dustbin—a fuselage here, a wing there, a like-new Merlin engine preserved as though waiting for such a rebirth. His cost was more than ten times that paid by the U.S. Army Air Corps in 1943 for a like model. Even so, his investment probably has a value double his cost. In the hot warbird market, *Mustangs* are highly prized. Clear testimony to *Mustang* superiority—in performance, handling qualities, and just pure sex appeal—lies in the fact that there are at least five times as many P-51s in flying status today as any other World War II fighter-type aircraft. So great is the demand for these peerless performers that there are two shops in California that produce for-real, full-size *Mustangs* from scratch at a rate of three or four a year.

Why are the truly dedicated aviation aficionados so in love with the *Mustang*? I was about to find out. On a clear, cloudless day in August, "Lady Jo" was lined up with eight other P-51s on the tarmac of Santa Maria Airport. "Lady Jo" is slightly different from your standard civilianized P-51. Many have squeezed a jump seat behind the pilot where a second occupant can ride, but that's all. Daryl Bond, its creator and owner, wanted more. With the help of his friend and fellow *Mustang* buff Ron Hackworth, who is a Douglas Aircraft veteran, he expanded the space for the second seat into a rear cockpit complete with dual controls and flight instruments. The canopy was stretched but not heightened.

Slithering into the rear seat is quite an acrobatic maneuver. This was especially true for me. A spine-crushing event after encountering high-tension power wires in the course of a soaring contest in New Mexico a decade earlier had left my lower half paralyzed for six weeks, followed by an enduring numbness in the feet, something like wearing ski boots all the time. Trying to act as though septuagenarians routinely do this sort of thing, I entered head first through the narrow opening between the forward canopy bow and the rear cockpit instrument shroud. Somehow I ended up facing forward in the rear seat. The rudder pedals had already been adjusted to accommodate my vertically deprived condition. Once strapped in tightly, I donned the hard hat lent by Ron, hooked up the audio, and checked the intercom.

"All set back here, Daryl."

"Roger."

One flick of the starter switch and the Merlin roared into life. On takeoff, the unique whine of the Rolls-Royce engine with the prop in fine pitch informed all within earshot that there were a lot of horses, 1,600 to be precise, propelling that *Mustang* down the runway. But "Lady Jo" tracked the centerline of the Santa Maria runway without a wobble and in less than 1,000 feet was airborne. A *thunk, thunk* beneath my feet informed me the wheels were in their wells. Objects on the ground shrank quickly into toylike proportions. Our rate of climb was half a mile per minute—not dramatic in the jet world but for War II fighters, very good indeed.

"Give it a go," from the front cockpit.

"I've got it," I said, as I grasped the stick and put my feet on the rudders. Leveling out at 6,000 feet, I essayed two-g turns left and right. From the very outset it was clear, this is one nice airplane.

"Mind if I stall it ?"

"Go ahead."

Power back to idle, hold the nose and wings level. Watch the airspeed bleed down—100 miles per hour, 95, 90, 88, 86, 84, 83—light aileron ripple, 82—a shudder, stick all the way back as the nose fell straight through without a hint of wing dip. Now, power up and pull into a left climbing turn, 60-degree bank angle, check for other traffic—all clear—pull back without watching the airspeed, a shudder as the stick hit the rear stop and the nose again fell through with wings steady as a rock. A glance at the airspeed showed 80 miles per hour. Nose down, power back, and roll into a gliding turn to the right. The same docile behavior. Adding climb power, I returned to 6,000 feet and accelerated to 240 mph. A barrel roll to the left, a slow roll to the right. I felt as though I had been born in this cockpit. Nose over to a speed of 280, stick back to four g's, then full throttle as I pulled into a half loop. As the nose touched the horizon on top, I executed a half roll to wings level and noted the course reversal was almost exactly 180 degrees. Don't press your luck.

"O.K. Daryl, your airplane."

"Got it."

We were nearing the Pacific coastline. Daryl rolled into a dive, pushing the airspeed well above 300. We leveled out parallel to the coast, perhaps a hundred yards from the shoreline and thirty feet above the wavetops. With nothing else to do I tried to count the string bikinis on Pismo Beach, but I ran out of fingers before we ran out of candidates. Daryl chandelled up steeply, turning to the east. There was the Santa Maria Airport less than ten miles inland.

Back on the ground, my once paralyzed legs with still-numb feet found a kind of free floating exuberance. At last I'd had a hands-on understanding of the *Mustang* mystique and was experiencing the euphoria of the teenager who has just been warmly kissed for the first time by his true love. I had enjoyed a long and close relationship with the *Sabres* and knew them to be sprung from a very special heritage—a bloodline of champions. More than thirty-five years since my last *Sabre* flight, I had just experienced a brief tryst with its sire. The long-dormant affection for the perfection I had for years suspected lay there burst into a special rhapsody of redoubled respect. The redoubtable, albeit taciturn, Slim Lindbergh, after his first flight in an early Mustang, pushed his talent for understatement to the limit when he reported, "It is an excellent plane—among the best in the world today."

When this country faced its first great challenge, there was that small cadre of giants—the drafters of the Declaration and the framers of the Constitution—who understood leadership and seized the helm of our infant nation. Similarly, as the threatening clouds of World War II darkened our future, if not our survival, there was a bubbling of aeronautical creativity at a place called North American Aviation. In a sense it was akin to the renaissance of the arts as Florence emerged from the Dark Ages, and to the dominance of the graceful and speedy clipper ships in the middle of the nineteenth century. As the clipper ships were quickly superseded by the greater expediency of the smoke-belching steamers, so the dominant *Mustang-Sabre* heritage of fundamentally great lines of natural grace fell to the limitless possibilities of computer-generated responses—responses that are infinitely more immediate than any human reaction and wholly indifferent to once-sacrosanct demands for now outmoded concepts such as good hands, eagle eyes, and lion hearts.

All of which would have been considered pure persiflage in the fall of 1947, as the North American team sweated to ready its entry in the posterity sweepstakes. In fact, they were wholly unaware of any such race. It was enough to be preparing with their usual insouciance the best possible next-generation fighter for the

U.S. Air Force. If it happened to overtake some hokey little research craft that had to be carried aloft in the belly of its mother ship, that was no concern of theirs.

As it turned out, the *Sabre* was indeed a worthy successor to the *Mustang*. By every standard it was the best fighter plane of its era. Measured by the immutable record of combat, in terms of aircraft shot down, against the best the enemy had to offer, the MiG-15, the *Sabre* enjoyed that eight-to-one (or was it ten-to-one?) advantage in the Korean conflict. This overwhelming demonstration of air superiority was without question the decisive reality that saved South Korea from being taken over by the Communist invaders. Another measure of the remarkable worldwide esteem afforded the swept-wing champion is that thirty-seven nations adopted the *Sabre* as the top-gun fighter for their national arsenals. For the United States, the North American Aviation team that made it all possible will remain a historic national treasure.

4 A Tale of Two Aces

From Wilmington, Delaware, to the Mojave via Pearl Harbor and the South Pacific

For Second Lieutenant George Welch, fighter pilot, U.S. Army Air Corps, the expected Sunday sleep-in after a late and boisterous party at the Wheeler Field Officers' Club would have to wait. The *crump, crump* of the bombs outside his window at the Wheeler BOQ, and the all-too-infrequent rattle of small-caliber return fire put his sorely tested yet still off-the-scale intellect on instant alert. Rushing to the window, he saw the billowing smoke from burning aircraft and the red meatballs on the sides of the attacking Japanese aircraft. His close friend and fellow fighter pilot Ken Taylor stood beside him, transfixed, but just for an instant. Both men swiftly threw on whatever clothes were closest at hand. Ken recalls he ended up wearing the tuxedo trousers he had worn the night before. Saturday nights were more formal in prewar Honolulu. Welch paused at the BOQ office telephone to call the duty

NCO at Haleiwa to have him ready their aircraft with fuel and ammunition. Then together they dashed to Ken's car for a swift drive to the auxiliary field at Haleiwa where their P-40 fighters had been pre-positioned for some gunnery training in the coming week.

Wheeler to Haleiwa is only ten miles as the crow flies but there are a few twists in the road leading through the fields of sugar cane and pineapples to the small grass strip on the northwest shore of Oahu. Thankfully, the road was clear. Ken Taylor recalls seeing speeds as great as 100 miles per hour in the course of the mad dash. At least once they were fired upon by the Japanese attackers. Two P-40s were already turning up, their crew chiefs standing by the cockpits, as Welch and Taylor spun onto the runway and screeched to a halt beside the ready fighters. In an instant, para-chutes were buckled on and the two pilots had vaulted into their cockpits. Donning soft helmets with earphones and goggles, they fastened their seat belts. Experience would later teach them that a few deep breaths of 100 percent oxygen does wonders in clearing the cobwebs of late-night overindulgence. On the morning of December 7, youth, adrenaline, and raw courage would have to do.

Welch was first to motion the crew to pull the chocks and, without waiting for engine or cockpit checks, roared down the run-way. Taylor was but a couple of minutes behind him. But two min-utes on the morning of December 7 on Oahu made a lot of difference. Welch did not have to climb very high to find the enemy, nor look very hard. The meatball emblazoned on the sides of twenty or more Japanese dive bombers (later known as *Vals*) over Barber's Point were picked up by Welch as the Japanese pilots pushed over for their dive on the Marine airstrip at Ewa. Charging his four .30-caliber guns, he attacked the dive bombers and sent a *Val* crash-ing to the ground. One of his guns jammed; and, as he pulled up off of the targets, return fire from one of the enemy tailgunners sent an incendiary round through his aircraft just behind the seat.

Climbing above some low, scattered clouds to check his aircraft, he noted with some satisfaction that Ken Taylor had also splashed one of the *Vals*. Unable to clear his balky gun but finding no other problems, he pushed over to attack another *Val*, apparently heading back to the Japanese task force. This hostile bird was quickly dispatched and splashed into the ocean a mile or so off the West Coast of Oahu. Meanwhile, Taylor also had shot down another of the attackers. The rest had disappeared.

The two P-40s were near Wheeler Field and almost out of ammunition. They landed to refuel and rearm. The field was a mess. The big hangars were ablaze and a number of parked aircraft had been torched, but for a moment there was a lull in the action. Dedicated crew chief Staff Sergeant Cecil Goodroe had sped back from Haleiwa and was waiting on the ramp. Welch stayed in the cockpit as the P-40B was refueled and rearmed. The jammed gun resisted all efforts to unblock its breech. Welch waved the crew away, restarted his engine, and blasted down the runway for takeoff just as another wave of attackers swooped in from the opposite end. Among other things of interest, they were seeking to get a P-40 in their sights. It was Ken Taylor, taking off in the opposite direction. Welch persisted in his takeoff, receiving three enemy rounds in his fighter during the ground roll, but none was critical. He chandelled up as his landing gear retracted, then dove on Taylor's assailant, shooting him down in flames.

He spotted another attacker seeking to retire to his aircraft carrier somewhere to the west. It was the fourth Japanese aircraft to fall to Welch's guns that day, or so the official record reads. Ken Taylor attests that in fact at least two additional victories belong to the feisty young fighter pilot out of Wilmington, but they crashed too far out to sea to be confirmed. Then there was one of the *Vals* that possibly had been hit by ground fire. It appeared that the pilot sought to dive into the power plant at Wheeler Field, kamikaze-fashion, as Welch took up the pursuit. Later in the war, more glory-hungry fighter pilots would have claimed such crashes as personal victories even though no shots were fired. Welch was indifferent to personal scores.

Taylor, who was wounded in the arm by the attacker Welch scraped off his tail, himself had two official victories on that day destined to "live in infamy." Like Welch, he had landed for fuel and ammunition and, despite his wounds, had made his second flight. He recalls scoring hits on two others in the final wave of that day as the pilots of Nippon retired from the fray. In his view they were more than probables but could not be confirmed. Gun camera film had not been loaded for those December 7 flights.

Both Welch and Taylor refueled and rearmed after their second flights and took off a third time, but by then the retreating attackers were out of reach. Those third flights may have been a special but unwitting act of courage. Unknown to them, one of their squadron mates had been brought down by nervous American gunners at Wheeler Field, an early victim of friendly fire.

Earlier that Sunday morning halfway round the world, the skies were clear and cold over a fighter base north of London as two RCAF *Spitfires* lifted off the runway and climbed eastward toward Belgium. There were reports that the Germans had launched an improved version of the Messerschmitt 109, and the fighter forces of Great Britain wanted to know more about it. As the two *Spitfire* pilots approached the coast of Belgium, they were pounced upon, and the wingman was quickly dispatched in flames. The flight commander also was in serious trouble and desperately dove to shake off his attackers. He was heavily hammered by his assailants. One of the Messerschmitt pilots later observed that the *Spitfire* pilot had slumped over his controls—unconscious or dead. His fighter did not burn but slid to a halt onto the Belgian beach near Breedene. Nazi soldiers appeared on the scene and pulled the pilot's body from his aircraft. He was Fuller Patterson, an American and an early boyhood hero of mine.

Fuller was the original golden boy—scholar, athlete, leader, and restless searcher for new challenges in most any field at home and abroad. He first attended my old school, St. Christopher's in Richmond, and then moved to rival Woodberry Forest some sixty miles to the northwest. He was an honor student at Princeton and an Olympic-class pole vaulter in an era when records attested to the athleticism of the vaulter rather than to the peculiar structural dynamics of the pole. He earned his civil pilot license while at Princeton. During his second year at Harvard Law School, Fuller abruptly abandoned academic pursuits to assist in Britain's desperate battle for survival. In April 1940 he went to Toronto and joined the RCAF. Six months later he earned his RCAF wings, finishing at the top of his class. The RCAF insisted that he remain as an instructor. He was not happy about that. When the second American Eagle Squadron was formed in March 1941, he insisted on a transfer and was granted permission to join, showing up for duty in April. At the time of his demise, he had baled out of flaming *Spitfires* twice, crashed once, and had two forced landings.

Not long before his final flight, he had written in a letter home:

> If this is where I get mine, up there where it is cold and clear, on a battlefield where the dead don't lie about and rot, where there is no mud and no stench, where there is moonlight by night and stars, and in the day the wizardry of intriguing cloud formations, and a blue sky above where a man is free and Jerry take the hindmost; if I get mine up there, there must be no regrets. I would have it that way. It is unfortunate that those of us who love life the most, the very ones who so keenly seek to live the fullest life possible, must take the long chances that in so many cases cut it short. We are not blind to the odds against us; true, we laugh at them or think lightly of them, but that is because we would have it no other way. I pity those, who in living, live in fear of death.

Fuller's last mission against the Nazi onslaught occurred on December 7, 1941. He was twenty-six years old. Before the remains of the gallant *Spitfire* pilot could be laid to rest, ten hours westward in the Pacific the clarion call to fill the insistent demand for heroes from the willing reservoir of our nation's youth was being sounded. It was still an era when virtually the entire nation would treat with utter loathing any who shirked that call. It would seem that true heroes never die; they just pass the torch.

In the immediate aftermath of the Pearl Harbor attack, assigning blame took a rear seat to selecting heroes. Senior staff on Oahu wanted to award the two young second lieutenants the Medal of Honor, but when a review was made in the lower echelons it was decided that this was too great an honor. After all, those crazy fighter pilots had acted without orders. Besides, the United States was not at the time in a state of war with Japan. They were decorated instead with the Distinguished Service Cross, which ranks just below the star-spangled sky-blue ribbon. The ceremony took place at Wheeler Field on January 8, 1942.

In an interview a few months later, on May 19, Welch stated that "Fighter Command called us (at Haleiwa) and requested (?) us to take any pursuit (that is, fighter aircraft) we had and proceed to Barber's Point at 8,000 feet." There may be those who question whether such a communication constitutes an unequivocal order. On the other hand, many might agree that any fighter pilot who got airborne that day to challenge the treacherous attackers deserved something more than just a medal.

Ask Pete Everest about George Welch. "You mean 'Wheaties'?" he will ask. Then with half a smile and a slow shaking of his head, as if seeking a phrase to encapsulate the incredible—"One crazy-ass guy." Now, Pete isn't exactly any run-of-the-mill used car salesman. An Air Force brigadier general, retired for a decade or so and living in Arizona, he flew fighters for the Army Air Corps in the Pacific and claimed one victory before being bagged himself, surviving the experience to spend the balance of the conflict as a prisoner of the Japanese forces in China.

In 1950, Lieutenant Colonel Everest showed up at Edwards Air Force Base as a test pilot and soon was head of the Fighter Test Branch. By 1952 he had become director of Experimental Flight Test, succeeding the renowned Colonel Fred Ascani. A major named Chuck Yeager became Everest's deputy and close friend. On May 25, 1953, Pete was chase pilot for George Welch's first flight in the YF-100A *Super Sabre*. He lost a two-beer bet to Welch when George took the *Super Sabre* supersonic in level flight on its very first flight. As if to emphasize his point lest historians ignore the event, as they had his similar invasion of the supersonic regime more than five years earlier, "Wheaties" did it again on the second flight of the same *Super Sabre* prototype, later that same day. Just imagine—taking a brand-new prototype fighter through the sound barrier on its very first flight, and then, before the sun went down, doing it again on the second flight. Makes faster-than-sound seem a fairly pedestrian venture.

Supersonic excursions were by then getting to be a trademark with the North American test pilot. Witnesses on the ground, at least those living in the Antelope Valley, were beginning to associate the double crack *ba-boom* that on occasion rattled their crockery with technological progress. There were at least a couple of spectacular boomers still ahead for Welch. But it is those earlier sonic signatures that Wheaties laid on the Joshua trees and sagebrush of the Mojave Desert floor that are of most interest to aviation buffs and serious aeronautical historians, especially the ones that occurred early in October 1947.

Nevertheless, the example Welch set in the YF-100, that of going supersonic on the first flight of a newly designed fighter, became an event essential for entry into the new era, which was soon reaching well beyond Mach one—essential but not necessarily sufficient to claim the next big production contract. Thus, less than nine months following Welch's supersonic first flight of the

Super Sabre, the dean of the fighter fraternity and chief test pilot for Lockheed Aircraft, Tony LeVier, flew a supersonic outing for the XF-104 *Starfighter* on its first flight with an afterburner installed some time after February 7, 1954, which marked the first

George Welch in flight gear standing in front of the F-86, 1948. *Courtesy of the San Diego Aerospace Museum*

flight with a non-afterburning engine. That date is believed to have been February 28, 1954, on which occasion, Tony upped the ante by accelerating the little "missile with a man in it" past 1,000 miles per hour—also a first for manned fighters. On September 29, Bob Little, chief test pilot for McDonnell Aircraft, flew the F-101A *VooDoo* past Mach one in level flight in its first time in the air. Six months on the heels of that caper, John Konrad, Vought Aircraft's chief test pilot, turned the XF8U-1 *Crusader* loose on its initial flight, on March 25, 1955. Like the *Super Sabre* and the *VooDoo* before him, his *Crusader* slid effortlessly past the Mach one mark while holding constant altitude. It was but ten days after the first anniversary of Welch's tragic demise that yet another advanced fighter prototype, the YF-105A *Thunderchief*, under the skilled guidance of Republic Aviation's test pilot Rusty Roth, demonstrated supersonic capabilities on its first flight, on October 22, 1955.

The first-flight supersonic daisy chain came full circle when Wheaties's successor as North American's chief engineering test pilot, Bob Baker, took the prototype YF-107A past Mach one on its first flight, on September 10, 1956. Perhaps it was a special salute to George Welch, who had issued the initial challenge to do it on the first flight in his *Super Sabre*. Some may even have recalled his earlier booming of the Mojave as he dove the simpler *Sabre* past sonic speed to rattle the dusty dude ranch known as Pancho's, but whether it was on the first flight or soon thereafter none can remember.

Next in line was the Convair YF-106, which the company's test pilot Dick Johnson flew for the first time the day after Christmas in 1956, and there the chain was broken. Unable to fully retract the nose gear, the new Mach two interceptor was constrained to fly below limit speeds for its first flight. That constraint was quickly remedied, and the delta-winged fighter slid easily past Mach one on its second flight. A similar glitch was encountered when Bob Little first flew the McDonnell XF4H-1 *Phantom* on May 27,

1958. He also had to be content with making his entry boom on flight number two. The ardor of announcing the first ascent of a new fighter with a big *ba-boom* over Rogers Dry Lake was cooled. Thenceforth, pragmatic heads prevailed, rationality returned to the development programs, and the safety gods were appeased. With the cutting edge of competitive exuberance quietly slaked by a new conservatism, the pioneer spirit surrendered with one more admission that élan must eventually give way to sound judgment.

Even so, history should not carelessly dismiss the quiet confidence, the cool competence of that particular sextet of test pilots—Welch, LeVier, Little, Konrad, Roth, and Baker. These were the pilots who in the very first flight of the prototypes of six brand-new jet fighters so assertively epitomized the early supersonic era of the 1950s, blithely zipping through the stonily mischaracterized "sonic wall" as they raced on to higher, faster milestones marking man's determined reach for the stars. The challenges to follow would lie more and more in the realm of the blistering heat that commenced rising to metal-melting temperatures not far beyond Mach two, and the growing necessity for electronic devices that respond far swifter than man and, when cleverly programmed, in a much smarter manner. Suffice it to note that the leader of the parade was North American Aviation's chief test pilot, George Welch, while closing out this unbroken string of first-flight *ba-boom*ers was Wheaties's successor at North American, Bob Baker.

It is no longer *de rigueur* to boom the countryside on the first flight of a new fighter. Indeed, it is not at all clear that a supersonic capability of any kind is a must for the fighters of the twenty-first century. After years of gestation the F-22 made its first flight in the fall of 1997, flew three or four flights, then was packed off for detailed studies of the data gathered and further ground tests. It has not yet flown faster than 300 knots. The highly touted B-2 strategic bomber, which soaks up close to two billion dollars per copy, is content to speed toward its targets at 0.7 Mach number.

The originator of the first-flight *ba-boom* tradition for new American fighters, George Schwartz Welch, was born in Wilmington, Delaware, on May 18, 1918. His birth certificate reads George Louis Schwartz, Junior, son of George Louis Schwartz and Julia Welch Schwartz. George senior was a research chemist with the Du Pont Company. His great-grandfather had arrived in the United States in the 1830s. He grew up in Seattle and graduated from the University of Washington, as did his bride, who was of British ancestry. During World War I and later, as the war in Europe was heating up for the second time, the German name and his sensitive position in a premier defense industry made him an easy target for paranoid spy-catchers. He was often accosted and, on one occasion, even jailed for a brief period before his credentials could be clearly established. The Schwartzes were determined that young George, along with brother Dehn, two years his junior, were not to be subjected to the mindless anti-German sentiment that was coked up during and immediately following the "war to end all wars" and was still a source of discomfort as Hitler rose to power. Consequently, the boys' last names were legally changed to Welch, and each carried the middle initial "S" for Schwartz. One story had it that the name was taken off a grape juice label. No one bothered to check the mother's family Bible. Certainly, after leaving Wilmington, George never discouraged speculation that he was in some way connected with, perhaps even an heir of, the grape juice magnates.

The elder Schwartz was obviously a well-regarded senior researcher with Du Pont. Both boys finished their secondary education at St. Andrew's, an Episcopal boarding school in Middletown, Delaware, where they mingled with du Ponts and the sons of other affluent families from along the Eastern seaboard. As at most prep schools of that era, athletics were given an importance almost equal to that reserved for academics. This was especially true for football. Since it was a small school, there were only fourteen members of the senior class that graduated in 1937. A sport that demanded eleven players put a strain on the St. Andrew's roster, even though in those days everyone played both offense and defense. Few excuses were accepted. George was only five feet eight inches tall and quite slender. Still, agile and fit, he was told to suit up for the team. An earlier childhood trauma induced him to complain, "I'll break my collar bone." In his first play from scrimmage, he met the team's hard-charging fullback head on and retreated to the bench holding his left arm. "I just broke my collar bone," he reported rather matter-of-factly and without a grimace. Clinical examination proved that to be the case. Thereafter, George was assigned waterboy duties in support of the St. Andrew's team. In his senior year, he was the team's manager.

For someone voted by his senior year classmates as their "laziest" member, George managed the academic hurdles of St. Andrew's easily. He was particularly adept in physics and chemistry. Looking back over more than fifty years, when asked to characterize the slight lad from Wilmington who had been nicknamed "cowboy," one classmate noted that George was, well, "messy." Did that mean that his clothes were frequently in disarray? No, rather that he was perhaps an infrequent bather. He also had the habit, disturbing to some, of lighting one cigarette from another.

In June 1937, Welch graduated from St. Andrew's School. He was nineteen years old. That fall he entered Purdue University as a mechanical engineering student. He was already itching to enter aviation and saw the military as the preferred route. The problem was that both the Army and the Navy required at least two years of college before he could become eligible for flight training. George was a better than average student at Purdue but he remained focused on getting into military aviation. Upon successful completion of his sophomore year, he applied to the Army's aviation cadet program and was accepted pending an opening. The war in Europe was heating up and many American youths wanted to join the fray, recognizing that it was but a matter of time until the United States would be a player in that struggle. Enlistments were up, especially for would-be aviators, where the waiting line was a long one.

As George returned to Purdue in the fall of 1939, Germany was completing its blitzkrieg of Poland in cynical association with the Russian Communists. Many of his peers were already in flight training with the RCAF in Canada and getting ready to join in the Battle of Britain. Impatiently marking time in his third year on the Indiana campus, George switched his course of study from engineering to science, perhaps in the belief that such courses might be more relevant to the meteorology and navigation he must cope with in flight training. He mastered the courses without difficulty. It mattered little. At the end of the first semester he departed for Randolph Field, having been sworn in as an aviation cadet in the U.S. Army Air Corps.

In February 1940 the so-called Phoney War was exposing the woeful inadequacies of French and British forces in Western Europe, allowing the Germans all the options they needed to coil and strike how, when, and where they pleased. At the same time, the Soviets had bitten off far more than they could chew in seeking what they had thought would prove an easy conquest of Finland. In the Far East, the Japanese were consolidating their hold on coastal China, while England and France sought accommodation with them. A fearful United States began to restrict its shipments of scrap iron and petroleum products, which had been supporting the Japanese war machine.

Upon winning his wings and a commission in January 1941, Second Lieutenant George S. Welch was assigned to the 47th Fighter Squadron based at Wheeler Field on the island of Oahu. The 47th had been activated in December 1940 with Captain (soon to be Major) Gordon H. Austin commanding. The squadron was initially equipped with eighteen Boeing P-26A and B aircraft. These open-cockpit monoplanes with fixed landing gear were replaced in May with fourteen Curtiss P-40B's, one P-40C, and fourteen Brewster

P-36A's. There were also an old Martin B-12A twin-engine bomber and an even more ancient Douglas BT-2B biplane trainer, assigned for target towing, instrument proficiency, and other liaison work.

Welch lived in bachelor quarters at the Wheeler Field Officers' Club. Fighter pilots, especially bachelor fighter pilots, were generally in great demand for the social whirl that the residents of Oahu used to mask their uneasiness at being on the ramparts for stopping further Japanese expansion in the Pacific. The recently concluded Battle of Britain had greatly burnished the image of all fighter pilots as a romantic, devil-may-care band of brothers who jousted with death from dawn through sunset. George was certainly not one to jeopardize such a view. He entered into the social activities on the island with an enthusiasm only slightly less energized than his determination to maximize his flying skills.

One evening there was a big bash at the Royal Hawaiian Hotel, but George was not on the list of invited guests. Undeterred, he donned his flight suit, drove his car to Waikiki Beach, buckled on his parachute, and slid quietly into the surf just west of the party. When he reached a point abreast of the Royal Hawaiian, he popped his 'chute and, silk canopy cradled in his arms, strode out of the breakers and onto the hotel's beachside dance floor, just as any fighter pilot would, especially if the party looked good from above and his engine sounded pretty rough anyway. He was the hit of the evening, but maybe somewhat less popular with the parachute rigger the next morning.

Going swimming in his flight garb seems to have been habit forming with George. When the squadron transitioned from the old P-26 fighters to the much better performing P-40 *Tomahawks*, the vintage BT-2B was still retained, principally for instrument proficiency flights. It was an underpowered two-seat biplane with fixed landing gear and uninspiring flight characteristics. As a matter of squadron policy, all pilots had to stay current in the BT-2B and occasionally share tow duty in this awkward beast, even though a somewhat less ancient B-12A twin-engine bomber had recently been added to the squadron's inventory. The twin was a much better towplane, but the cranky BT-2B was retained as backup and for remembering what it's like to fly in the murk on the gauges.

In the late spring of 1941, the 47th Fighter Squadron deployed to nearby Bellows Field for gunnery training. The ungainly BT-2B was deployed for support duties. To avoid the midday heat, flying started at 5:00 A.M. and was usually concluded well before noon. The balance of the day was clear for recreational pursuits. All personnel lived in tents pitched on the beach. At the completion of flying one day, the pilots were grousing about what a beast the BT-2B was to fly, and speculating as to why they should be burdened with such an antique.

Quietly contemplating this scene, Welch turned to his good friend and fellow fighter pilot Charlie Parrett: "Charlie, you're due for some instrument time." The two strode over to the big old biplane with squadron mate Ken Taylor. Abruptly, Welch pulled off his wristwatch and told Taylor, "Hold this." Then George and Charlie climbed into the ancient clunker, fired it up, and took off. Those on the ground watched as the BT-2B lumbered west over the ocean, then turned about from a couple of miles out and headed back toward the beach. The biplane appeared to be losing altitude. Its engine sounded rough and sputtery—or was George cutting the switch? Maybe a half mile out, the engine quit altogether. Turning to parallel the beach, the old bird contacted the water at very close to stall speed. When the wheels hit the water, everyone gasped as the tail rose and the fuselage pitched forward. It looked for sure that it would flip over on its back. That would make it very difficult for the two pilots, George and his buddy Charlie, to disengage from their straps before being carried down to the bottom, especially after a sharp slap on the head by the water. (Later, as the war got under way with considerable heat, the Navy devised the Dilbert dunker, which was a trainer designed to teach air crews how to get out of carrier aircraft that had flipped over on their backs, in just such a situation, when forced to crash land in the ocean. But the Army Air Corps pilots of the 47th Fighter Squadron had not been given that training.)

An audible sigh of relief escaped from the onlookers as the fuselage reached the vertical, all forward momentum ceased, and it then settled back into the water, rightside up. But George seemed to be hung up on something in the cockpit, and the airplane was sinking fast. The cockpit was disappearing below the surface as George and Charlie broke loose and started swimming for the beach. Half the pilots in the squadron rushed into the water to help pull them up onto the dry sand in their soggy flight suits.

Shaking off the water like a soaked puppy, the day's hero retrieved his watch from Ken Taylor, and, observing that it looked as though flying was finished for the day, he led the group to the mess tent. It might even be a good time for someone to buy a round of cold beer, or maybe two. Explanations could be presented later, if anyone up the line really cared. Obviously, a tough situation had been created by a sudden loss of power, not an infrequent circumstance in those days, and had been handled quite well by the future ace. It was two days after his twenty-third birthday. The remains of the old biplane were pulled ashore the following week by a salvage crew, perhaps because it presented a hazard to maritime activity. There wasn't much of value remaining.

Some kind of weirdo, that Welch? No doubt. But also decisive, bordering on the impulsive. At the same time George Welch was a very quick study, rapidly absorbing and sorting a mass of varied information and responding swiftly to master a new challenge, whether it be a Mach-busting new fighter or a bra-busting young nymph. The former was still a few years off in a most misty future. The latter proved an ever clear and present danger, both in the course of post-Pearl Harbor War Bond rallies and along Sydney's Bondi Beach during respites from the air battles over New Guinea.

A hasty cleanup of the debris left by the surprise attack, a brief time-out for funeral services and medal awards, then it was back to intensive combat patrols. Welch was flying almost daily, often two or three times a day and occasionally four flights in a single twenty-four-hour period. One night, according to his flight log, he encountered a Japanese flying boat. Whether it was shot down and if so by whom is not to be found in the records. His December 7 entries read, after the usual "combat patrol," only "the real McCoy." In February 1942 he flew thirty-four missions, accumulating forty-six flight hours without any reported enemy contact. In mid-May, it was determined by the powers responsible for such decisions that while awaiting a more productive closure with the enemy, when the Army Air Forces could be securely established on bases whence the Japanese advance toward Australia could be halted, George Welch, hero of Pearl Harbor, could make a greater contribution to the war effort by returning to the States and helping to sell War Bonds. It was a strenuous three months that established at least two things: George Welch was not the Air Corps' most effective public speaker, and there is a limit to the amount of adulation that even a virile twenty-four-year-old fighter pilot can gracefully absorb.

By mid-August he was more than relieved to return to his primary love—flying fighters. In September, his first full month of refresher flying out of Wheeler Field on Oahu, he flew forty-seven missions, accumulating nearly fifty-two hours. Mid-October found him once again in a real combat zone with the 36th Fighter Squadron flying P-39D's from the base at Milne Bay on the southeastern tip of the big island of New Guinea. At the end of November, the squadron was transferred to a field near Port Moresby. It is said by some of his squadron mates that George didn't always claim the aircraft he shot down, especially if there was only one in the course of a mission. However, on the first anniversary of Pearl Harbor, as a kind of reminder, Welch became a fighter ace with three confirmed victories—two *Val* dive bombers and one *Zero* fighter—giving him an official total of seven.

One of the problems for pilots of the 36th Fighter Squadron flying from Port Moresby in the sadly deficient Bell *Airacobras* was that the nearby 80th Fighter Squadron was flying the much classier Lockheed P-38 twin-engine *Lightnings*. When Welch inquired when the 36th might expect to move up to the superior P-38s, known by opposing Japanese pilots as the "fork-tailed devil," he was told that this would occur when they ran out of P-39s. Wrong answer. George Welch was becoming an expert at meeting the challenge of getting rid of inferior aircraft. Engine failures over the placid waters of Redscar Bay just northwest of Port Moresby became the order of the day and the despair of the squadron's maintenance chief.

Getting out of a "disabled" P-39 wasn't exactly a snap. For access to the cockpit, the little fighter had side doors with windows that rolled up and down like the ones on a hardtop coupe, only smaller. Even when the little *Airacobra* was sitting on the ramp, climbing in or out with a parachute strapped on wasn't all that easy. Airborne, once a door was jettisoned, there was the slipstream to contend with and then the wing. The leading edge of the wing was lined up with and just below the front edge of the door; for the most risk-free departure, however, the pilot would like to go beneath the wing. Otherwise, there was a strong probability he might be impaled on the horizontal tail. Thus, the procedure was to fall or dive from the cockpit toward the wing's leading edge and roll forward so as to drop below the wing and miss a painful encounter with the empennage. Not a really big deal—still, it was something to talk about during the evening beer call as pilots of the 36th Fighter Squadron sought better survival prospects by moving into a more respectable fighter. Discussion of the least hazardous technique for abandoning the noncompetitive P-39 got everyone's attention, especially if there happened to be present

someone who really understood the challenge and had successfully completed the maneuver.

The goal was made more difficult as a number of P-400s
started showing up in the theater. The P-400s were P-39s that had
been built for the RAF but which the British, despite their desperate straits, had turned down as inferior to their *Hurricanes* and
Spitfires. So these second-rate fighters were divided between the
Russians, who very much liked the *Airacobra*'s 37-millimeter gun
for low-altitude tank busting, and the U.S. forces in the southwest
Pacific, where they were used to intercept air assaults by the Japanese on New Guinea and northern Australia. Official Army Air Force
historians would later admit that "the *Airacobra*, even in a good
state of repair, was unable to meet the Japanese fighters on equal
terms."

Crazy-ass fighter-pilot behavior encompassing a certain
survivor's instinct governed the forced attrition of the P-39s. The
squadron maintenance boss more and more found himself winc-
ing as his *Airacobras* started reporting in on their return from
missions against the Japanese, anticipating an increasingly frequent "Mayday, Mayday," followed by "engine quit" or "out of fuel"
and "bailing out along the beach just south of Moresby." The "engine quit" excuse was a black mark on his job performance record,
whereas "out of fuel"—well, that was pilot error, wasn't it? Even
so, the proximity of the superior *Lightnings* on the adjoining base
and the steady stream of replacements for them informed pilots of
the 36th Fighter Squadron that soon their tired steeds could be
handed over to the training squadrons for the Aussies in Queensland
or just pushed back into the bush along the fighter strips of southeastern New Guinea. Who could blame them for inventing a method
of accelerating their transition to a superior mount? The more
than occasional and quite unceremonious parachute leap from a
smoothly functional, albeit overmatched, P-39 above the placid
waters south of Port Moresby would be followed by a silken,

smooth descent, a short paddle in the yellow life raft, and a brief hike to the air base. It all seemed less hazardous than risking an encounter at lousy odds with the more agile *Zeros*. With a little luck, a harbor patrol craft would pick a pilot up, often before his raft was inflated, and give him a much swifter ride to the port. It was clear that the transition for the pilots of the 36th Fighter Squadron from *Airacobras* to *Lightnings* would take but a few months.

For George Welch, then a captain, the transition would have a special dimension—romance. And there was nothing quite so romantic as wartime Sydney. Bereft of their young men by the empire's demands for Australian and New Zealand (ANZAC) forces in North Africa, Sydney was filled with gorgeous, healthy, tanned young ladies desperately lonely, anxiously seeking all the promise of the haunting wartime melodies of the era—"Bluebirds over the White Cliffs of Dover," "I'll See You Again," "Good-bye Sue," "Coming Home on a Wing and a Prayer," and the rest. In the last week of February 1943, George departed for Australia with thirty days' leave. He had flown 258 missions, 139 since returning from the War Bond trip. With seven confirmed victories over enemy aircraft in aerial combat, he was a bona fide ace. He wore the Distinguished Service Cross, second only to the Medal of Honor. Australia was filled with Yanks—Yanks on their way to the combat zone, Yanks on leave, Yanks in hospital, Yanks on their way home, and Yanks AWOL, determined never to leave such a paradise. And there were many anxious mums, especially those with radiantly nubile daughters.

For George Welch, certified hero, a special path was cut. From his arrival he had introductions to the top echelons of the social whirl, and he sorted it all out very quickly. His Air Force buddies regaled him with the free beer and easy conquests to be found in the pubs of King's Cross. But George had already zeroed in on a much classier act lodged in a very upscale section of Sydney: short, trim, with dark brown hair and sparkling dark-brown eyes topped by heavy eyebrows, and beneath, a mischievous smile that seemed to say most anything you wanted it to say. Indifferent to fashion, she dressed casually and gave little thought to her makeup. Her name was Janet Williams. George and Jan met during the early part of his Australian leave. It was late summer "down under" and the beaches were magnificent. She loved diving in the brilliantly clear coves around Sydney and spearfishing just beyond the breakers. He was an eager pupil. She regaled him with tales from the Great Barrier Reef, and he was determined to share that experience with her. It was as if they had known each other forever and no one else in the world mattered. The intervening conflict up in New Guinea and beyond—it would play itself out one way or another. No need to talk about it right now.

What mattered for the moment was the Great Barrier Reef and how they might get there for a few days of fabulous diving before George's leave expired. Somehow they cadged enough gas coupons and made it to Townsville, in the center of the barrier reef coastline. Townsville was also adjacent to a large operations base for U.S. and Australian fighters. George had it figured that they would play out his leave on the reef and he would check in when it expired at the American detachment at Townsville, where he could arrange transport back to his unit at Port Moresby.

Life on the reef was a huge slice of indulgence being greeted on successive days with even greater unfathomable wonder, coupled with the magic of exploding passion that remained blessedly too brief for the inevitable faultlines to show. It was a period blissfully lost in time. But that's not the way the Army Air Corps saw it. George was over leave—AWOL—and that meant a court-martial. When he floated in off of cloud nine at the Townsville facility, the colonel in charge was ready to put him in the stockade. After all, this was wartime. George got on the teletype to Port Moresby, the telephone to Sydney. He explained that the boat that was to have picked them up from their island on the reef was two days late, etc., etc. As the problem drifted higher up the chain of command, cooler heads came into play. The war was still young, experienced fighter pilots were at a premium, and bona fide heroes were not to be dumped unceremoniously into the brig. A compromise was reached. Welch would spend the final three weeks of April in Queensland assisting in the tactical training of Australian pilots. He would be flying out of Mareeba, near Cairns. Quixotically, he spent over a week back in Townsville showing the Aussies all about an Australian version of the Douglas SBD dive-bomber. Had Jan stuck around, just in case? War can be wholly bearable, especially when you're young.

George did return to his old squadron in May and resumed fighter sweeps to the east and the north. He was still flying the old *Airacobras*, but the continuing forced attrition finally paid off. In mid-May he was transferred to the 80th Fighter Squadron flying the P-38 *Lightning*. This was a vast improvement over his previous mounts. Still flying out of Port Moresby, the fighter sweeps grew longer, and time in the cockpit was often double that in the old P-39s. On June 21, George nailed two *Zeros* and was credited with a third as probable. Then on August 20, during a five-hour mission escorting bombers over Weewak, Welch shot down three *Tonys*. These single-engine fighters were the only serious attempt by the Japanese to use liquid-cooled engines. The *Tony* very much re-sembled the *Mustang*, but it was a resemblance in appearance only. Engine reliability for the *Tony* remained a serious problem for its entire service life.

Two weeks later, George closed out his combat career in an-other remarkable long-endurance escort mission to Weewak. This time three *Zeros* fell victim to his guns plus a *Dinah*. Of the *Dinah*, William Green, the famous chronicler of combat aircraft of World War II, writes: "One of the cleanest and most efficient warplanes to see service during the Pacific War, this beautifully contoured monoplane was regarded as the masterpiece of the Japanese air-craft industry." A high-performance twin-engine aircraft very similar in characteristics to the *Lightning*, the *Dinah* was originally outfitted for reconnaissance. Later, against the B-29s, it was configured with guns as an interceptor. The *Dinah* that fell to Welch's guns that September morn could run but not fight.

Before the middle of September, George began to realize he had a serious health problem. He had recently been promoted to major and had the seniority to keep his name off the schedule for the long escort missions. But the fever and nausea persisted. He flew a short local mission in a P-39 and tried again the next day in an old P-40. On this second attempt to shake off his bug, he abandoned the flight after twenty minutes and checked in with the medics. He had a full-blown case of malaria. George's war was over. Since December 1941, he had flown 348 missions and shot down at least sixteen enemy aircraft. The facilities on New Guinea were crude at best and the weather swampy. The Pearl Harbor hero and triple ace was evacuated to the 118th General Hospital, Sydney.

It is not clear whether it was the much improved weather, the advanced clinical capabilities at the hospital, or the social environment that was responsible; most probably it was a happy coincidence of all three. In any event, George made a rapid recovery. Jan was in frequent attendance. After a debilitating couple of weeks, the fever abated and a modest appetite returned. As flesh returned to his frame, George regained his penchant for mischief. Although not yet discharged as a patient, he felt good enough to sneak away from the ward one day, borrow an old biplane trainer from the Aussies, and beat up a nearby beach where Jan was getting a bit of sun. Not long thereafter, on October 23, he apparently felt very good indeed, since that was the date of the Welch-Williams wedding in Sydney. Major and Mrs. George S. Welch, U.S. Army Air Corps, returned to the States, where, after home leave, exhaustive debriefings, and a number of bond rallies, George found himself stationed in Florida in an air tactics development and training operation. The war was just beginning to heat up for the Americans and the demand for morale boosters on the home front was high. There were many calls for the young hero to make public appearances, and the Air Corps made sure George was available.

When not on tour, Welch was flying a wide range of fighters and other combat aircraft. It was in the spring of 1944 that Welch was visited by Ed Virgin, chief of Engineering Flight Test and chief engineering test pilot of North American Aviation. As noted earlier, Welch had been one of two fighter pilots recommended to Dutch Kindelberger by Hap Arnold when the North American leader was looking for a test pilot to inject combat smarts into new fighter design. The other candidate, Fred Borsodi, had turned down the North American offer. George accepted with a genuine sense of challenge. Within a few weeks he had moved to Los Angeles with his new Australian bride and was busily engaged in the flight testing of new variations of the *Mustang*.

From Hamlin, West Virginia, to the Mojave via the Air War over Europe and Wright Field

Having just signed on with North American Aviation as an engineering test pilot, I was making my first visit to the company's operations at Rogers Dry Lake's North Base, a kind of annex to the burgeoning Edwards Air Force Base flight test complex. It was June 17, 1954. I had arrived in a *Navion* with Ray Niles, one of North American's transport pilots, who gave me an en route checkout in the mysteries of flying the little four-place piston-powered aircraft. Convinced that postwar America would feature an airplane for every household, North American had sunk a bundle into the development of the *Navion*, but the huge market failed to materialize. The upscale end of the single-engine personal aircraft market that did evolve was captured by the slicker, faster Beechcraft *Bonanza*. Besides, there is a fundamental incompatability between production methods, marketing techniques, and costs associated with advanced military aircraft and those for light personal models. Beechcraft understood that; North American did not.

An oft-repeated story about the *Navion* relates how an auto industry friend of Dutch Kindelberger, the founder and chairman of North American, asked if Dutch could let him have a new *Navion* for cost. "You bet," Dutch replied, "how about $20,000?" That was more than twice the price being asked by dealers but a very close approximation of its cost. After abandoning the *Navion* as a commercial venture—actually, the project was sold to Ryan Aircraft in San Diego, where it was equally unsuccessful—the company held on to several of the highly utilitarian aircraft to provide transport for people, papers, and small packages between the Los Angeles plant at the LA airport and the desert test sites.

Climbing out of this neat air taxi at the company's North Base facility, I crossed a short stretch of the shimmering lake bed, cement hard in the mid-June sun. The great peanut-shaped expanse of perfectly flat landing surface stretched for over ten miles in the north-south direction and up to five miles east to west. The beige clay surface, smoothed by the winter rains, had long since been baked dry by the desert sun. In the process, the top layer had shrunk to leave a crazed surface—millions of tiny, irregular cracks a quarter to a half inch wide. For even the smaller aircraft tires, it was like a billiard table.

Coming out of the North American hangar was George Welch, then the company's senior engineering test pilot. He was wearing a faded light-blue flight suit and a head full of Shirley Temple blond curls. I suppose in time I'd get used to them. Mind you, this was 1954, not 1965.

"Want a look at the one-oh-four?" he asked.

I fell in step beside him. The Lockheed XF-104 *Starfighter* had flown for the first time in mid-February, but it was still shrouded in secrecy. Unlike the post-Vietnam era, in the midfifties when the

United States had something good our press didn't hand it to the Soviets on a platter because that little old lady from Dubuque had an inalienable right to know all about it. I was quickly learning, however, that in the tight fraternity of experimental pilots there are few secrets. When the job is to expand the limits and to increase human understanding of the physical world, and when your all-too-frail, thinly encased bit of protoplasm is snugly strapped to the tool that is the cutting edge for achieving that expansion, a newly encountered phenomenon, quirk, buzz, or flight-control anomaly is not a matter to be kept secret from other pilots working in the same regime, even though it may be for a different company. Such communications could save an irreplaceable prototype —or your life.

The Lockheed hangar was just a couple of hundred yards across the glimmering dry lake from the North American facility on Edwards North Base. The doors were open. Inside, Herman "Fish" Salmon, veteran Lockheed experimental test pilot, greeted us. Fish and his boss, the renowned Tony LeVier, had done virtually all the flying on the prototype *Starfighter* up to that time. On the morning of our visit, Tony was back at the "Skunk Works," where this latest advance in aeronautical technology had sprung from the creative genius of C. L. Johnson, better known as Kelly.

With no small measure of pride, Fish led us over to the new bird, soon to be dubbed by some insensitive journalist "the missile with the man in it." Even then too many reporters were conjecturing that, in due time, more probably sooner than later, missiles and other manner of unmanned vehicles would replace pilots for all but the most mundane of missions. At that time, professional pride coupled with distrust of a vacuum-tube-dependent technology gave us strong confidence in our job security. Now, nearly fifty years later, I'm not so sure.

Already standing by the sleek new fighter in the shade of the hangar was a man of medium build. He was carefully examining

Captain Charles E. Yeager at the October 1948 First Anniversary celebration of his 1947 supersonic flight, held at Lambert Field, St. Louis. *Courtesy of Archives II, College Park, Maryland*

the razor-sharp leading edges of the unbelievably thin, straight stubby wings. His Air Force flight suit carried faded gold major's leaves embossed on leather and sewn to the shoulder straps of the coveralls. The high forehead that receded on either side of a curly brown widow's peak was liberally sprinkled with freckles.

"Chuck, meet Al Blackburn. He's our new pilot."

The outstretched hand was also freckled. Square and strong, it might have belonged to a blacksmith, or just a good ole country boy from West Virginia. The piercing blue eyes really danced, and the smile that creased his face was as broad and warm and honest as any I can remember. I felt I was being welcomed by the mayor of Muroc into a hallowed company. And in a way, it was kind of like that.

Even before author Tom Wolfe ensconced Chuck Yeager atop the ziggurat, he ranked high in the pantheon of fighter jocks and experimental pilots. As a leatherneck, I was almost ready to concede that he might be nearly as good as Marion Carl, who also had distinguished himself both in combat (eighteen and a half victories as a Marine fighter pilot in the Pacific) and in test flying (a world speed record in the experimental Douglas D-558-1 *Skystreak* and later assaults on speed and altitude marks in the D-558-2 *Skyrocket*). Yeager had recently flown the XF-104 and was excited about its promise—an operational fighter that would be truly supersonic—indeed, one that was predicted to be capable of twice the speed of sound. Before the end of the year, he was scheduled to leave the test center at Edwards for an F-86 *Sabre* squadron in Europe, but he was already looking forward to the day an aircraft like the F-104 would be available for the operational forces.

The *Starfighter* is really a different kind of beast, he warned me. Pull the throttle back too far in the landing approach and you're going to make one big hole about a mile short. The tiny wing, razor-thin and sticking out only seven and a half feet from the fuselage, depends on a generous supply of high-pressure air from the engine compressor. This air is blown over the wing flaps to generate the extra lift required to keep the airplane aloft at the relatively slow speeds dictated for a safe landing. Slow for the F-104 is 180 knots, or more than 200 miles per hour. Boundary layer control is what the engineers call it. Diminish that flow of air directed over the wing flaps, which happens if the engine power is substantially reduced, and, in this new breed of high-performance bird, gravity is going to win the struggle between squeaking it onto the runway and suffering a shortfall that might compress your hips to somewhere up around your jawbone.

Tony and Fish had pretty well wrung the XF-104 out. They had taken it to a maximum speed of 1.85 Mach number, or nearly twice the speed of sound. There was no doubt that when the new J79 engine, recently developed by General Electric, replaced the less powerful Curtiss Wright J65 in the prototype, the airplane would easily exceed Mach two. In fact, Tony later told me that the only reason he didn't get to Mach two in the X-model was that he ran short of fuel. Even the early, low-powered version was still accelerating at Mach 1.85, a not-so-quiet tribute to Kelly Johnson and his "Skunk Works" team.

Fish told us that the handling qualities displayed by the silver sliver of an aircraft were superb, especially in roll. With its tiny wings there was little resistance from the air to inhibit the roll rate, which was probably the quickest of any fighter since the old Grumman F-8F *Bearcat*. However, Tony had encountered one rather nasty problem the first time the XF-104 was flown with large auxiliary fuel tanks attached to the wing tips. Initially these big, streamlined cylinders, each capable of carrying 170 gallons of jet fuel, had no aerodynamic surfaces to provide stability. When LeVier took this configuration to a speed of 400 knots, the wing-tank combination went into a classic case of flutter. Such an aeroelastic phenomenon more often than not proves to be a terminal dysfunction for the aircraft, and too often for the occupant as well.

Tony relates that the wingtip tanks were oscillating through an arc of 30 degrees and he was certain the aircraft was about to self-destruct. Never, he says, was he so close to seeking the safety of his parachute. But his instinct for finding the narrow path to survival, so finely honed over his thousands of hours of air racing and test flying, came together with the structural integrity of that deceptively thin but strong wing, which carried seven spanwise spars rather than the single spar normally found in more conventional designs. Very deliberately, Tony retarded the throttle while gently pulling back on the control stick for the purpose of slowing down and at the same time gaining altitude. In the event one or both wings did come unglued, he would have a little extra sky beneath him for his 'chute to open. Happily the flutter ceased as the airplane decelerated, and both pilot and craft were safely, expeditiously, and oh so carefully returned to the smooth sunbaked surface of Rogers Dry Lake. The addition of some stabilizing tail feathers to the tanks and beefing up the attachment fittings on the wing tips solved the problem.

After Lockheed's experimental pilots had identified most of the major problems with the revolutionary new fighter and had approved the fixes devised by the company's engineers, Yeager flew the XF-104 to make an initial evaluation for the Air Force. His enthusiasm for the potential of the new design generally matched that of the company pilots. Perhaps the *Starfighter* reminded him of the similarly straight-winged but not so slim *Glamorous Glennis*.

On the solution to one basic problem, however, there were strong differences of opinion between the company pilots and the Air Force evaluators. The problem was "pitch-up" associated with the T-tail configuration of the airplane. The horizontal stabilizer of the F-104 is mounted high on the vertical fin. As the pilot pulled back on the control stick to raise the nose of the airplane, there was found to be a point at which the nose continued to rise even though the pilot released his back pressure and pushed forward on the stick to stop it. This "pitch-up" was more often than not followed by entry into a flat spin. Recovery from a flat spin cannot normally be effected through manipulation of the usual flight controls.

Exploration of stalls and spin recovery techniques is done in the course of the company's experimental flight-test phase of all new fighter aircraft. During these tests, a spin chute is invariably mounted in the tail of the test aircraft and is sometimes supplemented by solid propellant rockets in the wing tips and nose or tail to help stop the spin rotation and get the nose down so that normal airflow can be reestablished over the wing and control surfaces. Having found the spin chute to be the only sure way to recover from the pitch-up maneuver, both Tony and Fish were convinced that the best solution for production versions of the *Starfighter* would be a device in the control system that would shake the stick as the aircraft approached the pitch-up regime and actually push the stick forward should the pilot persist in pulling back toward the point of no return. Yeager felt that Air Force fighter pilots are sufficiently well trained to avoid pulling into the pitch-up regime and argued strongly against "garbaging up" a nice flying airplane with gimmicks in the control system. He was certain such overengineering would degrade the excellent flying qualities of the F-104.

This was one that Yeager lost. The shaker-pusher was eventually designed, tested, and installed in the production aircraft as they started coming off the line in late 1956. The device has unquestionably saved the lives of many young *Starfighter* pilots around the world, few of whom sport the Yeager panache. Reinforcing that decision was the tragic loss, in February 1956, of Air Force test pilot and Korean War ace Major Lonnie Moore. Lonnie was lost in a pitch-up-related crash right after liftoff in an F-101 *VooDoo* at Eglin Air Force Base. The F-101 had a T-tail similar to that of the F-104.

I recall sharing the cocktail hour with Lonnie at Patmar's, the traditional watering hole for North American test pilots in that era. It was near the Los Angeles airport. Lonnie was about to leave for Eglin, where he was to join the team testing the *VooDoo's* operational suitability. We argued the potential hazards of pitch-up and the pros and cons of stick shakers. I probably didn't help my side of the argument by pointing out that the story of the Navy's great success in the recent war was that their weapons—warships, aircraft, submarines—were designed by geniuses to be operated victoriously by kids off the farm. Like Yeager, Lonnie wanted no device in the control system that could veto the pilot's command. After all, he was, by God, one helluva fighter pilot. Yeager's much later encounter, in 1963, with loss of control as a result of pitch-up in the NF-104A—a special model with augmenting rocket power (but no stick shaker/snatcher)—would occur at very high altitude. Even so, he barely escaped—and less than unscathed. That ejection and his subsequent collision with the separated seat and its still burning ejection rocket fuel was perhaps his closest brush with the Grim Reaper. Lonnie was not so lucky. Hardly a week after his arrival at Eglin, he encountered his first and only *VooDoo* pitch-up. It occurred on takeoff and the aircraft splattered in a fireball. But we do learn. Like the production F-104s, all F-101s delivered to operational squadrons were equipped with stick shakers and pushers.

My first encounter with Yeager was friendly and professional. He didn't seem to take offense that North American would hire a Marine pilot to test aircraft for the Air Force. Marion Carl had no doubt earned for the Marines a small corner in Chuck's private ready room for test pilots.

Welch and I headed back to the North American hangar at North Base.

"Nice guy," I observed.

"Yeah, and a good stick and rudder man." Welch paused, then decided to elaborate. "We often have to ask the Air Force for a chase plane. Whenever you do that, hope they send Chuck. Whatever the purpose of your flight—structural demo, spins, flutter test—Yeager will stick with you like glue. He has the knack for putting his airplane just where you'd like him to be without your even asking. It's a great talent."

A North American F-86 *Sabre*, on the left, extends its speed brakes in order not to overrun the Bell X-1A, a later, faster version of the Bell X-1, as the two aircraft join up over Rogers Dry Lake. *Courtesy of Archives II, College Park, Maryland*

The purpose of my visit to North Base was to fly some angle of attack calibration flights on an old F-86A, which was being used on a project to develop a new gun sight. I had not flown the *Sabre*, but it was virtually the same as the prototype XFJ-2B for the Navy that I had flown a number of times back at Patuxent River. The details of the test are immaterial. I had never been supersonic. In view of the crowd I was running with, I wanted to remedy that circumstance as expeditiously as possible, but on first examining the test plane on the ramp, I wasn't so sure. It wasn't exactly what you might call band-box new. There were the odd bumps here and there for special camera mounts and the paint scheme was pretty tired. The good news was that there were no drop tanks. There were some data to be gathered at 35,000 feet, whence I had to return to terra firma. The shortest distance was still a straight line, wasn't it?

I got the angle of attack measurements, then climbed on up to 40,000 feet just to make sure. The old girl could make it almost to 0.90 Mach number on the level. I rolled over onto my back and pulled through to the vertical at full power. Before I got to 35,000 feet I was at 0.98, feeling but a twitch of wing roll passing through 0.95. Then the Mach needle flipped to 1.02 and I was a Mach-buster. I throttled back and pulled level below 30,000 feet. In decelerating back to subsonic the wing action was more of a snatch than a twitch, but still quite manageable. Not really a big deal, but nice to know the basic design had not surrendered much to age. Coming nearly seven years after the premiere event, though, it was a bit of an anticlimax. But I was glad to have been there. Emulating Yeager, I made a quick check and, sure enough, my ears were still in place.

Having initiated myself into the Mach-busters club, I was feeling somewhat elated, even a bit ego inflated, and for no good reason. It can prove hazardous to any pilot's longevity, and even a professional embarrassment. Landing to the south on Muroc Dry Lake offers ten miles of hard-baked runway. No need to make a carrier approach out of it and try to catch the first wire, as the Navy's hotshots would characterize it. But no, I had to put it down right at the north end of the landing surface. I had been coming down in a steep descent with the power back in idle and, as I rounded out for touchdown, all of a sudden I noted I was going to end up short—in a ditch that had been cut along the north edge of the dry lake for drainage. No problem, just add a little power. Right—only I was in a very early F-86A with an engine that responds very slowly to power requests from the cockpit. I advanced the throttle as quickly as I could without sending the tailpipe temperature over the red line. I was almost in the ditch, holding the nose up just a few knots above the stall, when the engine took an extra gulp of fuel and provided enough push to switch vertical velocity from minus to plus and permit me to clear the ditch and plunk the old *Sabre* down on the first fifty feet of smooth lake bed.

All of that was more than forty years ago. Only recently has my interest in the Welch-Yeager saga been reignited. Maybe someday it will be fully understood why so many of our real heroes come from the backwoods, the small towns, the family farms of our great country. Fascination for that reality led me recently on a trek through the "hollers" of West Virginia, on a kind of pilgrimage to the birthplace and hometown of Chuck Yeager. I was joined by my best friend, patient wife, and most cogent critic, who assumed the additional role of navigator. Turning southwest with our nation's capital at our backs, we rolled down the wide valleys and beside the even ridges known as Shenandoah and Blue, respectively.

The giant hands that shaped those ridges and valleys running generally in a southwesterly direction from upper New York state through Pennsylvania, Maryland, and Virginia, on down into eastern Tennessee, seem to have lost patience as attention was turned to the southeastern regions of West Virginia. Instead of regular ridges and richly soiled valleys, it appears that whatever rocks and other material the master contourers had scooped up to form their orderly procession southwestward had here been unceremoniously dumped in random heaps to make up the wild geographical cacophony locally known as the "hollers." The slopes of the hills are so steep and the valleys so narrow that sunrise may not happen before ten o'clock, and the shadows of the evening arrive at three in the afternoon.

About sixty miles past Roanoke, we halted our southwestward slide along the valley, turned to the northwest, and penetrated the southern boundary of West Virginia at the Bluefields—there's one in each of the Virginias, with their immense marshaling yards for assembling the seemingly endless trains carrying the coal that powers much of our eastern seaboard. About thirty miles of winding through the hollers and we came upon the town of Welch. A pure coincidence, the name cannot be traced to the North American test pilot, but, less than sixty miles to the north as the crow flies—more than one hundred if you're limited to the roads that bend to the undulating contours—lies Yeager Airport serving Charleston. Although its population is less than 60,000 and shrinking, it is West Virginia's largest town. And Yeager Airport is named for the renowned U.S. Air Force brigadier general.

We decided to pay a visit to Welch Municipal Airport and were glad we did, for several reasons. The airport directory informed us that the facility was three miles southeast of town. A kindly villager offered more explicit instructions, with an expression on his face that seemed to say, "Sure, I'm happy to tell you how to get there, but would you tell me why you want to go?" All of which made Donna a little uneasy but only strengthened my determination to make the visit.

The route was not exactly the Dulles Access Road, but there were the occasional wider spots where two cars could miss each other if the drivers slowed down and were careful. It wasn't paved, and it ascended quite steeply. No one had mentioned that the airport was on top of the mountain. Fortunately it was not raining and the traffic was—well—nonexistent. Still, I was glad to be driving a Jeep with four-wheel drive. We broke out of the wooded ridges onto the clear, open, and quite evenly flattened mountaintop, reminiscent of the Schwäbische Alb region of Germany, where the glaciers some eons ago leveled and cleared the summits, leaving the valleys fully forested. There were two well-kept homes on the mountain, surrounded by brightly blooming flowers. Across the road was a large and healthy looking vegetable garden. Beyond lay the airport. A gate across the road was locked, but access on foot was possible. Donna said she would wait in the car.

The runway, all 2,700 feet of it, ran east and west with sharp dropoffs at both ends. Taking off to the west, the runway arced close to 20 degrees to the left about a third of the way from the east end. The macadam surface had seen better days. There were a half-dozen or so small hangars on the field. The roofs of two had collapsed. The windsock was sockless. Walking to the east end of the runway, I looked down into the valley. A former open pit mine and its tailings had been recontoured and planted. Except for the nearby highway, it seemed as though man had hardly been on the scene at all. The environmentalists should be pleased. The runway sloped slightly to the west, then evaporated as the terrain dropped steeply into the town of Welch. In the largest hangar by the entrance gate I could make out a couple of small aircraft, but the doors were locked. I was alone on the airport. As I wandered back to the car, I saw that Donna had company. She was in animated conversation.

I was introduced to Sam Hazzard, the manager of Welch Municipal Airport. He was also the chief flight instructor and head of maintenance. That day he was busy tending his vegetable garden. Sam owned several aircraft, including a four-place Cessna and, until recently, a Piper *Cub*. I fly the *Cub* for towing gliders. Also it's a great trainer. I asked why he had gotten rid of his.

"I didn't," he replied. "It almost got rid of me."

A couple of years earlier Sam was taking off in his *Cub*. There was a strong wind out of the west, so, without the extra weight of a passenger in the rear seat, he was able to climb rather steeply. He turned to the south and throttled back when there was a *pop* and fire started coming out of the engine cowl. Sam pulled back the mixture control to shut off fuel to the engine, which meant that the engine promptly quit, but the fire did not. Putting the nose down to maintain flying speed, he reckoned he might have just enough altitude to get back to the runway for a downwind landing.

Meanwhile, the fire was getting hotter. Flames were flickering back into the cockpit. Sam put the airplane into a slip to keep the flames out of his face, but that meant he had to surrender precious altitude fast, too fast to be able to make it back to the airport. He leveled the wings and suffered the flames now licking at his hands. It looked as though he would be too low to top the rise at the end of the runway. Then he remembered that the west wind was strong. Blowing against that slope, it created a lot of upward-moving air. Soaring pilots use the same phenomenon to keep their gliders aloft for hundreds of miles where the ridges have better organized continuity.

As he approached the face of the ridge he turned north, with his right wing almost brushing the trees. Suddenly he felt a surge as the upward-rushing air lifted his craft until it was level with, then above, the runway. But, dear God, he was burning up! His shirt was now on fire. He quickly turned to the runway heading and again slipped the *Cub* to touch down on the macadam surface. The entire nose and front seat of the aircraft were now engulfed in flames. Sam hit his brakes, but he was going downwind. How did the saints endure such pain! With the plane still moving, he stood on the right brake, turning the *Cub* to the south. Now the wind was on his right side. With one sweep of his charred hands, he unfastened his seat belt and shoulder harness, flipped the handle on the cockpit closure, and rolled out of the burning airplane onto the strip. His clothes were still afire.

Sam's survival was anything but certain as he drifted in and out of consciousness from his bed of intense suffering at the local hospital. However, his subconscious or his superconscious being—let the reader make the choice—was indeed alert. He clearly recalls taking his case to the highest authority.

"Lord Jesus," he pleaded, "I'm not ready yet. I have too many pieces of unfinished business. Give me one more chance and I will be a true Christian soldier for the rest of whatever time you and the Father may allot me."

The doctors may have wanted to give up, but Sam did not. Many weeks and a half-dozen skin grafts later, he returned home and, true to his word, told his pastor of his born-again experience. In further fulfillment of his promise, he gave witness to the congregation the very next Sunday.

Sam's biggest piece of unfinished business was his grandson. To say that youngster was the apple of his eye is the ultimate understatement. The young fellow had been living with his mother in Roanoke, but there was some gang involvement that was not at all healthy, so Sam brought him back to his home in the little town of Kimball in the valley on the east side of Welch Municipal. With the move came the opportunity to absorb a more enduring code of values. It was a highly successful change of scenery. Not only did the boy do well in school but he also got involved in Boys' Nation and became a leader among his peers. In his junior year in high school, he was elected the Boys' Nation governor for the State of West Virginia and sent to the national convention in San Diego. That trip had set the stage for a serious challenge to the young man's heretofore cheerful, confident, and optimistic worldview. At San Diego he was selected as a candidate for national president of Boys' Nation. One of only two running for this prestigious position, he was defeated.

He came back home angry and embittered. "Granddad," he said, " there was no way that crowd was going to elect a black to be their president." Granddad was just recovering from his trial by fire and knew he would have little chance to relax.

Sam concluded his tale of never-ending challenge, shrugged, and with a shy smile asked, "But what brings you folks to Welch Municipal?"

I told him about the two fighter aces and the duel in the Mojave sun for the Mach one crown, about how our pilgrimage to the Yeager origins at Hamlin had been enhanced by the discovery of Welch and its airport so eerily nearby. We just had to have a look.

Sam smiled again. "There's more coincidence in these hollers than you might know," he offered. "Just fifteen miles west of Welch is a little town of Iaeger. It's not spelled the same but it's all the same family. Folks in West Virginia don't fuss too much about spelling. I heard the Yeagers up around Hamlin had a feud with their cousins down here in McDowell County. Feuds aren't too strange in this part of the world. Just go on up to Logan and Mingo for the real thing. By the way, the Iaegers say their name means 'hunter.' Kind of fits our hero, I guess."

"Even more than you think. It also means 'fighter pilot.' "

I noted that we'd better move on if we were to get to Hamlin before sundown—by way of Iaeger, of course. Sam said we should come back with more time so he could give us an aerial tour of McDowell County in his 172. That remains on our list of "to-dos."

Going back through the town of Welch, we found a Iaeger Motors, but, no, there were no Iaegers still with the company. Rather eerily we discovered a number of autos with license plate holders that read "Iaeger Motors" on the top and "Welch, WV" at the bottom. There was a widow Iaeger living a few blocks away from the auto agency, but she was getting pretty old and quite forgetful. We pressed on to the town of Iaeger, only about a quarter the size of Welch and quite devoid of any monuments to the differently spelled Yeager so profusely celebrated hardly fifty miles to the north.

Follow the hollers we did. This led us to Logan, a town about the size of Welch and the county seat of Logan County. Just to the west lay Mingo County, and scattered around the hills of both were to be found at one time lots of Hatfields and a host of McCoys. How many survived the famous feuds that raged between the two families is not clear. During our brief visit the streets of Logan seemed quite busy and peaceful. We heard not the first crackle of gunfire. But then we departed long before sundown.

Hamlin was our destination. As we drove north from Logan, the steep hills and narrow hollers tended to flatten out into more rolling country known as the Allegheny Plateau. Approaching Hamlin, we drove along the Mud River. It appeared to us that the stream had gotten a bum rap. Having grown up on the James River near Richmond, which was generally believed to be too thick to drink and too thin to plow, I thought that in comparison the Mud seemed sparkling clear. A large sign at the entrance to town read: "Welcome to Hamlin, Home of Brig. General Chuck Yeager, USAF, First to Break the Sound Barrier." I looked at my navigator. "Golly, we sure don't want to rain on that parade." She thought for a moment, then offered a solution.

"Why not just modify the sign slightly to read 'First USAF Pilot to Break the Sound Barrier'? Shouldn't require a new sign. The town budget can probably handle it."

Just across the street was a large multibuilding complex that looked like a college campus. A big sign informed the curious that they were looking at the General Charles E. Yeager Training Center, offering vocational training for those youngsters not headed to college. Moving through the center of town we passed the Bobcat Restaurant on Main Street. For a moment, it was like going back to the thirties. A few Model A Fords would have completed the illusion. Continuing to the Hamlin High School just a couple of blocks away, we got out to inspect the statue out front. At first glance, it looked like a generic aviator in flight suit with a parachute over his shoulder and a hard hat in his hand. On closer examination we learned that it was indeed "Charles E. Yeager" because it said so in the inscription on the statue's polished stone base. By walking around the monument, one could read of all his significant exploits and awards.

The school was closed, so we retired to the Bobcat Restaurant for lunch. It seemed to be after the normal lunch hour. Anyway, we were the only customers there. The proprietor, Sherrill Lovejoy, came over for our order. In response to our expression of interest, he explained that the Hamlin High School athletic teams were known as the Bobcats, hence the restaurant's name. Sure, he knew Yeager, had been in the class ahead of him in high school. No, he hadn't seen Chuck in a long time, but his first cousin had brought in the fresh pastries earlier in the day. She'd baked them herself—made really great cream pies. There were still a lot of live Yeagers around town, and many earlier family members are to be found in the large Yeager family plot at the cemetery atop a hill above Hamlin with a commanding view of the town and the surrounding countryside. Albert Hal and Susie Mae Yeager, Chuck's parents, along with his older brother, Roy, and baby sister, Doris Ann, have been laid to rest there. If resting is the aim, along with providing a place for quiet contemplation by loving survivors, the bucolic vista from the Hamlin graveyard is certainly special, and most assuredly preferable to the freeway rumble at Forest Lawn or the deafening roar of full-throttle jets over Arlington.

Back at the Bobcat Restaurant we discussed with Sherrill the elevation to icon status of Chuck Yeager. Was there any evidence during his Hamlin days that he would become an international figure? Well, not really. Was he an outstanding student? A great athlete? About average. Absent the war, where would Chuck be today? You know, he had this good sense for mechanical things. If your car broke down, he could fix it. Outboard wouldn't start, he'd get it running. Had he hung around Hamlin, more than likely he would have ended up running an auto repair shop here in town. And he'd be a legendary hunter and fisherman. He was one hell of a shot, and he had this special instinct for knowing where the fish were. Apparently he still does.

Sherrill Lovejoy had also served in the army in World War II, but not in aviation. He'd served with Patton's 9th Army, first in North Africa, then in Sicily, Italy, southern France, and Germany. He was at the Battle of the Bulge. He ended up a platoon sergeant in a heavy weapons company. I suppose he had the usual collection of Purple Hearts, unit citations, and theater ribbons, perhaps even a Distinguished Service Cross. He didn't say. He was most happy to have come home to Hamlin in one piece. In addition to the Bobcat, he ran a furniture store and a drug store. Lean, healthy, and hairless, he looked substantially younger than his seventy-plus years. One could not but wonder whether, if he had traded his M-1 rifle for a P-51 *Mustang*, he would have come home to Hamlin in 1945.

Yeager's true birthplace was the tiny town of Myra, West Virginia. The Yeager home in Myra no longer exists. Myra, just a few miles east of Hamlin, consists of a two-story cinder block building about twenty-five feet wide by thirty feet long. It contains a post office, a general store offering everything from flashlight batteries to fishhooks, snuff to baby powder, and an apartment on the second floor for the postmistress and the store owner. The old Yeager home? It was up the first holler just past the post office, but it's not there anymore. Some seventy years ago, Hal and Susie Mae moved their growing family to a big four-bedroom home on the hill in Hamlin, by way of brief sojourns in the hamlet of Hubble and a smaller house in Hamlin.

Although it is but thirty miles by the back roads from Hamlin to Charleston, there is a time warp of sixty years dividing the two communities. Yet there is a link that promises to be durable. Crossing the Kanawha River into Charleston, the bridge is named for Chuck Yeager. Perhaps it is the span he flew beneath in the course of the celebration when the airport was named in his honor. That little caper caused much consternation among the pleasure crafters fishing beneath the bridge. Some swore he brushed their whip antennas. Any other pilot would have been hung out to dry for that bit of adolescent indulgence. After all, the war was over. Still, it's not every day you get a whole airport named in your honor, an airport that boasts the sixth longest runway in all of West Virginia. For the state's golden boy, cut him some slack. By comparison, Welch Municipal has a runway but half as long and but partially surfaced. Its tumbledown hangars cannot compare to the well-manicured turf and modern terminal at Yeager Field. Besides,

Welch Municipal is not named in honor of the Pearl Harbor hero. It simply seems an interesting conjecture that it could be. The relative status of the two contemporaneous Mach-busters in history seems to match too closely the condition of these two airports. Is it possible that there are still a few who treasure truth more than what is declared to be politically correct?

From Charleston, we drove southeast and crossed back into Virginia at the Greenbriar; from there it was nearly a straight shot along the Shenandoah Valley northeast back to our northern Virginia home. Meeting people like Sam Hazzard and Sherrill Lovejoy made the trip worthwhile. The many Chuck Yeagers encountered along the way added to the challenge of getting the story down in a truly objective manner. I often wonder how many historians lined the banks of the Rubicon.

5 / Events, Markers, Milestones, and Records

Keeping track of history can be quite a challenge. This is especially true in the world of the aeronautical achievements of an earlier era. One can only wonder whether the ancient, yellowed archives a full half-century old will be replaced by the Internet for the researcher of 2050. Will that make the researcher's life simpler? Surely it won't be nearly as exciting or half as much fun. The problem is that too many of those yellowed archives are being lost. For a brief period, I had access to the historic files of North American Aviation while they were still indexed and open to researchers in the old Inglewood offices. Then, in 1992, those records were loaded into two big seagoing-style containers and trucked to the company's operations at Seal Beach. With the acquisition of North American by Boeing, those containers became the property of the Seattle colossus. Their future is uncertain. Perhaps 10 percent have historical value, but who has the resources to sort through it all? I was able to recover most of the weekly summary flight-test reports of the 1947–1948 period. These were the routine submissions to the Air Force prepared by North American's engineering flight-test management. I was told that the reports dictated by George Welch on the blue Dictagraph disks employed by North American for that purpose were stacked in one of the files. These may still reside in one of those two containers, if they have not already been hauled to the dump. They might prove useful for making the case for Welch and his XP-86 in the supersonic sweepstakes. They could not prove he was not the winner, since he was under orders from the secretary of the Air Force to hold a tight rein on his *Sabre* and may have been discreet in his flight-test reports. Also, the two Welch sons, especially the younger, who was but a toddler when his father was killed, have a very real desire to hear their father's voice as it was recorded more than fifty years ago.

The central focus of this bit of aeronautical history is the time and place of the first *ba-boom* unleashed by a manned aircraft. But how would one characterize such an event? Certainly it's not a record—records are precisely measured in time and space. But the speed of sound: If it's hot, it's high; if it turns cold, noise moves more slowly. If not a record, then, it is surely a milestone. In moving from a standstill to Mach two, unless the quantum physicists have been very busy, most vehicles must go past Mach one. Thus, in going up and down the speed chain, Mach one—and two and three—serve as milestones of that progression, and regression. Going supersonic for the first time is clearly an event, an aeronautical event, just as the Wright brothers' first flights are memorable, historic events. But I must admit, I can never remember which of that illustrious pair did it first. They did it on the same day, and whether it was Wilbur, then Orville, or Orville, then Wilbur, just doesn't seem to matter very much. In the supersonic event, was it George, then Chuck, or Chuck, then George? Looking at the record, it could have been Welch by a fortnight or Yeager by four weeks. Or, as this presentation would suggest, it could have all happened on the same day—just like the first flights of those Wright brothers.

September–October 1947

INTO THE STARTING BLOCKS

The first XP-86 aircraft, Army Air Force serial number PU597, was rolled out of the North American plant at Los Angeles on August 8, 1947. After engine tests and other ground checks, it was disassembled and trucked to Muroc Army Air Field, where it arrived on September 10. As it was being prepared for flight, the ground crew made a number of engine runs. On the evening of September 16, during a full-power check of the turbojet powerplant, one of the ground crew, Mike Bricka, got too close to the inlet. He was sucked into the throat of the brand new *Sabre* and fatally crushed. It had taken a long time to educate people who work or wander around propeller-driven aircraft to avoid walking into the vicious arc of those swiftly rotating Grim Reaper blades. Turbojet inlets were a less obvious but no less fatal attraction. Soon there would appear open-mesh metal screens to be placed in front of those inlets during ground operations. They also served the function of blocking the ingestion of ramp debris that does damage to the engine's innards.

The price of progress? Learning the hard way? Ground crew, spectators, stunt pilots, test pilots—some put themselves in harm's way; others, innocent bystanders, get an early call to shuffle off this mortal coil. Often it seems that the most careful, the best prepared of our explorers get knocked out of the race by a cruel trick of fate, while the most extravagant, spotlight-loving risk takers survive disaster after disaster, if not wholly unscathed, then wholly unhumbled. Just put all the aircraft on the ground, stop all the motorcars, let everyone slow his pace to a walk, and all that human carnage would cease. Perhaps we would simply starve to death or die of boredom—but almost certainly in a pollution-free environment with little risk of bodily harm from our own inventions.

It seemed unlikely that George Welch was going to die of boredom. He had just completed the spin demonstration of the XSN2J, a new high-powered advanced trainer for Navy carrier pilots. Its performance was better than that of the P-40 fighter he had flown to meet the Japanese attackers at Pearl Harbor. In those days, the Navy got serious about spin demonstrations. Two, six, eight, or more turns might be required, depending on how promptly the aircraft recovered when antispin controls were applied. And once the customer was satisfied that the new trainer candidate was well-behaved in normal spin recoveries, do it all over again from inverted entries—that is, with the aircraft upside down.

With the first flight of the *Sabre* delayed, George was called on to investigate some high-speed propeller vibration problems encountered in the P-82 *Twin-Mustang*. Coming too late for World War II, where its performance would have paid handsome dividends, especially for long-range escort, the *Twin-Mustang* saw limited duty in Korea. In 1947 its jet successors were just beginning to take center stage.

The P-82 tests were a diversion for Welch, in view of the frustrating delays in getting the new *Sabre* into the air. The word from the X-1 camp was that Yeager had come very close to going supersonic on his September 12 flight. Surely on the next flight he would push it through; but strangely, the X-1 flights that had been going up every other day were postponed. Rumors of a serious pitch control problem drifted out of the Bell camp. There was evidence of a lot of scrambling. Chuck was pressing Jack Ridley, the one man on the X-1 team in whose hands he'd entrust his life. He wanted Ridley's assurances that changes had been made and that the changes would work. He wanted no more of running out of pitch control at 0.94 Mach number. Welch could only smile as these tales leaked out of softly traded confidences at Pancho's bar and in boudoirs. Maybe he could put his swept-wing beauty out front after all, in spite of the *Sabre*'s recent tragic delay.

With no other flights scheduled while he awaited the *Sabre*, Welch divided his time between Muroc and the engineering offices in the Inglewood plant, situated on the south side of the Los Angeles Airport. At the desert base, he spent a lot of time in the *Sabre*'s cockpit and observed the flight-test crew as they checked out all the aircraft systems and the special instrumentation for this dramatically sleek advanced new fighter. In LA, he talked to the engineers who had created it—Larry Greene, Ed Horkey, "Stormy" Storms, and others—men he had grown to trust. And he spent time with the guy who had been responsible for cutting out the pieces and putting them all together on the shop floor—Walt Spivak.

George had then been with North American for more than three years. He had joined the company in the middle of 1944 at the height of the war and the peak of demand for North American's prime product, the P-51 *Mustang*. The demand was not only for more of the war's top fighter but also for improved performance—faster, higher, farther. In addition, a reconnaissance version of the *Mustang* designated the F-6D was in the works. He'd been there only a month or two when Fred Borsodi visited from Wright Field and showed his film of shock waves on a *Mustang*'s wings as it dove at max power straight down from 40,000 feet. Theodore von Karman, the legendary aerodynamicist from Cal Tech, was there for that screening, and it's important to note von Karman's observation that when the entire aircraft, not just the air accelerating over the thickest part of the wing, went supersonic there would be shock waves sent to the ground. He theorized that people nearby on the ground would hear and feel the passing of that pressure pulse. Listening intently to all this were Ed Horkey, a former student of von Karman's, as well as Stormy and Larry Greene, who were leaders in the aerodynamics section of the advance design group at North American.

Welch carefully stored all these impressions for a later date. He was certain they would be useful. Already there were reports of German jet fighters. The first American jet—the Bell P-59—was less than inspiring, but in the fall of 1944 the Lockheed P-80 made its appearance. North American was scrambling not to be left behind. Several jets were on the company's drawing boards. The measures of a fighter's effectiveness in combat, assuming agility to the limits of human tolerance, were faster, farther, and higher. Propellers were like clumsy clubs as they approached the speed of sound. If real progress were to be made, the sonic regime must be traversed. Turbojet or rocket propulsion offered the only solution.

Meanwhile, there was a war to be won. George had come to North American to fly, and fly he did. He liked to fly; it was what he did best. He joined the company as an experimental test pilot in the middle of July 1944, and for the balance of that year he flew engineering test flights at an annual rate of 486. After ten years in that profession, in his last one he was averaging 420 flights per year. Over time, his average test flights per year numbered 342. More often than not, his flight logs show he was in the cockpit conducting flight tests on Christmas Eve and New Year's Eve. If not, he would be found taking to the skies on the mornings of those holidays—often a tougher challenge.

By the latter part of September 1947, Welch had paid his dues and won the respect of his engineering colleagues at North American. He had been honored by the assignment to fly—indeed, to be the project engineering test pilot for—the company's newest entry in the world's fighter sweepstakes, the XP-86 *Sabre*. Already he sensed a new challenge, one bigger than facing off against insuperable odds at Pearl Harbor or triple acing the Japanese competition before the war was half over. It would be an event on a par with the Wright brothers' first flight and Lindbergh's solo passage over the Atlantic. Evidence of its importance could be gained by the attention and investment given to the little orange-colored rocket ship being lumbered aloft with growing frequency by its B-29 mother ship from the main runway at Muroc Army Air Base. Everyone knew that this represented a substantial national effort, bringing together the resources of the U.S. Army Air Corps, the NACA, and the Bell Aircraft Company to launch the first manned aircraft designed specifically and solely to fly faster than sound.

Then, on September 18, 1947, Stuart Symington was sworn in as the first secretary of a brand new Air Force. Suddenly the Mach-busting mission became the Holy Grail of this junior service in a new military triumvirate; at least, it would be for those who played the Washington game and the small group around the X-1 at Muroc. And as it would turn out, it was the fledgling Air Force that would understand better than the Army or Navy how to survive and gain the dominant role in carving for itself the lion's share of attention and budget. Partly it was because the wild-blue-yonder boys had more pizzazz and sex appeal than the mud-spattered doughboys or the too-long-at-sea sailors. And partly it was because the developing Cold War focused so much on the rapidly moving, technologically dominated long-range weapons of mass destruction in which the Air Force played the ascendant role.

These political nuances were totally lost on George Welch, but not the reality of the challenge. The more he got involved in the development of the *Sabre*, the more he was convinced that he could capture the laurels of a first supersonic flight for North American Aviation. There were the Borsodi film and von Karman's tearful welcome to that visual confirmation of his theory. George Gherkens, a senior aerodynamicist with North American at that time, recalls Welch's reaction to that film and the subsequent discussion. "Going supersonic is really no big deal," he had said with a shrug. "What's to be afraid of?" That was in 1944.

More than three years later, he was frustrated by the delays but more eager than ever to cop the prize. He had seen the competition. Maybe it had made sense in 1943 when NACA's John Stack at Langley had sold his wind-tunnel-in-the-sky concept to obtain funding for the X-1. But the real world had caught up with the chubby little research ship that required the services of a former nuclear bomber to lift it to its destiny. Besides, George had had a much too highly personal look at the *Airacobra*, Bell's contribution to the war effort, to believe that the Buffalo crowd could ever get out ahead of the creative team that had given birth to the *Mustang*. Its next-generation successor, the swept-wing *Sabre*, looked to be moving at supersonic speed just sitting on the tarmac.

Casually making his rounds at the Inglewood plant, George stopped by for a visit with Walt Spivak. The Spivak persona was outwardly tough and obdurate in the formal meetings concerning his responsibility for getting the new *Sabre* assembled and readied for flight. One-on-one, he and Welch had an easy relationship seasoned by mutual respect and certain trust that shared confidences would not become hangar gossip.

"Come in, George. Have a seat." Walt pushed aside some revised production schedules and looked up. "What's on your mind?"

Dropping into a chair across the desk from a smiling Spivak, Welch lit a cigarette. "Nothing specific. Looks like we'll be ready to fly the new *Sabre* pretty soon. Just thought I'd like to have your take on what to expect. It's quite different from anything we've built in the past. Any special features that give you a bit of heartburn?"

Walt looked over his shoulder at a large three-view drawing of the *Sabre* tacked to the wall behind him. "I suppose the leading edge slats are the trickiest part of the design—combined with the swept wing, of course. I'd have a good bit of altitude when you unlock those slats for the first time. Aero tells me they have them just right, but then they get some new wind tunnel data and make some changes. I expect we'll be fine-tuning those babies well into the flight-test program. But that's what you get paid for, isn't it?" Walt had a really warm smile.

Overhead shot of the first XP-86 on the ramp at the Los Angeles plant of North American Aviation, September 1947. *Courtesy of Archives II, College Park, Maryland*

George stumped out his cigarette. Walt could tell he had something else on his mind. "The slats operate only in the low-speed regime, or high-altitude, high-g situations. I was thinking more about the high-speed end. How tough is this prototype?"

"If you fighter jocks don't try to pull eight or ten g's, it'll be OK. Tony Weissenberger has done some truly imaginative structural design work to maintain torsional stiffness in that swept wing without adding a lot of weight. The flight controls are all well balanced. The flutter people see 650 knots as well within the envelope."

"We can wait to pull the wings off later in the program. Look, Walt . . ." Welch gazed around. No one outside the glass walls of the office was paying any attention. They had work to do. Spivak ran a taut shop. His people were all on tight deadlines. Even so, George lowered his voice. "Horkey, Stormy, Larry Greene—they all say this *Sabre* will slash through the so-called sound barrier. The consensus is that a full power dive from 35,000 feet will do it. Any special problems from your perspective?"

Walt wasn't smiling anymore. "Take it easy, George. You haven't even got the first flight under your belt yet and you're already talking about busting the sound barrier."

"But, Walt, you should see the funny little skyrocket Bell's going to use to do the job. They have to use a B-29 to get it up to altitude and once it's there it has about three minutes of fuel to zoom through Mach one. What in the hell good is that? The German rocket planes at least took off from the ground and they had guns in them—even shot down some of our bombers. Seems to me it's in the Air Corps' interest—hell, it's the U.S. Air Force now—to bust through for the first time in its new fighter. It sure in hell is in North American's best interests."

Walt could see he was getting in over his head. "I'm not so sure. Don't you think you ought to ask the Air Force?"

"Don't worry, Walt. It was just a passing fancy. We'll probably never have a shot at it. I hear it's only a matter of a few days until Bell's rocket ship will whistle through. But thanks for the confidence builder on the *Sabre*. If it does break, can I bring it back for a new one?"

"Sure, George." Walt paused. With his sports jacket and bow tie, Welch looked like some college sophomore. He had that funny smile on his face that seemed to say "I can do anything and get away with it." Walt wanted to stay in the loop. "Let me know how it's going, George. This is a really big one for North American."

Lighting another cigarette, the test pilot said, "You can count on it." He meant it. Walt was a special resource. With a quietly satisfied smile on his face, Welch wandered off in the direction of the engineering offices to look for the aero people—the ones who predicted how high and how fast a new fighter might fly. He was in luck. Stormy was huddled with Larry Greene over a drawing board. They were clearly pleased to see him.

"How come you're not in working garb?" More often than not George wore his flight suit when he visited the engineering offices.

"I wanted to get the feel for being a hotshot executive. Besides, you guys haven't got anything on the ramp for me to fly."

The drawing on the board had been the subject of discussion. It depicted the horizontal stabilizer trim device, which offered an optional pitch control mechanism that the test pilot wanted to know a lot more about.

"Is that the pitch trim system?" Welch pointed to the drawing.

"Yeah," Stormy answered. "We were just discussing whether we may have too much speed in the actuator. You can determine the right setting for takeoff from your taxi tests. Then maybe it's best not to make any changes until you're comfortably airborne. Once you have a little altitude, make changes with momentary blips. Then hold it down for a couple of seconds to check the maximum rate of change in each direction. It's really not for the low to medium speed range that we designed the system this way."

George broke into a wide smile, then quickly went poker-faced. "Really, tell me more."

Larry Greene broke in. "It's not something you're going to want to worry about on the first flight."

"Let's talk about it anyway."

The two aerodynamicists traded glances. Stormy picked up the theme. He was the more impulsive of the pair, but sometimes it was necessary to clean up behind him. Larry knew how to do that.

"George, as you have no doubt heard, we think this *Sabre* is going to be a real barnburner. Larry's spent an awful lot of time on the original German analytical data and wind tunnel test results for their swept-wing designs. His facility in German put us ahead of some of the others in the game. Also, we've done a bit of wind tunnel work on our own. We're almost certain that top speed at altitude will be better than 0.9 Mach in level flight. At that Mach number, the center of lift is going to start moving aft on the wing. You're going to have to pull back on the stick and start trimming . . . but very carefully. Changing the angle of the whole stabilizer at that speed and a changing Mach number could get pretty tricky."

George wasn't going to worry about trim sensitivity when he was closing in on the real heart of the matter. His juices hadn't been flowing like this in a long time. He inwardly chided himself to play it cool. An amused nonchalance was his style. Rather off-handedly, he inquired, "So I'm doing nine-tenths at, say, 35,000 feet and push the nose over into a 25 to 30 degree dive. What then?"

Larry couldn't contain himself. "By 30,000 feet, you're supersonic."

"What's the risk?"

Larry kind of shook his head and threw up his hands. "Look, George, we really don't know. Our best guess is that it's not very great."

It was Welch's turn. "My guess is virtually zero."

Stormy was a real crapshooter, especially if he knew the dice were loaded on his side. But he was also a damn good engineer. "What makes you say that, George?"

"Last month I spent the night at Deming, New Mexico. Ever been there?"

The engineers shook their heads.

"It's a few miles west of Las Cruces. I'd never heard of it either. I was taking the new Navy trainer back to Patuxent for the final demonstration. I had been shooting for El Paso but ran a little short of fuel and landed at Deming. Spent the night there. Ran into some interesting rubes at the bar that evening. You guys know what's going on in that part of New Mexico?"

The two engineers shook their heads.

"Listen up. Las Cruces is where they're putting together the V-2 missiles brought in from Germany, and north of there is the Army's White Sands Missile Test Range, where they fire them. They've been doing it for more than a year. At least one blasts off each month. Sometimes they launch two or three a month."

Stormy was getting impatient and started to fidget. Welch grasped his arm. "Hear me out. Deming is not much of a show town. The guys go hunting in season. The flicks are several years old. Dullsville, believe me. But then the V-2s started blasting off. Apparently it's quite a show. Fourth of July times a thousand. Some of the town's people work on the base. Enough to get advance notice. First they started driving onto the base and that was OK, but the more creative started getting positioned atop the San Andres Mountains on the western edge of the base and downrange from the launch sites. Visibility in New Mexico is forever, makes the Mojave seem like smogsville. I talked to several guys there in Deming who had witnessed two or more of these launches. A really dramatic blastoff, then the missile, which stands more than forty feet tall on the launch pad, starts arcing toward them. Situated some 3,000 or 4,000 feet above the blastoff, at first they're looking down on this monster. But not for long. Quickly the missile zooms overhead and goes downrange to the north and as high as a hundred miles.

"On occasion things get screwed up. This past May, one of these monsters headed south rather than north. Some kind of guidance problem. It boomed along for eighty to ninety miles, then crashed into a hillside just south of Juarez in Mexico. No one hurt, but close to a disaster. Apparently, it hasn't happened since. But that's not the point. What's important is that these big babies really move."

Impressed but detached, neither Stormy nor Larry made the connection. Hell, the Germans had done that thousands of times. George paused. There was more. "You gotta hear this! Twenty to thirty seconds after each launch, as the V-2 passes above them, the ground observers there on the mountaintop are hit by the blast of the shock wave. A big *ba-boom* just like von Karman predicted. Hell, that V-2 is bigger than the *Sabre*, or the X-1 for that matter, and it slides through the so-called sonic wall as routinely as a surfer riding a big wave at Malibu. On the flight from Deming to El Paso, I detoured north near the White Sands launch pads. There was a V-2 sitting on its tail getting readied for launch. That's not some toy you might expect to find under the Christmas tree. It's really big!" George paused to light a cigarette. "I don't know what Yeager's waiting for, but I'm ready."

Some of the other engineers started to drift over to the trio, sensing the conversation had turned to something other than plans for lunch. George thrust his hands up, palms outward toward his two cohorts as if to dump the challenge in their laps. "Think about it. We should be ready to fly next week . . . and thanks for the heads up on trimming the stabilizer. I've got to go talk to the flight test guys." And he was out of there.

Stormy and Larry looked at each other, started to shake their heads, then broke into barely contained laughter. Without waiting around to reveal the source of their mirth to their approaching colleagues, they decided to break for lunch, recognizing that in a rather nebulous manner they had just become uninvited coconspirators.

The following Monday morning, September 29, the number one XP-86 prototype (now Air Force serial number 45-59597) was ready for test at the North American flight-test facility at Muroc. The program for the day was high-speed taxi tests. The pilot was to evaluate ground handling characteristics, nose wheel steering, wing slat operating characteristics, and control effectiveness. These ground runs would be made on the Muroc Dry Lake first at 90 percent power, then a second run at full power. Welch showed up early, wearing his trademark sky-blue flight suit and carrying his bright orange crash helmet, custom molded by the eminent Dr. Lombard. (A former Air Corps flight surgeon, Lombard had made special studies of the optimum shape and energy-absorbing materials for these hard hats. He turned his research into a tidy little business. His helmets were light, comfortable, and effective. Each was molded to fit the skull of the wearer. One of them saved my life some years later when I crash-landed a *Sabre* in rough desert terrain. My head, protected by a Lombard helmet, was bashed hard and repeatedly against a test camera mounted on the radar scope.)

Side view of the first XP-86 *Sabre* on the North American ramp at Los Angeles Airport in September 1947 just prior to being disassembled and trucked to Rogers Dry Lake in the Mojave Desert for its first flight on October 1, 1947. *Courtesy of the San Diego Aerospace Museum*

All was ready, and Welch strapped into the cockpit. An external power cart provided the juice to start the engine. An increasingly shrill whine of the compressor combined with the rumble of ignition from the burner cans indicated a good start. George gave a thumbs-up to say he was happy with the cockpit engine readings. The external power plug was pulled and the wheel chocks removed. North American engineering flight-test mechanic Bob Cadick was at the wheel of the yellow pickup truck with two large yellow-and-white checkered flags attached to the rear of the cab. The truck would parallel the track of the *Sabre* across the dry lake bed to allow the film folks in the back to obtain movie coverage of the taxi tests. There were also two large fire extinguishers strapped to the sides of the truck.

The tests went without incident, and Welch got a clear picture of what horizontal stabilizer trim setting he should use, at least for the takeoff run. For each test the *Sabre* was accelerated on the dry lake bed until nose-wheel liftoff was clearly achieved, then power was cut back to preclude becoming fully airborne. With nothing but good results to report, George taxied back to the company hangar. It was not yet ten o'clock. The late September sun was just beginning to heat the hard clay surface of the world's greatest natural runway as the test pilot brought the aircraft onto the tarmac in front of the large Quonset-style structure that served as shelter from an autumn sun that could still be brutal by noontime. Sliding back the canopy, George shut down the engine as Cadick chocked the wheels and dropped the step that unfolded from the left side of the fuselage.

"Well, Wheaties, how'd it go?"

Handing the mechanic his helmet and knee board, George unbuckled his parachute and slid out of its shoulder straps. Standing up in the cockpit, he felt with his left toe for the spring-loaded step fairing a couple of feet below the canopy rail, then swung his right foot onto the leading edge of the wing, and his left foot onto the cable-suspended fold-out step. He was back on the ground.

"Everything looked and felt good to me, Bob. How'd it look from the truck?"

"Solid as a rock."

"Well, we'll see what the data show, but she sure wanted to fly. Time to get this thing airborne."

There was a small puddle of fuel under the fuselage behind the wing. "Hope that doesn't create any problems that can't be fixed in a hurry," Welch remarked as he retrieved his hard hat and knee board. "See you at Pancho's?"

"Hard to say. We may be working late." He looked at the fuel leak. The instrumentation people were already pulling the cameras and oscillograph out of what would be the gun and ammo bays in the production *Sabres*. The data they contained would be processed and analyzed at Muroc. For the taxi tests it was all pretty simple.

SABRE *DANCE. FIRST FLIGHT*

George had driven his own car up to Muroc very early. He had fallen into the habit of rising with the dawn—sometimes even before sunrise, as was the case that Monday. He had recently acquired a postwar MG roadster that he liked to drive, especially over the mountain roads. It seemed like an extension of his own fingers and toes. This was before the era of freeways. His Brentwood home was a stone's throw from Sunset Boulevard, which flowed not straight for any meaningful stretch, and the same was true heading north on Sepulveda as it threaded the coast range. The San Fernando Valley was straight and dull until just past Van Nuys, where it became necessary to climb and twist through Soledad Canyon, and suddenly the whole Mojave Desert stretched out like a splotched beige quilt. Straight north, then a right turn at Rosamond, and Muroc was but fifteen miles away. With heavy concentration and light traffic, he could make the hundred-mile trip in ninety minutes. It was his plan to stay until the first flight was behind him. Jan was seven months pregnant with their first child and was glad to have him out from underfoot. Her doctor was also married to an Australian, and the two young women had become close friends.

In the desert, George would usually stay at Pancho's Fly Inn, later to be named the Happy Bottom Riding Club. It comprised some four hundred acres bordering the Muroc Air Base on the south. In addition to rooms there were suites, a restaurant, bar, swimming pool, riding stables, and an air strip. Many of the North American crew would show up—Ed Virgin, Roy Ferren, Bob Cadick—as well as members of the X-1 team—NACA leader Walt Williams, Jack Ridley, and Chuck Yeager of the Air Corps/Air Force, and Dick Frost from Bell. Of course, there were the usual bevy of Pancho's down-on-their-luck ladies who added their own leaven of lust and lustre in more or less equal measure. Pancho herself was unique. Born of wealthy and distinguished forebears, she chose to wear trousers, ride horses, and fly airplanes. She resembled a Roseanne before plastic surgery and ended up being married four times. Her real friends included Jimmy Doolittle, Chuck Yeager, Buzz Aldrin, and many of the Hollywood set, for whom she had done the stunt flying in the early days of aviation films. Her conversation was punctuated with obscenities that would make the saltiest boatswain's mate blush.

Among the ladies at Pancho's, George had formed a special relationship with one Millie Palmer. A larger-than-life brunette, Millie was quieter and more serious than most of the other girls. She knew what was going on in the rest of the world and could talk about it rationally. When George and Millie had dinner together at Pancho's, he drank less and got to bed earlier. Also, Millie was aware of all the competitive egos caroming off the bar and diving board and corral gates at the Happy Bottom. She had a first cousin who was a staff sergeant flight engineer on a C-54 cargo plane based at Hamilton Field near San Francisco, which had the responsibility for logistically supporting the X-1 program. That meant a lot of flights between Muroc and the Bell Aircraft plant at Buffalo. More often than not the sergeant would check in with Cousin Millie when at Muroc. On occasion, riding with the sergeant would be an illustrious Army two-star based in the Bay Area. This was Major General Joe Swing, a paratrooper who had fought one helluva war in airborne operations in the Pacific that earned him a chestful of medals. Swing had a special affection for Pancho's.

Monday evening after the XP-86 taxi tests, George Welch was at Pancho's having dinner with Millie. He was quietly pleased with how well the first outing had gone. A first flight on Tuesday was problematical. There were still a number of ground checks to be completed and strong west winds were predicted for the afternoon. Early morning in the desert is typically calm. The best bet was for an early to midmorning takeoff on Wednesday. He noted that the X-1 crowd looked pretty glum. The little rocketship hadn't flown in more than two weeks. Millie reported the rumor that Ridley was working on giving Yeager more pitch control through the trim mechanism originally designed as a ground adjustment. She didn't exactly say those words but used her hands to represent the X-1's tailfeathers, much as the NACA engineer had done for her the night before. Welch smiled. She sounded almost like Larry Greene, who had foreseen the same problem for the *Sabre* months earlier.

In any case, it looked as though the X-1 might be flying again as soon as Friday, according to the Bell people. Millie's cousin had just brought the C-54 in from Buffalo that afternoon. Would the next flight go for the big casino? Some people thought that entirely possible. Welch looked around. No one was paying any attention to them. He lowered his voice. "It looks as though Wednesday is my big chance. A supersonic dive is for sure not on the flight card for the first flight, so I'll have to do it without recording data. Still, it's agreed that I'll pull up the landing gear. Just to get a feel for how it flies in the clean condition. Without making a record in the usual way, you'll have to be my data bank. If on Wednesday morning you hear a sharp boom like a clap of thunder, be sure and write it down—what it sounded like, what time, reaction from others, stuff like that."

"Don't do anything dumb."

"Not to worry. The North American bunch is really first class and they're not ashamed to take technical help from outside experts—like the Germans or von Karman, even the NACA."

"I'll be alert. Want to give a demonstration of what to expect?" Millie knew all the right moves.

"Not here." He smiled and called for the check.

The first flight of the XP-86 did indeed take place on that Wednesday morning. The takeoff was from the lake bed to the south. Winds were calm. George climbed with full power to 10,000 feet above sea level. That meant 7,700 feet above the Mojave desert floor. On his wing was Bob Chilton in a P-82 *Twin Mustang*. The right cockpit of the dual fuselage fighter was occupied by a cameraman. As he went through 10,000 feet indicating 160 knots, George retracted the landing gear, or at least he moved the cockpit gear handle to the up position.

Bob, who was also a North American engineering test pilot, slid in beneath the *Sabre* to have a closer look.

"Your main gear doors aren't shut, George."

"I'll put them down and try again."

"The mains are down now, but the nose gear is only about half way there."

George would worry about the down side later. He wanted to get the aircraft cleaned up. He came back to half power on the jet engine and slowed to 140 knots. Again he put the gear handle in the up position.

"Looks all up and locked now," Chilton reported.

George advanced the throttle to maximum thrust. "Don't go away, Bob. I just want to feel it out a bit." The *Sabre* zoomed up and away. Holding 300 knots, the climb rate was close to 5,000 feet per minute. In a little more than ten minutes he had reached 35,000 feet. Leveling out, the test pilot smiled as he watched the indicated airspeed accelerate to 320 knots. He estimated that should be 0.90 Mach number. He had been heading east and was just passing over

El Mirage dry lake. Rolling into a 40 degree dive, he turned to the west. His aircraft was pointing directly at an isolated group of buildings several miles south of Rogers Dry Lake that made up Pancho's hacienda. The airspeed indicator seemed to be stuck at about 350 knots. The *Sabre* was behaving just fine. Then, at 29,000 feet, there was a little wing roll. Correcting the roll, George pushed into a steeper dive. The airspeed indicator suddenly jumped to 410 knots and continued to rise. At 25,000 feet, he pulled the Sabre into level flight and reduced power. The wing rocked again and the airspeed jumped from nearly 450 back to 390. Observers on the ground would have seen the graceful swept-wing jet pull up into a big barrel roll to the left followed by one to the right. They were not unlike the victory rolls used in the recent war by returning fighter pilots to let their crews know they had bagged yet another enemy aircraft.

The number one North American XP-86 with George Welch at the controls in slow flight over the Mojave Desert, October 1947. Note that wing leading-edge slats are partially open. *Courtesy of Archives II, College Park, Maryland*

"Where are you, Chilton?"

"Circling over El Mirage at 15,000. Everything OK?"

"Couldn't be better. Be with you in a minute."

Work was being done on the configuration of the speed brakes, so they had been disabled for this flight. He would have to swing wide for his join-up with the chase plane. It was easier to spot against the azure sky than looking down onto the desert, so George continued his descent to 14,000 feet as he approached El Mirage and thus spotted the unmistakable twin-fuselaged P-82 in a left turn. He slid under and joined up on Bob's right wing.

"Still looks to be all in one piece."

Trying to restrain his jubilation, Welch noted with understatement, "Not a bad airplane."

"There's still the matter of an uneventful landing. Let's have another look at that landing gear."

Welch slowed the Sabre to 150 knots and pushed down on the gear handle. The main gear snapped into place without any problem, but the nose gear, as before, trailed at a 45 degree angle.

Cycling the gear several times didn't help, nor did the emergency gear extension pump. Some discussion with the engineers on the ground yielded little except that George was in no mood to bail out. He pushed over to 170 knots, then pulled up briefly to three g's. No luck. Finally, fuel running low, George made a long, straight-in approach for a landing to the north on the lake bed. His speed was on the high side, about 120 knots, as he touched down very smoothly. Bob Cadick had the pickup, with warning flags flying, tracking on the left side of the *Sabre*. The cameraman was in the back, along with two others from flight test just in case. George had trimmed the stabilizer to the full nose up setting. He held the nose off as long as he could. As the speed slowed to 77 knots, the nose gear snapped into the down and locked position and almost simultaneously the nose gear tire contacted the lake bed.

As the *Sabre* taxied carefully over the short distance to NAA's North Base hangar, someone was clicking a mike and intoning, "Lucky! Lucky! Lucky!" Must have been George. Perhaps "double lucky" would have been more appropriate. Takeoff to touchdown, this first flight of the XP-86 *Sabre* had lasted one hour and eighteen minutes.

Before he left for LA to brief the *Sabre* project people, George put in a call to Millie. She was more excited than he'd ever known her. "It was just like you said, baby. *Ba-boom*! It nearly bounced me out of bed. And I wasn't the only one who heard it. Pancho is really pissed. You know how nuts she is about Yeager. Her story is that the boom stuff happens all the time. Says it comes from some mining operation up in the hills east of Pearblossom. But nobody else recollects ever hearing one. Not like that boom you lowered on Pancho's habitat this morning."

"Let her have her way, Millie. Make it our secret. After all, the Air Force pays our bills. At least for now keep it under your hat. I'll be back next week."

As he hung up, Welch couldn't suppress a smile. In his innermost thoughts he was conversing with von Karman: "It was just as you said, Professor. Just as you said." And he couldn't help wishing that Fred Borsodi were on hand to witness the playout of his early speculation with the professor on sonic shock wave propagation. "Thanks, Fred, wherever you are."

PERSISTENT BOOM MEISTER

It wasn't long after the first flight of the XP-86 on October 1, 1947, that Welch dropped into Horkey's office at the Inglewood plant. He wanted to talk about his recent flight and some "funny" readings in the airspeed indicator. He had made a straight-out climb to more than 35,000 feet. Then, turning back toward Muroc Dry Lake, he had begun a full-power, fairly steep descent.

"I started at about 290 knots,"Welch was explaining to Horkey. "In no time I'm at 350. I'm still going down, and I'm still accelerating, but the airspeed indicator seems stuck like there's some kind of obstruction in the pitot tube. I push over a little steeper and by this time I'm going through 30,000 feet. All of a sudden, the airspeed needle flips to 410 knots. The aircraft feels fine, no funny noises, no vibration. Wanted to roll off to the left, but no big deal. Still, I leveled out at about 25,000 and came back on the power. The airspeed flicked back to 390. Whadya think?"

"What did the flight recorder look like?"

The self-deprecating grin that was uniquely Welch masked any hint of conspiracy on the part of the test pilot. "It wasn't on the flight card. I was just feeling it out, so I wasn't running the camera. You know how brassed off the instrumentation guys get when I run out of film for the landing. Anyway they said there wasn't anything wrong with the airspeed system. They checked it out after I landed."

"You may be running into some Mach effects. Doesn't seem like you're getting into any kind of trouble. Next time you're up that high, have another look," Horkey suggested. "Meanwhile, I'll talk to Ray Rice and Atwood about getting NACA to help us out. You know they have that fancy new radar theodolite at Muroc that can tell us how fast, how high, and where you are within a gnat's ass. But we have to get on their schedule. They may even want us to help pay for their new toy."

George smiled again. He knew that the new NACA equipment was being used to track Yeager's flights in the X-1. He also knew that North American didn't have a prayer of getting on the theodolite until Yeager had done his thing. George was on his own, but it wasn't a new experience for him. Without enlightening Horkey about Millie's testimony, he strolled over to an empty office to check in with Dutch.

Now, nearly fifty years later, sophisticated instruments displaying the speed of an aircraft in terms of Mach number are as commonplace in jet aircraft as simple airspeed indicators were in the cockpits of the forties. The first Mach indicators consisted of a red-and-yellow striped needle added as a second hand on the airspeed instrument. When the white needle on that instrument advanced to coincide with the striped Mach needle, the airplane was going at the limit Mach number for that aircraft. I recall such an instrument in our postwar F4U-5 *Corsairs*, for which the limit Mach was 0.76. For the production F-86A *Sabres* the limit was set at 0.95 Mach number below 25,000 feet, but not above 580 knots indicated airspeed, which meant that limit Mach number at sea level was 0.88. Although these early production *Sabres* also had what are today conventional Mach meters, none of the three XP-86 prototype models had either type of Mach measuring instrument on their cockpit panels during their early flights. Nor for that matter were such sonic gauges included on the photo panel mounted in the gun bays to record various measures of aircraft performance for later analysis by the flight-test engineers.

Thus, the only signal to the pilot that the XP-86 was going supersonic was the hangup, then jump, in the indicated airspeed. And this would occur at various airspeeds depending on the altitude and temperature at which Mach one was exceeded. Those on the ground in the vicinity of where the nose of the *Sabre* was pointed would be informed of the event by the as-yet-quite-unfamiliar *ba-boom*. It was a sound like a stuttered clap of thunder and occurred only when the shock waves formed by a body moving at supersonic speed struck the ground.

EARLY STORK BUT CLEARLY SUBSONIC

There was a lot of work to be done on the number one XP-86. The nose gear extension mechanism had to be strengthened. The nose gear door had been damaged. The reason for the main gear doors not fully closing on the first try had to be found and fixed. Meanwhile, some flight-test work could still be done but only with the landing gear in the down and locked position.

The second flight took place on October 9, with the landing gear bolted down. A latch was secured over the cockpit control so inadvertent movement of the handle to the gear-up position was not possible. Low-speed stability and control checks were conducted and stalls in the landing configuration were investigated. Maximum altitude was 12,000 feet. The flight lasted forty-three minutes.

George was getting very fond of the *Sabre*. Like the *Mustang*, it had delightful handling qualities. The anticipated problems of uneven operation of the aerodynamically actuated slats on the leading edges of the wings had not materialized. Stalls so far were docile with no pitch-up or rolloff. Considering the wholly new swept-wing design, the engineers had done one splendid job. Still, George was getting restless. Two days after his first flight had rattled Pancho's place, the X-1 had gotten back into the air. There had been a three-week hiatus in X-1 flights up until then. Reports from the usually reliable sources indicated that Yeager was still hung up on a close approach to the supersonic goal but had yet to push through. Certainly there had been no detectable boom laid on the base to affirm such an event.

The rocket ship had gone aloft again on October 8, the day before the *Sabre*'s second flight. The dejection of the X-1 crew at Pancho's that evening said it all—a little bit closer but not there yet. The following day, as Welch made his turn over the base prior to landing from the second flight, he observed that the orange research aircraft was being towed to the fueling pit. Bell must be feeling the pressure. He'd like to lay at least one more boom on the base before Yeager's entry in the record books was officially documented. He would have leaned on the crew a little harder after shutting down had not a different priority taken charge.

Bob Cadick chocked the wheels. Then, as the whine of the unwinding turbine diminished enough to permit a vocal exchange, he shouted, "Check in with Roy Ferren, pronto. You've got a message from home. . . . How's the aircraft?"

"No squawks. Let's get the gear fixed so I can take it where it's designed to go. I see the X-1's going to fly tomorrow."

"We're bustin' our butts as it is trying to keep the inspectors happy. We know we're number one, and we're just as anxious as you are to let the world know. Here, give me your hard hat and 'chute. I think you'll be taking the *Navion* to LA. It's all ready."

The inspector system at NAA was a good one. No aircraft left for a flight without an inspector's stamp of approval. The inspectors worked for quality control and the head of quality control reported to the company president, Lee Atwood. If an inspector thought a tire was too worn or had a cut he didn't like, that tire was changed. An oil leak that was worrisome? It was going to be fixed. The inspectors worked alongside the rest of the flight-test crew. Usually they were highly qualified aircraft technicians. But sometimes when the heat was really on to get a flight off, it might seem as though the inspector was being a nitpicking obstructionist. It rarely, if ever, turned out that way. Those guys really took their responsibilities seriously.

On the occasions when I found myself in a hospital ward as a consequence of having to bail out under adverse conditions or being compelled to ride one down onto rough terrain, I learned that I could expect at least two phone calls—one from Lee Atwood, because that's the kind of leader he was, and one from the inspector who had released the aircraft for flight with his stamp on the inspection sheet, just to assure me the aircraft was completely up to snuff when he signed it off. We really counted on the inspectors.

There was no way we could do a meaningful preflight on our own. Our trust was well served.

Roy Ferren was waiting by the *Navion*. "Jan's gone into labor. She's at the maternity ward at St. John's. Thought you'd like to check on her. Probably quicker to land at Santa Monica. Give us a call when you know how it's going."

"Holy cow, the baby isn't due until December. Thanks, but I think I'll go into LA. My clothes and car are there. I'll call you from the hospital. No problems on the flight in the *Sabre*. It was right on the money. How about getting the landing gear fixed?" It was not yet noon as the test pilot climbed into the *Navion*. He'd be with Jan in less than two hours.

Before 2:00 P.M., George strode into Jan's hospital room at St. John's maternity ward. She was propped up in bed and beaming.

"Hello, Ratty. How does it feel to be a daddy, love?"

George awkwardly embraced her. She pulled him to her and gave him a long kiss. "He's a wee one, less than three pounds, but he's going to be just fine. He's in the premie room right now until he gains some weight and they're sure he can breathe on his own. It's just down the hall. You can wave to him through the window. But no hurry. His eyes aren't open yet. Sit down and tell me about your new *Sabre*. Have you laid any more Guy Fawkes eruptions on the godforsaken Mojave?"

"I got the second flight in today but with the landing gear locked down. A good flight but nothing fancy."

"How's the competition?"

"Yeager flew yesterday and it looks like he'll be going again tomorrow. He still seems to be hung up on a pitch control problem. Most people think Al Boyd has run up the caution flag. You know— new Air Force, new responsibility—don't want to be caught running into a speed trap. But Jack Ridley will coach Chuck through it. He's a pretty clever guy."

"Tell me again, Ratty, who was recording your big event?"

"Not really recording it, Jan. It was Bud Poage's friend Mona. She's one of Pancho's girls. Buddy told her to be alert for the boom signal on the morning of the first flight. She said it almost knocked her off her feet. Other people at Pancho's heard it too. Pancho's pretty unhappy."

"Couldn't happen to a sweeter lady." Jan spoke "lady" with a broad Australian accent.

"Take it easy on Pancho, sweetheart. For all her foul mouth, she's got one helluva big heart."

"And a barn full of floozies ready to warm the bed of the first hotshot test pilot who's feeling horny."

"Not really like that, sweetheart. Bud and Mona are getting married. They're nuts about each other. I'm going down the hall and take a look at our new son. What will we name him?"

"Giles. I rather like Giles, don't you?"

"Yes, Giles is fine." George started toward the door.

"Ratty?"

"Yes."

"I'm going to call Mum in a few hours. Giles is her first grand-child. May I tell her?"

"Tell her? Tell her what?"

"About your breaking the sound barrier. Making the big boom."

Welch shrugged. "Sure. Why not? Just tell her to keep it under her hat. I don't want to get Dutch in any trouble, although Sydney's not in the normal food chain of the gossip gobblers. And, Jan . . ."

"Yes?"

"Give your mum my love and tell her your being a mum makes you even lovelier than ever."

"Thanks, Ratty. I needed that."

She'd invented the nickname Ratty when George was hospitalized in Sydney with malaria. The high fever had wasted him to skin and bones. The skin was drawn tight around his nearly fleshless face, sharpening his nose and accenting his cheekbones.

His prominent eyeteeth were much more evident, almost like fangs. The high fever kept his hair matted with sweat. She kept kidding him that he looked like a half-drowned rat. Hence, it was Ratty and it stuck, but only with her. If others used a nickname it was Wheaties, from a long-forgotten puff-piece paean to the Pearl Harbor hero on a cereal box.

Later, as morning arrived in Australia, Jan was on the telephone to her mother in Sydney.

"Hi there, Mum. How does it feel to be a grandmum now? . . . Yes, almost two months early. A wee lad, not yet three pounds, but they tell me he's going to be fine. George is here. He just went off to see about taking me home. . . . He's having quite a month. Last week he took their new jet supersonic. It's a first! . . . No, not for George, for the whole bloody world! . . . Yes, Mum, it's bigger than Pearl Harbor. . . . But listen, it's all very hush-hush. Not a word. . . . Sure, tell Pop if you like. . . . Jimmy's OK, but do keep it in the family. . . . I'm telling you, Mum, it's not a family secret, it's a military secret."

Many years later, Jimmy Williams, Jan's younger brother, would recall that phone call telling of George Welch's supersonic flight. He remembered hearing of the event because Jan had called to announce his nephew's birth, which had taken place on October 9, 1947. In the course of that call she noted incidentally that George had broken the sound barrier. His mother couldn't discern whether Jan was more pleased with the new baby or George's latest aerial exploit. He also remembered his mother had warned that George's supersonic flight was very hush-hush.

FURTHER FLIGHTS OF FANCY MACH WORK

The news from the flight of the X-1 on October 8 was that it had pushed but a few knots past the speed of the previous flight on October 3—to 0.925 Mach number, as compared with 0.92 on the earlier outing. But on October 10, Yeager was sure he had "done it."

Jack Ridley had worked his magic on the horizontal stabilizer trim mechanism and Chuck was certain he had popped through. The entire X-1 flight-test team was at Pancho's that Friday evening waiting for the data reduction people to show up with the official figures. Chuck and Pancho were huddled in a corner. The X-1 pilot had a furrowed brow. He was trying to explain to Pancho that he might not have been pointing toward the Flight Inn when he finally pushed through the big barrier. That might explain the absence of a boom earlier in the day, when he was virtually certain he had finally made the first supersonic flight. When Pancho pointed out that Welch had sure made one helluva boom on his probe into the supersonic more than a week ago, Yeager insisted that it was just a fluke. Pancho arched her brows and noted that, no matter, it had sure heated up a stable full of fillies at her hacienda.

Then the data sifters showed up—half elated, half despondent. Yeager had gone a lot faster than ever before. He had come as close as you can get and still not have made the ultimate penetration. The most careful analysis showed that on the morning's flight, the X-1 had attained a maximum Mach number of 0.997. Another pint of rocket fuel and it would have slid through. Even so, no boom is no boom.

It was a Friday evening. Some of the crew would be working over the weekend, but it would not be an all-out effort. It was the consensus of the X-1 team members that Tuesday could be the big day, no earlier. Bob Cadick, sitting at a nearby table with Bud Poage and Mona, smiled as he sipped his beer. The North American team would be working all weekend. The *Sabre* should be ready to suck up its landing gear and get back into this duel in the Mojave sun, perhaps as soon as Monday. Since any excursions of the XP-86 "into the unknown"—as some were characterizing it—were unrecorded for reasons of company discretion, the only measure of satisfaction that NAA protagonists could take was from the reality of the booms so indelibly recorded in the memories of Pancho's ladies.

Leaning close to Bud and Mona, Bob whispered, "It looks as though Tuesday is shaping up as a busy day for you boom detectors."

Bud could only smile and add, "Wheaties says if these clowns are really shook up about the dangers of going supersonic, they should go to White Sands and watch the V-2s as they routinely boom the desert there in New Mexico. Those big mothers slide through the sonic wall like a flat stone skipping across the mill pond. And they do it with aerodynamic controls. The big wall's a bunch of phony baloney."

They had been joined at their table by Joe Swing, who interjected his take on the supersonic challenge: "Don't knock it. The myth of the wall is important to the Air Force. They can probably keep the hero list high while assaulting the dread sonic wall with fewer casualties than the Nazis suffered piercing the Maginot Line. Meanwhile, the romance potential should be undiluted. The important thing is to keep the secrecy wraps tight. That way rumor and leaks can be appropriately adorned."

Swing was an Army two-star who knew whereof he spoke. He liked it at Pancho's. Stationed in the San Francisco Bay area, he occasionally hitched a ride to Muroc, on a C-54 Air Force cargo plane flying out of Travis Field in support of the X-1 program. During the war, he had gotten to know George Welch in Australia, renewed that acquaintance at Muroc, and consequently met a number of the NAA flight test people.

Bud ordered another martini. "How come you're so smart, General?"

"Hanging around this place is like taking a graduate course in seductive cynicism. Not clear it makes you any wiser, but maybe a bit more careful. In any case, that young fella Yeager is one talented professor. Or maybe creative thespian is a better term."

Clearly events were progressing inexorably toward the big climax, the ultimate *ba-boom*, the official canonization with cannonade accompaniment. October 14 was chosen to be the Guy Fawkes Day of aeronautical advancement for the jet era. What could be more important for a brand-new Air Force than to blast a hole through that formidable sonic wall? The focus was more and more on the coming Tuesday. To zoom into posterity, the X-1 had but to add two miles per hour to its recorded and documented speed of the preceding Friday—and for sure it must make the requisite boom, else the maids of Pancho's would not anoint a new ascender to the Machbuster's pedestal. One could not ignore the special ardor already accorded the creator of the undocumented "unofficial" boom emanating from the North American *Sabre* more than a week earlier.

Not only was there talk that Yeager and the X-1 might make it official, though classified, on Tuesday, but there also was further rumor that the *Sabre* was not to be outclassed. It, too, would be making some booming statements that were not to be ignored. What an honor for the Mojave Desert to be so dramatically located for that ultimate experience of the decade—full exposure to the first sonic boom from a manned aircraft in the history of the world! The fall of 1947 in the Mojave was an incandescent time to be alive— for the crazy-ass pilots and for the lovely, loving, and hopeful ladies who attended their safe return from the outermost reaches of man's other desire. So soon after the war, it was akin to the euphoria of victory but blessed with much smaller casualty lists.

Early Monday morning, October 13, Welch called Roy Ferren from his Brentwood home to check on the status of the *Sabre*. Roy reported that it would be ready first thing Tuesday morning. Having brought Jan home from the hospital over the weekend, George wanted to stay in Brentwood on Monday to line up the necessary household support for the balance of the week. In particular he wanted to extract the maximum commitment from Clara, the couple's Jill-of-all-trades, and to make sure all was well with Giles in the special ward for premature infants. He assured Roy that he would be at Muroc early Tuesday morning.

"That should work just fine," Ferren replied. "By the way, George, LA is insisting that the next two flights be made with the gear down."

"Well, there's plenty of gear-down testing to be done." George's mind was working at warp speed. Why were they doing this? Was the Air Force making sure there would be no more surprise, albeit unofficial, booms? "Uh, look, Roy . . ."

"Yeah, George."

"Whatever test configuration is called for tomorrow, I don't want to make any more flights like the last one with the wheels bolted down. We can focus on the gear-down tests for the next two flights, but I want the option to retract the gear if I need to. With the wheels down, that thing glides like a rock. Should there be any trouble with the engine, I may have to pull up the gear to make it back to the lake bed. I'd hate to have to bail out."

"Not to worry, George, the crew worked over the weekend. The new nose gear actuators have been installed and the linkage for the main gear doors have been adjusted. We've had it up on jacks. Everything works like it's supposed to."

"Thanks Roy. I'll fly the *Navion* up—be there early in the morning."

Hanging up the phone, Welch chuckled aloud.

"What's up, Ratty? The last time I heard you laugh like that you were either getting ready to fly under the Sydney Bridge with the *Airacobra* or beat up Palm Beach in the *Tiger Moth*. I forget which."

"It's something like that, Jan," George replied, as he wandered into their bedroom. "The Air Force doesn't want anyone raining on their parade, especially not one of their contractor pilots. Sounds as though someone in the X-1 camp at Muroc has bitched to the Air Force head shed that the new *Sabre* is flirting with—maybe even through—the sound barrier."

"If I remember correctly, you were an Army Air Force fighter pilot. Major Welch, wasn't it?"

"It's not just that. The government—Air Force, NACA, the taxpayer—has spent a bunch of bucks on this Bell X-1 rocket ship for the sole purpose of exploring the challenge of going supersonic with a man along. Of course, the V-2s have demonstrated thousands of times that it's really no big deal. They may not carry a man along, but they are a lot bigger and twice the weight of the X-1.

"Even so, suppose a new fighter comes along, say a *Sabre*, which is the greatest fighter of the decade, carries six guns and bombs, and makes the United States *numero uno* in the world of air combat. And incidentally this *Sabre* can also take its pilot supersonic and does it even before the supposedly advanced-technology rocketship. Or even a day or two later, or a week or two later, for God's sake. It still makes the government look like a bunch of spendthrift idiots."

"What else is new?"

"Yeah, but they don't like to get caught at it. One thing's for sure. We're not making any booms with the landing gear down. Someone with a lot of clout in the Air Force told the company not to fly the *Sabre* with the gear retracted until further notice. It's strictly a matter of safety, of course. They want their inspectors to check the fixes on the nose gear extension rig. The way it's filtered down to flight test is that the next two flights will be entirely with the gear down."

"They can't keep this kind of thing secret forever, can they?"

"In a way they can. Both projects are classified SECRET. The lid can be kept on for some time and then selectively released. First the X-1, then some months later the *Sabre*."

"But how are they going to hide those booms?"

"You do listen to me when I talk in my sleep, don't you?"

"I especially liked the tales of the V-2 in New Mexico. So you'll be leaving early in the morning. And you'll find an excuse to pull up the landing gear and zoom high enough to make a slumber-shattering dive on those crazy lazy daisies at Pancho's. When are you going to lay a boom on Brentwood?"

Welch had a half smile on his face, a certain detached appearance that said he was contemplating Muroc, figuring a plausible strategy for taking the *Sabre* once again through the sound barrier.

"Oh, Ratty, I know you, love. Already you're in that bloody *Sabre*, making plans about how to stay out front without driving the Air Force bananas."

George laughed. "Actually, I was calculating that I could indeed make it to Brentwood, lay a boom on the canyon, and have enough fuel to get back to Muroc."

"Enough, you crazy bastard. You'd spook some of Liz's Thoroughbreds. That'd stir up a lot more trouble than any of those Air Force cadets could hand you." Jan referred to wealthy heiress Liz Whitney, whose canyon ranch was a few hundred yards above the Welch home. Liz had called Sunday afternoon to check on the arrival of Giles and to tell Jan that the Whitney mare, Blue Petticoat, was a sure thing in the sixth race at Hollywood Park on Tuesday. Reflecting on that tip, Jan thought it rather more likely she'd be laying her wager on *Silver Sabre*.

Early Tuesday morning, Welch taxied the *Navion* onto the ramp of NAA's hangar at Muroc's North Base. The XP-86 had already been rolled out. The crew thoughtfully had placed the sleek *Sabre* where it was shaded from the slanting rays of the recently risen desert sun. Also on the ramp was the P-82 chase plane. Fellow test pilot Bob Chilton would be flying chase again. He was standing beside the *Twin Mustang* with one of the company cameramen. They waved greetings as George stepped out of the *Navion*.

"Your 'chute's in the cockpit," Chilton shouted.

"I've got to pick up my hard hat. Be with you in a minute."

Chilton followed Welch into the pilot's locker room.

"The Air Force is kinda looking down our throats on this flight, aren't they?"

Welch nodded in agreement.

"Look, George, if you want to go off and freelance a bit, why not let me provide a bit of cover? If there's to be an awkward twelve to fourteen minutes of separation, we can at least confuse the folks on the ground with meaningless chatter. Like puffs of smoke from the tailpipe requiring careful inspection of the rear end. Or fluctuations in the hydraulic pressure that I need to check for leaks. You can even stretch out the test card, letting the narration trail the actual performance of the maneuvers. By the time they hear the boom, they may think it's Yeager."

"Good idea. Looks as though Yeager will be finally going supersonic today. I'd sure like to lay at least one more boom on the base before he joins the club. Not long before it'll be your turn, Bob. I'll look for you as before at 15,000 feet over El Mirage." Chilton was Welch's backup on the program. He would get a couple of flights in the *Sabre* just before the Air Force started Phase II tests in December.

The third flight of the *Sabre* lasted six minutes. The aircraft had hardly lifted off the lake bed when Welch noted that the airspeed indicator had failed. He brought the swept-wing fighter back safely onto the runway using his pilot instincts. The problem, apparently caused by the failure to reattach some tubing that had been disconnected during a preflight instrumentation calibration check, was fixed, and the *Sabre* refueled in thirty minutes. Before nine o'clock, Welch and his chase plane were back in the air. In twenty minutes George had climbed to an altitude of 10,000 feet and run through all the lateral and directional stability tests called for on the test card, but he had reported the results via radio to the North American flight-test engineer at Muroc on only half of them.

He retracted the landing gear and waited for Chilton to slide underneath to check on his gear doors. Bob gave him a thumbs-up and Welch advanced the throttle to full military power. During his climb to 37,000 feet, George kept reading out the results of the tests not yet reported. As he reached his altitude goal, 2,000 feet above his starting point for his successful sound barrier penetration of nearly two weeks earlier, he once more rolled into a dive of at least 40 degrees and again he headed westward with the nose of his *Sabre* pointing directly at the Happy Bottom Hacienda. On the way down, he called out the results of the next-to-last test point on his card.

Once again he experienced some wing roll as his airspeed indicator hung up and then popped through to the greater, supersonic readings. Because he had started higher, the Mach-related transients were less pronounced than on the first flight. Instead of a gentle, throttled-back recovery as before, George left full power on and performed a four-g pull-up, little realizing that this would greatly increase the impact of the shock wave aimed at Pancho's place. He carefully throttled back and called off his last point on the test card as though he had just completed it. Turning eastward toward El Mirage, he looked for the *Twin Mustang*. For a moment, looking into the sun, he mistook a big, black four-engine plane for Chilton. At least it was black underneath, with an orange blob in its belly. It was the Air Force B-29 laboring aloft with the fully fueled X-1 safely tucked in its tummy, en route to a date with destiny. Chase pilots Dick Frost and Bob Hoover were clawing skyward from below to fly chase for Yeager in their now-obsolete P-80s.

As George swung around to join up with Bob Chilton, he mused: "Yeager has had twelve flights in that truly freaky research bomb and may make it to supersonic speed for the first time today. I'm on my fourth flight in the *Sabre* and have already boomed the valley twice. The X-1 has been flying for over twenty months to get there. Two weeks have expired since the first takeoff for the *Sabre*.

Case closed." Slowing to 160 knots, he held his breath and moved the landing gear handle to the down position. The three landing gear lights went to amber to say the wheels were in transition to the down and locked condition. Then the main gear lights showed green. The next several seconds were the price the adventurer pays

George Welch in the XP-86 dives for the lake bed to conclude his second flight of October 14, 1947, as overhead Chuck Yeager fires the X-1 rockets for his historic flight past Mach one. *Painting by Morgan Wilbur*

for leaving the path of the rules-keeper. After those several seconds, which seemed so agonizingly extended, the nose gear light turned green and Chilton slid under for an up-close check just to make sure. As he slid back out to his normal position on the *Sabre's* wing, Bob gave a clearly happy thumbs-up. George hoped the cameraman had left his lens cap on during the gear-up maneuvers.

Lining up for a landing to the south on the lake bed, George turned on the oscillograph and the photopanel so the engineers could have a good look at the *Sabre's* landing characteristics. He landed to the south because the cameraman was in the right seat in the P-82. With Chilton flying on his left wing to give the camera a clear shot, the morning sun would be lighting up the side of the *Sabre* facing the camera. The cameraman contemplated the unconsciously artistic canvas the polished aluminum *Sabre* made as it captured the deep azure of the clear desert sky on its upper surfaces and reflected the warm, bright beiges of Muroc Lake caressing its underside.

As the XP-86 slowed after touchdown on the dry lake, George made a wide U-turn and headed for North Base. Looking at his watch, he noted it was 10:25; he had been airborne on this second flight of the morning for over fifty minutes. He had shut down, dismounted, and was heading from the airplane toward the locker room to drop his 'chute and helmet before debriefing with the flight-test engineers when he heard a distant but distinct *ba-boom*. His watch read 10:30. Smiling, he was about to open the hangar door when Bud Poage caught up with him. Smothering his laughter, he declared, "That was pretty weak compared to the one you laid on about fifteen minutes ago, Wheaties."

"Who, me? Remember, I had my gear down for the whole flight."

"In a pig's eye! You must have knocked out a bunch of windows at Pancho's place."

"You don't suppose Yeager did it twice in one flight?"

"You mean you're not going to take credit for this one, either?"

"No way that swept-wing beauty can manufacture shock waves with the gear down. You trying to get me fired, old buddy?"

Poage knew, Welch knew, and both knew the other knew. Let the rest of the world anoint their alternate heroes. Putting his thumbs up, Bud smiled. "Don't give it a thought. You know where to find me if you need to."

"See you at Pancho's tonight? I expect I'll be flying again early tomorrow."

The orange X-1 was circling the lake bed for a landing.

"Doesn't stay up very long," Bud remarked. "Yeah, I'll be there. By the way, that Yeager has a real big pair of brass ones. Story is he flew today with two busted ribs. Cracked them in a full gallop collision with a closed corral gate at Pancho's Sunday night."

"See you later . . . and Buddy. . ." George hesitated an instant, then realized nothing further need be said, smiled, returned the earlier thumbs-up, and turned to walk into the hangar where he would regale the flight-test people with tales of a fifty-one-minute flight in the beautiful new *Sabre* with the landing gear extended. He'd brought back a bundle of good data recorded on the photopanel and the oscillograph in the airplane's ammo bays—and had deftly dispatched another data burst in a more direct fashion. The latter had reached the ground with greater energy perhaps than he had intended and in a form they had not yet learned to interpret. Still, the subsequent but softer boom that had followed from Yeager's differently directed shock wave out of the thinner atmosphere some 12,000 feet higher probably meant that Welch would be able —on the record—to retract the *Sabre*'s landing gear on the next flight.

ON THE RECORD AT LAST

A security clamp was immediately placed on Yeager's penetration of the sound barrier. Consequently, a celebration at Pancho's was out of the question. Instead, the X-1 team started their whoop-de-do at Yeager's house and later, when Yeager ran out of booze, they adjourned to Dick Frost's. The price might be high, but for that one triumphal evening, broken ribs were something the hero of the moment could think about tomorrow. As proof that the newly minted icon was truly relaxed that memorable evening, he flipped twice zooming his motorcycle to and from Frost's house without benefit of illumination—the bike had no light. If this aggravated the rib injury, it is not to be found on the official record—or any record, for that matter.

It's not that Pancho's closed down for the evening. The North American crew showed up if only to get a reading from their own highly sensitized boom detectors in residence at Pancho's. Both Mona and Millie were on hand to provide clear authentication of the *ba-booms* that had truly rattled their cage. Especially the first one, which actually cracked a couple of large windows in two of the bedrooms facing to the east. George Welch and Bud Poage were making careful mental notations while ascribing all credit to Yeager and the X-1. Joe Swing was on hand again and found it passing strange that there were two *ba-booms* some twenty minutes apart. Didn't it take at least two days to get the X-1 ready to fly again? With only four minutes of fuel at best, it certainly couldn't make two *ba-booms* in such a short interval. Welch shrugged and suggested with a perfectly straight face, "Maybe a V-2 flew off course out of White Sands."

Joe Swing laughed. He knew only too well that choir-boy look that Welch could assume so effectively. While preparing for the arduous campaign to be supported out of Australia through New Guinea to the Philippines, the paratrooper general had been contemplating the bronzed long limbs gracing Australia's loveliest aquatic damsels at Palm Beach near Sydney. His pleasant detachment was interrupted when a *Tiger Moth* did a thoroughly professional beat-up job along the water's edge, driving some of the ladies into the surf while others sought to flatten their endowments into the sand to escape they knew not what—only that it was loud and low. It was George. Having wearied of a lengthy recuperation from malaria at Sydney's 118th General Hospital, he had taken leave of his sick bed without a formal discharge and bummed a ride to nearby Mascot Airfield. There he conned some of the RAAF people into letting him have the *Tiger Moth* for a refresher flight before he must return to the war, to once again join the effort to stop the Japanese hordes threatening Australia from the north.

Swing noted that one of the tanned lovelies was wholly unflapped by the crazy flathatter. Indeed, she stood and waved encouragingly to the little yellow biplane.

"You know this guy?" he asked.

"Of course, it couldn't be anyone else." And she went on to tell Joe Swing about George Welch. It turns out she knew quite a lot. She was Janet Williams, the Australian girl Welch would marry before he left the southwest Pacific. Before Welch and Swing departed from "down under," they would meet and find, despite the disparity in age, that they had a lot in common. It's entirely possible that the general showed up for the ceremony when George and Jan were married a week or two later. Swing had been in North Africa and Italy. He had helped plan the airborne invasion of Sicily. Now he was leading the 11th Airborne Division, getting ready for operations in New Guinea and airborne invasions of Leyte and Luzon. Welch, on the other hand, had completed his combat tours. After 348 missions and sixteen enemy aircraft "officially" shot down, his malaria attack spelled the finish to his war but not, as it turned out, to his flying career. It is more than a little ironic that Welch and Swing should meet briefly in Australia and then cross paths again at a place as improbable as Pancho's Happy Bottom Riding Club. Though it should not be overlooked that Joe Swing had been an outstanding polo player, there are few who believe that it was Pancho's horses that drew the general to her desert hacienda.

As one of the most creative developers of tactics and techniques for paratroop operations, Joe Swing had an abiding interest in aviation. Not a graduate of any formal flight-training school, he managed to became a pilot by assimilation. He conducted his own reconnaissance over Philippine battlegrounds at the controls of the small liaison aircraft assigned to his airborne division. At Muroc he was known to occupy the left seat, normally reserved for the plane commander, of a C-54 cargo plane operating out of Travis Field in support of the X-1 project. In addition to a Distinguished Service Cross, Distinguished Service Medal, three Silver Stars, two Bronze Stars, plus numerous lesser awards, his decorations included two Air Medals. A classmate of Dwight Eisenhower's at West Point ('15), he was said to have been a great athlete but indifferent scholar. Even so, out of a class of 164 cadets he finished thirty-ninth (Ike was sixty-third). During the Mojave Supersonic Handicap of '47, he was fifty-three years old. Handsome, tall, and fit, Joe Swing could stay out in front of most men half his age in any contest he might enter. After he retired in 1954 with three stars, President Eisenhower made Swing the commissioner of the Immigration and Naturalization Service. In that role, he served his country another seven years with a competence, integrity, and effectiveness that has been sadly lacking in the current policing of our increasingly porous borders.

But in his early days, Swing's career was marked by impetuous, even crazy, behavior. The record of his athletic prowess was marred by his absence from critical contests when excessive demerits required him to march penalty tours instead of donning the football pads to help stop such traditional foes as the Fighting Irish. In his most spectacular wartime triumph, Major General Joe Swing conceived, planned, and led the airborne operation that rescued 2,134 prisoners of war (three-fourths of them Americans) from the notorious Los Banos prison on Luzon. Parachuting with his troops some twenty-five miles behind enemy lines, Swing's 11th

Airborne Division brought all prisoners to safety—not one was lost—while virtually annihilating a Japanese force of some two thousand soldiers. The 11th lost two men.

The reports of this spectacularly successful, virtually casualty-free operation arrived on the desks of editors around the world on the same day they received copies of the flag-raising on Mount Suribachi, signaling the end of the intensely bloody campaign for Iwo Jima. Standing alone, the Los Banos rescue would have meant a certain Medal of Honor for Joe Swing. Overshadowed by the press-contrived flag-raising, a Distinguished Service Cross would have to do. The general did indeed have much in common with George Welch, even though George was twenty-four years his junior and a major, not a major general. At Pancho's, rank was left outside the door.

Welch did fly the *Sabre* on the next morning. The following week he made four flights, and the subsequent Monday he flew four flights in a single day. In a single week, he had flown eight flights totaling over six and a half hours. Whether or not George did any further "freelancing," as Bob Chilton characterized it, is not clear. From subsequent events, it seems possible that complaints from on high may have put a quietus on Welch's exuberant boom-bopping. If so, it was only temporary.

Immediately following his four-flight day of October 27, Welch surrendered sole possession of the *Sabre*'s cockpit to Bob Chilton for a couple of familiarization flights. Chilton was no shrinking violet. It is entirely possible he laid a boom or two on his own. Subsequently, Welch commenced a series of high-Mach dive flights—so labeled in his flight log. In the eleven-day period from November 3 through 13, he flew eight such flights. The most intensive aural assault emanating from the Mach-busting *Sabre* took place on November 4, when three flights totaling more than three hours in duration were flown to the quiet satisfaction of the North American team, people such as Bud Poage and Bob Cadick.

This persistent barrage of *ba-booms* at the Air Force test base finally precipitated permission to use the high-precision radar theodolite facility that had confirmed the reality of Yeager's climb to immortality. Welch's dives in the *Sabre* were measured on that range in the course of two flights that took place on November 13. His supersonic excursions were clocked as low as 1.02 and as high as 1.04 Mach number. The *ba-booms* were finally and officially acknowledged, but only under tight security wraps. North American flight-test reports covering these tests are asterisked with a notation that data concerning speeds in excess of 0.90 Mach number have been detailed in an amplifying document under a higher security classification. These amplifying data could not be found in the North American archives. In George Welch's personal, handwritten flight log, these flights are variously classified as "Hi Mach No. Dive," "Hi Mach Invest," or simply "Hi Mach." Between November 3, 1947, and the end of February 1948, Welch flew twenty-three flights in the XP-86 that are so characterized. Total flight time was more than twenty hours. Almost certainly each flight included at least one incursion into the realm of the supersonic. The average is more likely two or three per flight. Concurrently, he flew forty-five other engineering test flights, adding up to more than thirty-five flight hours in the *Sabre*. All sixty-eight flights were dedicated to the expeditious development of what was to prove the world's best fighter aircraft for at least a ten-year era. Additional supersonic excursions may well have occurred in the course of these other flights, which were not exclusively devoted to high-Mach investigations.

It should also be noted that during this same four-month period, an entire week was devoted to the Air Force's Phase II test and evaluation flights on this same XP-86. These flights were flown by Wright Field's XP-86 project officer, Major Ken Chilstrom, who was also Colonel Al Boyd's Fighter Desk chief. He flew eleven flights with a total of more than eleven hours' flying time from

December 2 through 8. With time out for the weekend on the 4th and 5th, he averaged better than two flights per day. On the sixth anniversary of Pearl Harbor he flew four flights, perhaps in recognition of the four victories George Welch scored that day in 1941.

By way of comparison, during that same four-month period the X-1 made seven flights, attaining supersonic speed on three of them, but no more than once per flight. Chuck Yeager was the pilot on all but one of these X-1 outings. Total time with rockets operating was less than twenty minutes. Total flight time free of the mother ship was less than two hours. At least three-fourths of the X-1 flight time was spent gliding to the lake bed without power. For those *Sabre* fans who would rather not take their shoes off, the four-month total for the XP-86 was seventy-nine flights and sixty-six flight hours. This amounts to eleven times the number of flights and thirty-three times the flight hours attained by the X-1 over the same period.

Ken Chilstrom gave a glowing report of the aircraft while flying it to a maximum altitude of 45,000 feet and a maximum Mach number of 0.9. Why didn't Major Chilstrom push the *Sabre* through the sound barrier? Quite probably because he worked for Colonel Boyd. Al Boyd kept a tight rein on Air Force flight-test operations. He had just carefully nursed Yeager through Mach one in the Bell X-1 after twenty-eight flights spread over a year and a half. He no doubt had difficulty even conceiving that a prototype fighter only two months past its first flight could be ready to explore the mysteries of the supersonic. He was a great friend of Pancho's and had no doubt heard the rumors of *Sabre ba-booms* that floated out of her hacienda. But recollect that the fall of 1947 was an era in which the sonic boom phenomenon was not yet broadly understood, even by many technically sophisticated people. Pancho had assembled some very nice young ladies, but none of them was a Cal Tech graduate. Moreover, such knowledge as might have surfaced as a consequence of Yeager's flight was still highly classified. Similar restrictions were strictly applied to any details of the *Sabre* dances.

Colonel Boyd was keenly aware of his route to stardom. He knew the X-1 program had special protection in high places. Being first to go supersonic was important to the Air Force. For the Bell Aircraft Company, it was absolutely vital. The only reason for the existence of the X-1 was to pave a way through the sound barrier. Millions of the taxpayers' dollars had been spent to make that happen. Now it had been done. For North American Aviation to come along and say "Hey, what's the big deal? Our new fighter does it as a piece of cake" certainly wasn't going to be helpful. The taxpayers had every right to say the X-1 was a big waste of money when a nifty new fighter showed with enthusiastic *ba-booms* that supersonic was a natural fallout from just building good fighters. The yet-to-be-defined importance of manned space exploits and the X-1's relevance to that adventure was still in the distant future. Al Boyd could see that it was clearly in the best interests of the USAF that the X-1 be unequivocally first by a considerable margin and that the *Sabre* rattling be quelled as long as possible to keep the press off the scent. His stars might depend on it.

The demands of national security made the task a relatively easy one. All supersonic events must be carefully cloaked in official secrecy. North American could take satisfaction in huge new orders from around the world for its *Sabres*. Medals and Collier trophies often as not were seen by the cognoscenti as political plums for the also-rans. The burgeoning balance sheet at North American and complete confidence in its competence would carry the company for a long time. Unable to compete in the business of fighters, Bell switched to truly subsonic helicopters and found a highly rewarding niche.

Dutch Kindelberger had visited Wright Field in September. In discussions with General "Bill" Craigie he had noted that his aerodynamicists at North American believed their new XP-86, just getting ready to fly in a week or so, would be able to go supersonic in a slight dive. Larry Bell had gotten wind of that and raised unholy hell at the highest levels in Washington. There were reverberations in Dayton. Al Boyd wanted to steer clear. He had his hands full managing the X-1 success. Thus, he was glad to note the 0.90 maximum Mach number limitation when he reviewed the agenda for the XP-86 Phase II tests to be flown by Ken Chilstrom. Scheduled for December, it would be completed in ten to twelve flights. In addition to the usual checks of performance, stability and control, and general handling, there was that clear limit on maximum Mach number. He had learned that the XP-86 did not have a Mach meter. Consequently, he had one of his flight-test engineers draw up a chart of indicated airspeed versus altitude at a constant 0.90 Mach number. The data came from a small black looseleaf notebook titled "Aerodynamics Handbook." North American's chief technical engineer, Ed Horkey, had given him a copy on his last visit only a couple of weeks earlier. Al Boyd had handed the resultant chart to Ken Chilstrom before he left to fly the Air Force's first evaluation of the new *Sabre*. The area of higher Mach numbers—those in excess of 0.90—was shaded in gray.

"North American still has a limit of 0.90 Mach on the *Sabre*. Let's be sure we leave it to them to open the envelope in the gray areas. And look out at the higher altitudes. Above 40,000, the difference between nine-tenths and supersonic is only 30 to 35 knots of indicated airspeed, so be careful up there. We've learned, sometimes the hard way, that above nine-tenths our airspeed indicators tend to hang up. Not our job to do the fancy stuff, at least not on this one."

Ken didn't click his heels and snap a fancy salute, but he would have gladly done a couple of backflips had he thought it would make the colonel any more content with his choice for this assignment. It was a fighter pilot's dream to be the first to fly the most advanced fighter in the world. He looked briefly at the chart the colonel handed him.

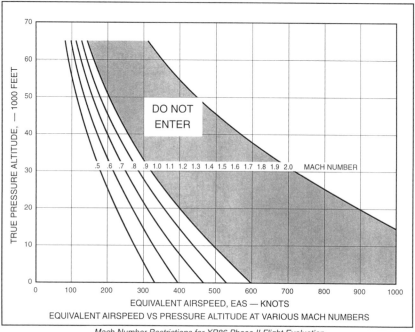

Mach Number Restrictions for XP86 Phase II Flight Evaluation
by USAF — Dec. 1947

"Don't worry, colonel. I'll keep it out of the gray, but I'll also find out everything we need to know to make sure this new *Sabre* is everything the Air Force is hoping for. I'll do my best to confirm it's at least as good as North American says it is, or find out the whys and wherefores of any shortfalls. Oh, and Colonel, thanks for the assignment."

Al Boyd smiled and slowly shook his head with that faraway look that indicated the unquestionable sincerity of his farewell wish: "I envy you on this one, Ken. I hear it's really a great new fighter."

Six months earlier, in selecting a pilot for the X-1, Al Boyd had sought the counsel of his deputy, Lieutenant Colonel Fred Ascani. Fred's choice had been Chilstrom. He had flown with Ken a great deal and found him to be smooth, smart, and unflappable.

Boyd had a high regard for Chilstrom, but he had recently flown quite a bit with Yeager and wanted to assign him to the X-1, saving Chilstrom for the *Sabre*. Ascani had not flown with Yeager but respected his boss's judgment. History left him with no regrets.

SHOW ME THE DATA

In the search for what went on between Wheaties Welch and his newfound swept-wing passion in those bright blue skies over the Mojave in the months before Ken Chilstrom arrived, perusal of Welch's personal flight log and study of the unclassified portions of North American engineering flight-test reports are helpful. Much additional information concerning what really happened high above Rogers Dry Lake, and in what sequence, that October and November more than fifty years ago has been gleaned from talking to people who were on the scene. One of the most knowledgeable of these has been Walt Williams.

Few people have understood as well as Walt Williams the challenge of testing new systems designed to rocket man to the outer fringes of the atmosphere and beyond. Early in 1947, he was sent to Muroc by John Stack, the legendary promoter of wind tunnels in the sky that evolved into the X-series aircraft. Walt's assignment was to manage the first such project, the X-1, as an annex of the NACA Langley Research Center in Tidewater Virginia. It was a tough assignment. Not only were the operational facilities primitive, with little shelter from the blazing desert sun, but in addition living accommodations for his team were distant to nonexistent. Walt accepted the mantle of responsibility not as a hair shirt but more as a determined visage he donned each day to identify for the team and other observers who was in command of that complex charge into uncharted territory. Later in his career, whenever tragedy struck the space program, such as the loss of Grissom, White, and Chaffee in the *Apollo* fire and the *Challenger* disaster, the first cry for help went out to Walt Williams. Even after he had joined the private sector, the call inevitably came and he made himself available. Senior management burdened by these mishaps knew that from Walt there would be no grandstanding, no self-serving fancy talk aimed to impress the news media—simply a no-nonsense, knowledgeable examination of the facts and an ungarbled report that would include a clear path for remedial action.

Thus, as gaps in memories and ancient archives hampered my exploration of long-ago activities at Muroc during that fall of 1947, I turned to Walt in California. It was but six weeks after the violent shattering of the freeway overpasses recorded as the Northridge earthquake of January 17, 1994. Walt's home was in Tarzana very near the epicenter. He welcomed my call and the opportunity to chat about those times long, long ago; and oh, yes, he and his good wife Helen had survived the crockery-rattling temblor unscathed in person or property. We met at the Market Broiler Restaurant in Tarzana for lunch. Walt was carrying an oxygen bottle and wore a nasal cannula to assist his breathing. A long bout with emphysema was taking its toll. Thirty seconds into our reunion, it was as if the tubes and tank had disappeared. He had learned to live with it, so let's get on with what's left.

I first asked about the earthquake. The reconstruction of the freeways and other structures was just getting under way. Ever the taker of relevant data, Walt had measured the accelerations, in pilot's lingo: the g's experienced by his home in the San Fernando Valley. In terms of damage potential for a domestic structure in Tarzana, they were clearly significant. For a feisty fighter pilot evading an enemy seeking his demise, it was a different order of magnitude. What was real and meaningful was that Walt Williams was still collecting and thoughtfully assessing relevant data, or in another sense—truth.

For a man of such instincts for what is true, it was a special pleasure to reflect on events at Muroc in October and November

1947. What was difficult might be validation of rumors and hearsay. No problem for Walt recollecting the details of the X-1 project and his data collection activities using the radar theodolite to track the *Sabre*'s "Hi Mach No." dives.

Going back to early 1947—he had arrived at Muroc in September 1946—Walt recalled the first boom leveled on the dry lake as Bell pilot Slick Goodlin did his crack-the-whip maneuver in the X-1 model with the thicker wing, pulling 8.7 g's at 0.80 Mach number. It must have been in February of that landmark year. It was a sharp crack, not the *ba-boom* that would later become so familiar over the Mojave. Careful examination of the data showed that the speed was pegged at the target Mach number of 0.80 but that the g loads had been applied abruptly, causing the overshoot beyond the

Less than seven months after the first successful supersonic flight by Chuck Yeager (left), two other Air Force pilots—Captain James T. Fitzgerald, Jr. (right) and Major Gustav E. Lundquist (center)—had taken the X-1 *Glamorous Glennis* past Mach one. *Courtesy of Archives II, College Park, Maryland*

targeted 8.0 and even more sharply reversed, overshooting to a negative 1.5. Even so, the maneuver met the requirements for the contractor's structural demonstration. So much for subsonic aural emanations.

After that, the skies were quite assuredly boom free until October. Yeager's historic flight of October 14 was unequivocally accompanied by a classic *ba-boom* as predicted by von Karman. Yes, it's true that before and after that well-documented event, the crazy bunch that assembled nightly at Pancho's spoke in muted tones of other *ba-booms* occurring when the X-1 was on the ground. The only other possible source among the new aircraft then operating out of Muroc was the sleek, swept-wing *Sabre*. Of course, one should not too casually dismiss the possibility of an errant V-2 from White Sands or aliens from other worlds. Laughing, Walt threw up his hands and demanded, "Show me the data."

He did most assuredly remember that his team tracked the *Sabre* on two closely spaced occasions some time in mid- to late November 1947. He remembered the time because it followed two X-1 events that were politically important. First, the Air Force wanted to have Yeager push the mark a little higher. Second, the number two X-1 had just been turned over to NACA, and the Langley leadership wanted to make sure one of their pilots became the first civilian to crack the sound barrier. To accomplish the first of these goals required seven flights subsequent to the historic October 14 outing before another supersonic event could be recorded. One failure after another plagued poor *Glamorous Glennis*. Finally, on the seventh flight following its first sonic penetration, Yeager again went supersonic, raising the mark to 1.35 Mach number at 48,600 feet. This happened on November 6. The aircraft would not fly again until mid-January.

The next wicket would prove a little stickier. NACA pilot Herb Hoover had been selected by the powers that bestow such legendary stardom to be the civilian Mach-busting pioneer. Unfortunately, on his first glide flight introduction to the X-1, flying the number two aircraft on October 21, Herb made a rough landing and broke the nose gear, putting the rocket ship in the repair shop until mid-December. Three months and eleven flights later, on March 10, 1948, Herb managed to fly the NACA X-1 supersonically to 1.065 Mach number, and thereupon became the first civilian pilot officially to break the sound barrier. This date set the long-delayed release of the XP-86's ventures past the sonic wall. It was deemed politically acceptable to announce that the *Sabre* had indeed gone supersonic as of April 26, a month and a half after Herb Hoover managed to struggle through. Welch made the first "official" flight in the number two prototype, the same aircraft that "Bee" Beamont would fly a month later to be the first British pilot to join the ranks of the anointed. None of the *Sabre* information was released until June. As we shall see, it is patently clear that George Welch had taken the *Sabre* supersonic at least two dozen times before the X-1 flight for which Herb Hoover was ensconced in the annals of aviation history.

I went over these early flights with Walt at lunch there in Tarzana that bright February afternoon in 1994. It was all familiar ground to him. He pointed out that his radar theodolite crew had finally responded to the North American request to clock the *Sabre* shortly after Herb Hoover's first glide flight in the X-1, when he busted the nose gear. Both X-1s were thus down for heavy maintenance and his people could focus on other demands for their services. I mentioned that North American flight-test reports indicated that the number one XP-86 *Sabre* with Welch in the cockpit made two flights on the speed calibration range on November 13, flights characterized in his log book quite simply as "Mach no." The flights were one hour and three minutes and forty-four minutes in duration. Walt said that sounded about right. He recollected that careful review of the data indicated maximum Mach numbers achieved were 1.02 and 1.04, but he couldn't recall in which order.

The accuracy of the range was a matter of great pride. He felt confident in their ability to measure speeds to one-thousandth of the speed of sound, or better than one mile an hour. In addition, he noted that there had been the increasingly familiar *ba-boom* signatures from the *Sabre*-generated shock waves. Walt pointed to the X-1 flight of October 10, when Yeager was certain he had exceeded Mach one, but careful sifting of the data showed a speed of Mach 0.997. Tantalizingly close, but no *ba-boom*. For the flight of four days later, the data showed 1.06, and there had indeed been a convincingly confirming *ba-boom*.

If these runs on his range were but repetitions of earlier high-Mach explorations, then wasn't it pretty obvious that Welch had taken the *Sabre* supersonic earlier, maybe even six weeks earlier? Walt could only shrug and repeat, "Show me the data." But Walt, a number of people heard the *ba-booms*. Walt looked to the heavens, threw up his hands, and litanized, "Show me the data." He did point out that his Tarzana garage was filled with personal files and records reaching back to those historic days in the Mojave Desert, but he doubted he would be attending to their codification anytime soon.

Little more than a year later, Walt Williams succumbed to his emphysema. Perhaps because he never sought it, he never received the broad national acclaim he deserved. In the eyes and hearts of those dedicated to greater professionalism and higher levels of safety in flight testing and space operations, his legacy lives on in lives saved and catastrophes averted, and, more important, in charting prudent pathways to ever higher speeds and more distant goals. The ultimate medals, the ceremonial trophies, were nice morale boosters to shore up egos and mend political fences. Walt knew who he was and what he was good at, and that was quite enough, thank you.

To separate what we know for certain from the purely anecdotal, the data, according to Walt Williams, showed rather unequivocally that the number one XP-86 *Sabre* prototype did fly faster than the speed of sound, to Mach 1.02 and 1.04 as measured on the Muroc radar theodolite, on the two flights of November 13, 1947. That is more than five months earlier than the "official" date for such an event announced by the U.S. Air Force, April 26, 1948. The formally sanctioned information was officially released in June 1948. Oddly enough, the "official" Mach-busting ceremony for the *Sabre* was flown by George Welch on April 26 in the number two prototype. Number one was undergoing the special instrumentation required for the *Sabre*'s structural demonstration. This official release was probably precipitated by the inadvertent supersonic announcement made on the radio by "Bee" Beamont as he became the first British pilot to break the sound barrier, on May 21, 1948, in the same number two *Sabre* prototype.

The structural demonstration is a program of intensive tests at maximum speeds and loads, conducted at high and low altitudes to prove the structural integrity of the aircraft under the ultimate conditions anticipated in combat. Satisfactory completion of these tests by the contractor is required by the Air Force before delivery of production aircraft to the operational forces. Conduct of these tests is a rigorous and time-consuming exercise. Almost invariably, structural weaknesses are uncovered. If not, the aircraft is most probably overdesigned and consequently heavier than need be. Thus, the buildup to ultimate loads is a careful one. The company, of course, takes great care to correct small defects as they occur and fervently prays that nothing catastrophic shows up. The project pilot for these tests is more than a casual bystander in ensuring that the best analyses back up all the whispered prayers. In August 1948, George Welch completed without incident the structural demonstration of the first model of the *Sabre*, which would become the F-86A. This cleared the aircraft for delivery to the operational Air Force in less than eleven months after its first flight.

But let's return to the hard data Walt Williams remembers recording. He knew for sure that his radar theodolite team measured the XP-86 at supersonic speed on November 13. It follows that the persistent high-Mach explorations by Welch in the *Sabre* prior to that date mean that without doubt he went supersonic on the flights of November 3 and 4 characterized in his log book as "Hi Mach No. Dive." As anyone who has flown those early *Sabres* can attest, if you took it to 35,000 feet or higher, then dove with full thrust, the aircraft was going to go supersonic. And, from the reports of Major Chilstrom on his Phase II tests in early December, we know that the prototype had a service ceiling of 45,000 feet, which made it all the easier. Later model *Sabres* could reach the supersonic starting as low as 25,000 feet, as Welch frequently demonstrated to Air Force squadrons equipped with the first F-86As serving in Japan and Korea in the course of his confidence-builder trips during the Korean conflict. Early on, the sonic *ba-boom* became a Welch trademark.

SUMMING UP

We know beyond any reasonable doubt that Welch was taking the *Sabre* supersonic as early as November 3. But the reason for conducting those high-Mach exploratory flights in the first place was that he had complained to Ed Horkey about funny jumps in his air speed indicator before any "Hi-Mach No." flights were scheduled. That would mean that on one or more of the *Sabre* flights in October a supersonic excursion took place. For those who insist "Welch did it first," this would have had to have been on October 1, or on the fourth flight, prior to 10:30 A.M. local time on October 14. The second flight was made with the landing gear down and locked; the third flight was only six minutes in duration. Supporting the notion that Welch did in fact join the Mach-busters on October 1 is Jan Welch's call to Sydney on the 10th or 11th of October to report the birth of son Giles on the 9th, and incidentally to announce the hush-hush fact that George had gone supersonic. Jan certainly made that call before October 14.

Attesting to the belief that George did it before Chuck are the affirmations of Bud Poage, Bob Cadick, Joe Swing, several of Pancho's girls, and scores of others. Supporting that scenario are two aspects of the Welch persona. First, the guy had an intelligence that was off the scale. He absorbed a complex array of information and made rational assessments of their interactive meaning. He was wholly underwhelmed by the supposed terrors of supersonic flight. His sessions with Borsodi and von Karman and with the first-rate team of talented aeronautical engineers at North American, his observations of the V-2 and thorough knowledge of its easy romps from the launch pad to Mach four or more—all these convinced George that the challenges of piercing the dreaded sonic wall were trivial to nonexistent. This assumes, of course, that the designers had put together an aircraft to manage the well-identified shock waves already described by von Karman, and photographed by Borsodi, that could be heard in their greater-than-Mach-one manifestation by any and all who might be strolling in the Mojave when George Welch took the *Sabre* out for an airing.

Second, George was an incurably addicted prankster. Everyone at Muroc knew the do-or-die goal of the X-1 and the dedicated determination of the top-notch Air Force/NACA/Bell team to achieve that goal. So deep was their concentration that it is doubtful any one of them took seriously the trim little swept-wing *Sabre*, altogether agile and wholly independent of all the cryogenic and mother ship complexities of their own program. The graceful little North American jet hardly rated a backward glance.

How about looking back from fifty years, from the vantage point of supersonics as a commonplace but in a world where, then as now, political pronouncements, though they may change from day to day, are the closest one may hope to come to reality? Could anyone believe that a nicely competent but wholly apolitical company could mount a meaningful challenge in the supersonic sweepstakes to the massively supported—both technically and politically—orange rocket ship? You gotta be kidding! What could be more politically incorrect than to rain on their parade, to cop their prize with a loud *ba-boom*, then shrug it all off as just another of the incidental challenges that must be met, mastered, and put in its appropriate place en route to building better fighter planes? For the truly dedicated, it's not so hard to say—please leave the laurels to those who need and want them most, we have a job to do. Then laugh all the way to Pancho's to needle the old gal about betting on the wrong contender.

6 / Hindsight

The Supersonic
a Commonplace

From the Cockpit

After Welch and Yeager alternately dove and rocketed through Mach one, the race was opened for the next milestones along the way— Mach two, three, six, ten—even to orbit and beyond. Unheralded outside the tight fraternity of aviation pioneers and their entourage, first passage of these later, and in some ways more fearsome, markers carried little fame and virtually none of the great rewards heaped upon the man thought to have been the first fearless penetrator of the dreaded sonic wall. This may seem for those informed on such matters to be rather oddly perverse, since the thermal thicket awaiting pilots venturing very far past Mach 2.5 presents more seriously life-threatening obstacles than the dangers associated with laying a barely sonic boom on an Antelope Valley mink ranch. And in the very high-altitude, Mach two-plus world of an almost nonexistent atmosphere, inertial forces and gyroscopic couplings caused mysterious spontaneous gyrations of aircraft in response to seemingly imperceptible control inputs from the pilot. These wild tumblings could be quite disconcerting, and, if your luck ran out, fatal.

In the fall of 1953, six years after the Yeager-Welch contest, the double Mach mark remained unbroken. But Yeager, by then a major, was hot on its trail. The improved Bell X-1A rocketship clearly had what it would take. NACA was pushing the Douglas D-558-2 *Skyrocket* with research pilot Scott Crossfield in the cockpit, but whispered reports from the instrumentation people in the Douglas camp indicated that the *Skyrocket* just didn't have enough poop to push past the double sonic speed. Still, it had been coming heartbreakingly close. On October 14, 1953, the sixth anniversary of Yeager's historic single-Mach event, careful reduction of the flight-test data showed that Crossfield had taken the *Skyrocket* to a speed of 1.96 Mach number.

When the NACA leaders heard that Crossfield was trying to beat Yeager to Mach two, the order went out from Langley to cease and desist. NACA is for research; let the Air Force have the records, Scotty was told. He was not to be deterred. He shrugged noncommittally and quietly pulled in some markers from old Navy friends back in Washington. The NACA head shed released the restraints by indicating they would look the other way. The following month, on November 20, the *Skyrocket* was ready, but Crossfield was not. He was fighting a flu bug. The report of a lot of activity around the X-1A got his adrenaline flowing. It seemed to be a good antidote for the flu. In any case, despite his malady, he would orchestrate one of the best flight profiles of his event-filled career.

Dropping from the B-29 mother ship at 32,000 feet, Scotty fired the rocket engine and climbed swiftly to an altitude of 72,000 feet. From there, with full power thrusting the *Skyrocket* ever faster, he pushed over to level flight, went uneventfully past the once fearsome Mach one, and reached Mach 1.5 as he started a gradual descent. At 62,000 feet, the Mach meter read Mach two plus a little bit. A few seconds later, the rocket engine quit as its extra load of supercooled fuel was fully depleted, and the intrepid research pilot was slammed forward against his shoulder harness under a deceleration force of nearly two g's. To inform anyone who cared and might be able to see it, Scotty executed an exuberant barrel roll.

Painstaking sifting of the data revealed that the D-558-2 had indeed gone past Mach two in a shallow dive, to Mach 2.005 to be precise. It would be the only Mach two flight for the swept-wing research rocketship carefully crafted by the engineers at the Santa Monica plant of Douglas Aircraft. They had designed it to probe beyond the simply supersonic after that zealously sought event had been achieved a number of times by the X-1s, once by the D-558-1 *Skystreak*, and repeatedly by the growing breed of F-86 *Sabre* pilots who delighted in booming the homes of their girlfriends and the bases of Navy pilots and more mortal Air Force jocks still constrained to subsonic steeds. In fact, the top brass, anticipating the complaints of taxpayers annoyed by those clear sky thunderclaps, were limiting Mach-busting flight to remote areas. That Antelope Valley fur farmer was already threatening suit against the government for the wildly antic behavior induced in his mating minks by the all-too-frequent *ba-booms* being laid on their wire-enclosed habitat.

In less than a month following Crossfield's first excursion beyond the double sonic marker, there occurred a couple of abortive attempts by the Air Force to duplicate that feat in the X-1A. The first took place on November 21, the day after Crossfield had captured the mythical crown. This first shot made it to no better than Mach 1.15 and was characterized as a familiarization flight for veteran Bell rocket rider Chuck Yeager. It is somewhat ironic that simply going through the dreaded sonic wall had become hardly worth noting. The word was out at Pancho's Happy Bottom Riding Club that the *Skyrocket* had already doubled that mark.

Still, because the initially reported margin beyond the technologically meaningless Mach-two milestone was so narrow—only 0.25 percent—competitive juices were really flowing in the young fighter ace more recently anointed by Pancho and a number of his research pilot colleagues as senior seasoned honcho of that very small fraternity. Perhaps reevaluation of the data would show Crossfield had actually fallen short. Yeager had no intention of making that mistake. In fact, he seems to have set his sights on Mach 2.5, this despite the warnings from NACA scientists that some serious stability problems were to be anticipated were the X-1A to be pushed beyond Mach 2.3. As we shall see, his hell-bent-for-immortality determination very nearly killed him.

To appreciate the stakes in this high rollers' game being played out in the stratosphere above the high desert of southern California, one should perhaps pause briefly to contemplate the flight—and aborted flight—records of the experimental airplanes American scientists and engineers had crafted to probe the unknowns of traveling at historically high speeds. The X-1A's thirty-month history from first flight to last is typical.

The first six X-1A flights were with Bell test pilot Jean "Skip" Ziegler at the controls. Number one, on February 14, 1953, was a pilot familiarization glide flight with successful fuel jettison tests. Propellant system difficulties precluded firing the engines on flight two. A false fire warning on flight three terminated that outing prematurely. Flight four was a successful demonstration of full-power operation with a maximum speed of 0.9 Mach number. On flight five, Ziegler noted elevator vibration at 0.93 Mach number and terminated the flight. On April 25 the same vibration was noted during flight six, but further exploration of this problem was abandoned because of an overspeeding propellant turbopump.

While these problems were being researched on the ground, Ziegler returned to the Bell plant at Buffalo to get ready for the X-2 flight tests. He was killed when the X-2 exploded in the belly of the B-29 mother ship over Lake Ontario. Further X-1A testing was turned over to the Air Force with Yeager chomping at the bit to catch Crossfield in the race for Mach two. Chuck's first X-1A flight did not take place until November 21, 1953, the day after Scotty had reportedly pushed the *Skyrocket* past that next milestone.

Getting all the pieces together for those experimental rocket craft along with their mother ships was quite a challenge. Thus, it was not until nearly two weeks later, on December 2, that the X-1A was ready again. This time, Yeager managed to nudge it up to Mach 1.5. Six days later, despite his aggressive fighter pilot determination, the maximum speed he could obtain was Mach 1.9. Four days later, throwing caution to the winds and bent on getting to at least Mach 2.5, Yeager chose to ignore the warnings of the NACA engineers. The redoubtable fighter ace pressed on to the top speed the X-1A would ever attain—a Mach number of 2.44. In the process he had climbed to an altitude of 75,000 feet. At that altitude the air is really thin. In a single cubic foot there is only 4 percent as much air as is to be found at sea level—not very much for the wings and control surfaces to grab onto. There, more than fourteen miles above the desert floor, all hell broke loose when, as predicted, the aircraft lost any semblance of stability and tumbled out of control, giving up some 40,000 feet of altitude before any possibility of recovery was regained. At 35,000 feet Yeager found himself in a subsonic inverted spin, and in getting there he had really taken a beating. The aircraft had experienced loads eleven times the force of gravity from most every direction. In his thrashing around the cockpit his head had hit the canopy with sufficient force to crack the inch-thick glass. Fortunately, his helmet was designed for such abuse.

Having allowed a competitive but poorly informed excess of testosterone to overrule the counsel of his well-instructed engineering teammates on the ground, Yeager very nearly carved out an untidy grave for himself in the desert that day. Highly intuitive stick and rudder skills came to his rescue. Returning groggily to the conscious world as the merciless wrenching between restraint straps and seat came to an end, he recovered from the inverted spin only to fall off into an erect one. No big deal that—straight and level flight was finally assumed at 25,000 feet. From there, return for a safe landing on the lake bed was an anticlimax.

This was the tenth and final flight for the X-1A for 1953. In 1954, fourteen flights would be attempted but only four would be even partially successful. On the last, with the rocket ship still suspended in the mother ship, a low-order explosion near the liquid oxygen tank encouraged NACA pilot Joe Walker to leap from the cockpit for the safety of the B-29's bomb bay. After an extended period of agonizing deliberations, the X-1A was unceremoniously jettisoned without its pilot for an ignominious splat in the desert.

Imagine, a total of but fourteen at least partially successful flights over an eighteen-month period—an average of one flight every thirty-nine days. It took seven flights to work up to more than Mach one and then just barely, despite the fact that its less capable predecessor, the X-1, had made a number of supersonic flights in the 1947–1951 era. For comparison, consider the inaugural flights of the North American Aviation YF-100A, a production prototype that flew in the same general time frame as the X-1A. It was the first fighter capable of supersonic speeds in level flight. George Welch took this initial prototype of the *Super Sabre* past Mach one during its first flight out of Edwards on the morning of May 25, 1953. He returned it to the skies over the Mojave again that afternoon, once more piercing the dreaded sonic wall and sending his signature *ba-boom* along the valley floor just to remind anyone paying attention that this supersonic stuff was old hat for North American Aviation—just take it as a given from the hero of Pearl Harbor. In its first two months of developmental flying, the first *Super Sabre* completed twenty-six flights with George Welch in the cockpit.

Before that, back in 1947, North American's experimental prototype XP-86 *Sabre* made its first thirty-four developmental test flights (including its first supersonic probes) in less than two months, occasionally making two or three flights in one day. All but two of these flights were made by George Welch. Toward the end of the Phase I developmental flight program, veteran company test pilot Bob Chilton made two test flights. The purpose was to make sure that Welch's glowing reports of the swept-wing beauty's flying qualities weren't exaggerated. Phase I was followed immediately by Phase II, flown by Air Force Major Ken Chilstrom—eleven flights in six days. Thus, forty-five test flights were flown in the number one XP-86, completing Phases I and II over a total span of seventy calendar days. Eliminating the weekends, that is fifty working days, or very nearly one flight per working day. Compare that with roughly one flight for every five and a half weeks for the rocket ships. It scarcely bears noting that neither the XP-86 nor the YF-100A had any need of a mother ship.

Returning our attention to the Mach two contest, on December 12, 1953, Yeager did quite aggressively push past Mach two, farther past than he should have, almost killing himself in the process, but not until Crossfield had already been there. So when Yeager showed up at Pancho's bar to claim his reward for going past Mach two, much as it pained her to deny his next ensconcement, Pancho noted that she had already paid off Scotty. First is first, no matter how slim the margin. And no matter that Chuck had pressed on beyond good judgment just to make an uncertain point, and nearly bought the farm along the way.

For all his skills in the cockpit, Chuck seems to suffer from a long-term memory deficit. A number of years later, he would pull the same dumb trick again, contrary to wiser counsel, and come even closer to a fiery embrace with the Grim Reaper—that subsequent event occurring in an NF-104, a nonstandard F-104 with an auxiliary rocket engine, a special airplane whose departures at high altitude were predicted to result in spins that tend to be unrecoverably flat. His book, the one called *Yeager*, tells all about it. Not noted in the book is that the NF-104 did not incorporate the stick-shaker/snatcher mechanism that has saved so many *Starfighters* and their pilots, a device for which an old pro like Yeager had little use.

It took a little over six years for the Mach meisters to push the event marker from Mach one to Mach two. A similar span of time would be needed to pass the next marker at Mach three. Again, a lot of personal rivalries, animosities, and egos would clash in an arena where corporate goals and a sometimes officious officialdom continued to make the playing field more than a little muddy. Moreover, unlike the phony sonic wall, getting up to Mach three presented real technical obstacles. Some referred to it as the thermal thicket.

Normally, when we want to cool things down, blowing cold air on the heated object seems a good idea, especially when that air is really cold, such as –65° Fahrenheit, the temperature of the air found in the earth's atmosphere at altitudes of 35,000 feet or higher. But it seems there's such a thing as blowing too hard. The fastballs of big league pitchers may reach a hundred miles per hour. Behind home plate, the catcher brings that sizzling missile to a halt in a fraction of an inch. It's a palm-warming experience. But suppose the ball were traveling 1,500 miles per hour. That is the relative speed with which a wing's leading edge encounters the molecules of our atmosphere when an aircraft is moving at Mach 2.2 at 35,000 feet or higher. Of course, those molecules are not nearly so heavy as a baseball, but there are many millions of them striking the leading edge every second. Note also that our physics professors teach us that the energy of any moving body is proportional to the square of its speed; thus the energy to be absorbed in bringing a molecule of air to a halt at Mach 2.2 is 225 times greater than that for stopping one going 100 miles per hour.

This large amount of energy is translated into heat. The temperature at the stagnation point of a wing's leading edge, where the airstream divides to flow above or below the wing, reaches some 320° Fahrenheit at Mach 2.2. That's about as hot as aluminum alloys can get without significant loss of strength.

For example, in flying the Lockheed F-104, unlike lower performing aircraft, I was instructed to focus my attention on the engine inlet temperature, not the tailpipe temperature. As the F-104 accelerates beyond Mach 2.0, its General Electric J79 turbojet develops thrust faster than the corresponding increase in drag on the airframe. The engine wants to behave more and more like a ram jet and must be throttled back before the stagnation temperature of the air entering the engine grows hot enough to cause catastrophic meltdown. Otherwise, thrust, speed, and inlet temperature would keep rising to the point of self-destruction. Obviously, an aircraft capable of slicing through the thermal thicket must be built of much sterner stuff than its slower predecessors.

In the late 1950s, three different approaches were employed independently to penetrate the thermal barrier. The U.S. Air Force was determined to have a Mach three interceptor and a Mach three strategic bomber. Both design competitions were won by North American Aviation. The interceptor, called the F-108, never got beyond the mock-up stage. The bomber became the B-70 *Valkyrie*. Two prototypes were built and flown to a stabilized cruise speed of Mach three. The structural heating problem was solved by using stainless steel honeycomb, but that technology presented many difficulties, such as pinholes that leaked fuel and a huge price tag. Tooling alone cost over $100 million (in 1958 dollars). Harrison "Stormy" Storms was chief engineer at North American's LA Division in the B-70 era. Some years later he confided to me that never again would he design an aircraft using stainless steel honeycomb. More fundamentally, war-gaming studies showed that even with a Mach three speed, the survival of the high-altitude bomber in a tough anti-air missile environment was highly improbable. Alternatively, there was no way the B-70 could have performed as a terrain-following penetrator.

The *Valkyrie* never went beyond the two prototypes. One was lost in a tragic midair collision over the Mojave that had nothing to do with any shortcomings of the huge, high-altitude Mach-three bomber. The surviving XB-70 went to NASA and flew a number of exploratory tests principally associated with the challenges of building a successful supersonic transport, especially those having to do with the public's tolerance for sonic booms. This huge relic of a once real Cold War can now be seen at the Air Force Museum at Dayton. But there's no denying that North American's B-70 had found a feasible, if impractical, method for negotiating and cruising along the thermal thicket. By the time its Mach three capability had been achieved, others had already been there. Indeed, there were two programs that preceded the B-70 that pushed into the Mach three-plus regime using a different technology.

The second approach to sustained Mach three and beyond was shrouded in the mysteries of the spook world. Even before Francis Gary Powers was shot down in 1960 over the Soviet Union, close observers of the U-2 operations knew that the United States would need a spy plane that would go much higher and far faster. Kelly Johnson was already at work on it at the Lockheed "Skunk Works." In April 1962, the first version of what would become the SR-71 *Blackbird* made its initial flight. Although wrapped in the tightest national security constraints, the *Blackbirds* quickly demonstrated the advantage of clearly identifying a talented team and turning it loose under a strict code of tightly guarded secrecy and a minimum of bureaucratic nonsense. Made primarily of titanium—some 93 percent of its structural weight—and crammed with the latest in cameras and electronic sensors, the SR-71 demonstrated an ability to cruise for great distances at Mach three and faster. Stagnation temperatures on the nose at maximum speed reached

625° Fahrenheit, yet sustained cruise for more than an hour and a half at those speeds and temperatures became almost routine.

However, the first aircraft to maneuver successfully in the thermal thicket, the first to make it through Mach three, and ultimately the fastest and hottest of the lot was, appropriately, a NASA-sponsored research craft. As with the X-1, which may have been the first to go Mach one (in October of 1947), and the D-558-2, which was certainly the first to go Mach two (in November 1953), the North American Aviation X-15 was rocket powered and was carried aloft by a mother ship, in this case a Boeing B-52. Consequently, there was no need to provide for air inlets, since rocket ships by definition carry their own oxidizer. Inlet design for Mach-three air-breathing aircraft is a very challenging task. This is undoubtedly the reason NASA chose rocket power for the X-15.

Before examining the forays of the X-15 into the world of Mach three and beyond, we should pause and make sure that there is a special place in aviation history for Air Force Captain Milburn G. "Mel" Apt. This able test pilot on his first flight in the Bell X-2 research craft on September 27, 1956, flew the swept-wing rocket ship in a flawless track of the prescribed flight plan, reaching a speed of Mach 3.2 in a slight dive at an altitude of 65,000 feet. There were ten seconds more rocket burn than anticipated by the flight planners. Consequently, the X-2 remained at a speed in excess of Mach three for that extra period of time. At burnout, Mel initiated a turn back to the Edwards lake bed. His roll input may have been more abrupt than was wise. In any event, all semblance of control was lost. The aileron deflection for the turn induced yaw and then pitch. A violent tumbling ensued, and Mel was knocked unconscious. When he came to, the tumbling was unabated. He jettisoned the nose capsule, which included the cockpit, but was again rendered unconscious as the separated capsule began to gyrate wildly. Unable to deploy his parachute, he was fatally injured as the capsule struck the ground. Recorders of aviation events and markers require that record-breaking aircraft be returned relatively intact to the earth with a living, breathing pilot so that any notable feat may be officially inscribed in the history books. Because of Mel Apt, when it is noted that So-and-So was the first pilot to exceed Mach three, there must be added the footnote: "and survived." Indeed, Mel Apt was the first pilot to exceed Mach three. He survived the event but not the landing.

Two X-2 research rocket ships had been built. As noted earlier, one had already been lost when it blew up in the bomb bay of its B-50 mother ship over Lake Erie on a captive test flight. The highly respected experimental pilot Skip Ziegler was standing beside the aircraft when the explosion occurred and was lost in the blast. A successful Mach three excursion would have to await the X-15.

On September 30, 1955, almost exactly one year before the Apt tragedy, North American Aviation was selected by the U.S. Air Force to design and build the X-15. The purpose of this exotic new experimental research aircraft was to explore the many problems of flying aircraft on the fringes of space. It was hoped it would attain speeds as high as Mach eight—and it came close. The unflappable Pete Knight took a much-modified model to Mach 6.7 just before the end of the program, although a lot of skin made from high-temperature nickle-steel alloy was burned off in the process. Pete's ultimate probe into the thermal thicket with the X-15 would take place on October 3, 1967, more than twelve years after the contract award.

An interesting event that accompanied North American's winning of the X-15 project was the departure of Scott Crossfield from the ranks of NACA experimental pilots at the Edwards facility. Scotty had played a dominant role in the experimental flight-test work that took place there during his relatively brief sojourn. His first flight out of Edwards in a research aircraft occurred on April 20, 1950; the last, as a NACA pilot, on September 2, 1955.

During that period, five hundred exploratory flights were conducted in X-series and D-558 research aircraft out of that facility. Scott Crossfield flew 181 of these flights, the balance being spread among other NACA, Air Force, and contractor test pilots. Including Scotty, there were an even two dozen of them. Crossfield flew slightly more than 36 percent of the flights in research aircraft launched from the famous test installation while he was there. This does not include the many models of military and civilian aircraft in prototype or production configuration that were also tested from the Edwards runways by these same pilots and a number of others.

While at NACA, Scotty had been a strong proponent of the X-15 as a research tool to explore extended supersonic flight deep into the thermal thicket. When North American Aviation won the contract to design, build, and test that exotic rocket, he signed on with the company as design specialist and project pilot. He hoped to be in the cockpit to push the X-15 out to its limits. Yeager had claimed the Mach one marker, and Crossfield had barely slid past Mach two while still with NACA. With Mach eight as a design target, the X-15 could conceivably put six more Mach laurels upon his brow. Alas, the system just doesn't work that way.

Early on in the program, North American was informed quite clearly that its responsibilities were to demonstrate the X-15's capabilities to Mach two plus a little bit. From there, NACA and the Air Force would be responsible for its operations, including selection of the pilots. Recollect that NACA had earlier been advised that Crossfield was to keep the D-558-2 in check until Chuck Yeager had a chance to whistle past Mach two in the X-1A. That was back in 1953, when Crossfield called on some old friends with political clout and beat Yeager to Mach two by three weeks.

The X-15 was a different matter. Now the thoroughly vetted pro was working for a big corporation whose bottom line could be affected if the rules weren't carefully followed. Scotty had worked hard to sell himself to North American as a two-for-one package—design specialist and project pilot. Once there, he gave full value and put in long hours over the drawing board, on the shop floor, and flying the simulator. A lot of time was spent with David Clark and his human factors experts in designing a pressure suit that would be a prototype for future space missions. He and project engineer Charlie Feltz became fast friends. They were frequently joined at their discussions by another close friend, chief engineer Stormy Storms. Late sessions frequently were adjourned to the nearest bar, continuing till midnight and beyond. The tough technical details became manageable. But for many test pilots and other testosterone driven leaders in their chosen field, the competitive game was paramount. Being out front was the whole ball game, especially if the guy nipping at their heels was out of his class and just might take the prize as a consequence of bureaucratic position rather than championship form.

The X-15 project pilots for the initial flights by the Air Force and NACA were Major Bob White and Joe Walker, respectively. White, a quiet, competent pilot, had been abruptly pulled out of the fighter section at the Air Force Flight Test Center to take on the X-15 in place of the ebullient golden boy Iven Kincheloe, who had died tragically in a freak F-104 crash at Edwards in July 1958. A Korean War ace, the fun-loving, articulate "Kinch" had it all. Many thought he was a cinch to become Air Force chief of staff one day. Bob White, on the other hand, was quiet, reserved, and studious. The press had loved Kinch and plastered his photograph in all the right publications. White would go on to be the first pilot to take an aircraft past Mach four, Mach five, *and* Mach six. The world of aeronautics, much less the great uninformed public, took little note nor long remembered. But the Air Force knew quality and kept Bob White moving up the promotion ladder to two-star status before he retired.

Between White and Crossfield there was an easy relationship. Bob was a good listener and Scotty had a lot of rocket ship flight-test experience to pass along. Crossfield and Walker—that was another story. They had served at NACA together for four years, flying many of the same research projects. They were totally different personalities and simply did not get along. Now with the X-15 getting ready to fly, it truly stuck in Scotty's competitive craw that after all his dedicated work to make it all come together, after a few run-of-the-mill demonstration flights, Joe Walker would take the X-15 out to its limits. It didn't seem fair.

He wasn't around when the XP-86 first flew, or when Yeager was officially declared the first to go past Mach one, but he had gotten to know George Welch—partly through direct contact, but with perhaps equal intimacy through those careful preservers of "the right stuff" who hung around Pancho's place. If Wheaties could break ranks and beat Yeager to the Mach one marker, why shouldn't he follow the North American tradition and cop the Mach three trophy ahead of Joe Walker? After all, it was kind of the way he got to Mach two first, and no one made any big fuss about it. Scotty had it all figured. He knew that once Walker got in the cockpit of the X-15, the opportunity to head him off before he made it at least to Mach three was poor to nonexistent. After Scotty left NACA, Sputnik was launched. It was in October 1957, and in October 1958 the National Advisory Committee for Aeronautics (NACA) became the National Aeronautics and Space Administration (NASA).

It was more than just a change in name. It was a dramatic shift in public affection as the fickle press switched its attention from the X-15 to the *Mercury* program. When kids go to the circus, they marvel at the skills of the acrobats as they toss each other from one trapeze to the other high above the crowd in the big top. But it is the death-defying feat of the mindless human cannonball blasted with a loud bang and much smoke from a hokey spring-loaded cylinder, fashioned to look vaguely like an ancient artillery piece, that leaves them awestruck. One's a trick any ape could perform. The other requires a lifetime of training and practice and split-second timing.

The powerful XLR-99 rocket engine ultimately destined to power the X-15 was quite a development challenge. It would not be available until eighteen months after the start of flight tests. For the initial tests two XLR-11 engines from the X-1 era were used to get the program under way. Together they offered but one-third the thrust expected from the bigger engine. It was not clear that it would be enough. However, when the first powered flight of the X-15 reached Mach 2.11, Scotty knew that, even with the smaller engine, the new research ship would make it past Mach three. The next flight he pushed a little higher and faster. On the third flight he was ready to push through Mach three when an engine fire required an emergency landing at heavy weight, resulting in a broken fuselage.

Joe Walker was badgering Scotty for a flight. The damaged ship gave Crossfield an excuse to put off the NACA pilot's introductory exposure to the exotic new bird. But Scotty saw the pressure building. If everything looked copacetic on the next flight, maybe, just maybe, he'd do a Welch. He knew damn well he was going to try. When he dropped from the B-52 mother ship for his fourth powered flight, Scotty climbed at full thrust to 65,000 feet and started to level out. As the speed built up to Mach 2.5 the wily pilot, instead of resuming his climb at that Mach number as the test card indicated, held the rocket ship level and observed the Mach meter build to a speed of Mach 3.1. As the X-15 sped southwestward along the test range above the Nevada desert, satisfied that the triple Mach marker was in his pocket, he once again pulled the nose of the aircraft up more steeply and watched the speed deteriorate back down to Mach 2.5. Soon thereafter, fuel depleted, the engines quit, and Scotty concentrated on setting himself up for a circling approach to a landing on the Edwards dry lake.

After the flight, Paul Bikle, who had assumed leadership of the NACA flight-test facility upon the departure of the indomitable Walt Williams, stopped by the pilots' locker room where Scotty was getting dressed.

"Looked like a good flight, Scotty. Anything unusual from your perspective?"

"Not really. Everything seemed pretty normal."

"Good. You know the ground-tracking radar guys had you pegged at Mach 3.1 while you were supposed to be in a steady two and a half Mach climb."

"Really, Paul. Are they very accurate?"

"They better be or we threw away a helluva lot of money."

"Gee, guess that titanium beauty is a lot slicker than we imagined. But that wasn't a part of the day's work that we were most interested in. It'll be a long time before they get around to reducing the data for that part of the flight. Unless, of course, you want us to have a special look at it."

"Naw, no way. Besides, no sense in getting Joe all bent out of shape. We just won't talk about it. OK?"

Scotty smiled half conspiratorially. He really liked this guy Bikle. "Yeah, just tell the radar guys they must have been out of calibration. We don't need any unhappy customers, do we?"

It was enough. He knew for sure and so did someone for whom he had a great deal of respect, not just for his technical smarts but also for his integrity and judgment. After all, Bikle understood about records. Just a year later on February 25, 1961, climbing in the Sierra wave near Mount Whitney, less than one hundred miles north of Edwards, Paul would set the absolute altitude record for sailplanes—over 46,000 feet—a world record that would stand for twenty-five years. On the same flight, he set a world record for altitude gained in a sailplane—more than 42,000 feet—which has yet to be broken.

Thus, Scotty had the Mach two trophy officially and the Mach three award in a special corner of his personal footlocker. It would stay there for a long time, but not even a straight guy like Paul Bikle could keep a secret forever—nor for that matter could Scotty. For Welch there had been the unmistakable *ba-boom* and Pancho's rumor mill. Joe Walker would "officially" exceed Mach three on May 12, 1960, on the fifteenth X-15 flight, some four months after Crossfield's "inadvertent" triple-Macher. Barely six years later, in June 1966, flying a promotional stunt for General Electric engines, Joe would let his F-104 slide too close to the downward folded wingtip of the B-70, striking it with his horizontal stabilizer. This caused the *Starfighter* to pitch up and, caught in the vortex from the *Valkyrie*'s wingtip, roll into the huge bomber's vertical tails. The little fighter's canopy was crushed with unsurvivable results. So the secrets must be preserved a little longer.

There you have a brief look at three assaults on the thermal thicket, three different ways of getting to Mach three and beyond. The somewhat remarkable aspect of all three, a common thread, is that as these aircraft sliced through the air after takeoff or upon being dropped from a mother ship, they were clearly subsonic and must therefore penetrate the sinister sonic wall if they were to get to Mach three. Yet nowhere do any of the reports note the first problem or the least concern for piercing the sound barrier en route to the greater challenge twice again as far on the other side.

In time, the truth will out. In October 1995, at Sun City, Republic of South Africa, the Fédération Aéronautique Internationale was holding its annual meeting, a movable feast. Known as the FAI, this highly esteemed organization is the ultimate arbiter of events, records, markers, and such having to do with aeronautical matters. They do this for the entire world. At Sun City, Scott Crossfield was presented with the FAI's gold medal, its highest award, for being the first person to fly an aircraft at a speed of Mach two and also the first to exceed Mach three (and survive). Probably there is no longer anyone at NASA, or at North American Aviation's successor (once Rockwell International, now the Boeing Company), who cares. But for some of the old grey eagles and the hangar gang who were a part of that illustrious North American team, the ones who occasionally assemble to compare PSA's and hip replacements, they probably knew all along. What good's a secret if everybody keeps it forever? Although six years separated each of the transitions from Mach one to Mach two and from Mach two to Mach three, in less than two years the next three milestones would be passed, all by the X-15 with Bob White in its cockpit. The heat of the research craft became dramatically higher with each advance. Dealing with it became an ever-increasing challenge. Although the X-15 was originally designed to reach Mach eight, the effort to attain that mark was halted with Pete Knight's flight of October 3, 1967, which reached Mach 6.7, the fastest the X-15 would ever fly. Despite the use of special ablative paint for better heat protection, it was becoming clear that sustained speeds much above Mach three simply require too much cooling to be practical. For this kind of high-speed operation on a sustainable day-in, day-out basis, it will undoubtedly make more sense to get out of the atmosphere and count on the transitional management of the intense but briefly experienced heat of re-entry at Mach twenty-five or so, as is now done routinely by the space shuttle.

Meanwhile, we should hear it for the White-Knight-Crossfield team of test pilots who helped craft the vehicle and explored the limits of atmospheric flight. Crossfield retired recently from a staff position on a congressional committee for research and development. For years he kept alive the concept of research for the exploration of very high-speed flight by manned vehicles, as most recently epitomized by an experimental aircraft that would take off conventionally, go into orbit, and return for a normal landing. It would be a single-stage-to-orbit vehicle embracing much the same technology as the Orient Express fancied by President Ronald Reagan. As so often happens, bad politics frequently gets in the way of good science, and corporate greed often overreaches common sense. Such programs, whose economic viability is not always apparent even to some of the more creative capitalist intellects, prove very difficult to sustain in a purely planning mode over a decade or more. They need a strong sense of national purpose, similar to John F. Kennedy's commitment to put a man on the moon.

The manned single-stage-to-orbit vehicle is like Mount Everest. It's out there to be climbed, to be built, to be done—if only someone can find the sponsor, the funds, the reason to do it in the first place. In retrospect, however, for the old Mach meisters of the post-1947 era, after the early X-1 and XP-86 probes through and beyond the "sonic wall," going supersonic had all the challenge of a daylight stroll in the park. If that stroll's with a boom box, be careful not to pass near the nursing mothers. So with supersonic flight, pilots must be ever alert not to break any windows or upset any endangered species. From the cockpit, the *ba-booms* are wholly inaudible. Only the jump of the Mach meter will herald the event. Of the 199 flights of the X-15, only two failed to go past Mach one, and they were both unpowered flights. If penetrating the sonic wall presented any concerns to the intrepid dozen who flew that remarkable research craft, history fails to record them. The same is true for the SR-71 and the B-70, although, in tacit recognition of the added drag at their air-breathing inlets, those two triple Machers dipped in their subsonic climbs as they reached roughly 35,000 feet and 0.95 Mach number to provide more push, so the shock waves could be swallowed and contained within their inlets as those aircraft slid through Mach one.

From the Laboratory

More than fifty years ago it was demonstrated that a manned aircraft could slip unscathed through the dread sonic wall. Almost immediately it became a matter of military doctrine that all combat aircraft must be supersonic capable—well, at least the fighters. Then in the midfifties, it was technically feasible to build Mach-two fighters. In the late fifties, we knew how to build a Mach-three bomber.

The British and the French stole the march on the commercial world with their Mach 2.2 *Concorde*. The United States announced that it would build a Mach 2.7 supersonic transport (SST) with double the *Concorde*'s accommodations for but one hundred passengers. Then the bills started coming in. Boeing had won the competition, but the company's leader, Bill Allen, breathed a sigh of relief when a presidential commission looking into the wisdom of a big U.S. investment in an SST said the program should be scrubbed. The commission was headed by former Pentagon genius and accounting whiz Robert McNamara. The eminently wise decision was reached for all the wrong reasons, but, no matter, Boeing and the U.S. taxpayer were off the hook. The British-French consortium inked its agreement for the *Concorde*'s development in 1962. The first commercial flight took place in 1976. Although many international airlines signed up to purchase this capability to nearly triple the cruise speed of their jetliners, by the time certification by French and British authorities had taken place in 1975, all but Air France and British Airways had dropped out.

A total of fifteen fully certified *Concordes* have been built. Even though passenger fares on this one-class airliner are substantially greater than first-class prices on the subsonic jets, the development and production costs have never been paid. The two airlines, until recently state-owned, barely recover operating costs. The money-losing service remains available as a matter of national prestige.

Several years ago the *Concorde* coalition was approached by
Federal Express. The package carrier wanted to lease several
Concordes in a freighter configuration to provide superior delivery service between Europe and the United States. The negotia-
tions broke down when the *Concorde* group refused to guarantee
support of *Concorde* operations for at least ten years. By then the
technology on which the aircraft is based would be forty years old.
Surely we can do better than that. It's like Cessna resuming production on the even more ancient *Skyhawk*, first introduced in the
early 1950s.

Apparently the military has also given up on the speed chase.
In its vision of the future for both fighters and bombers, the macho mantra is stealth. The most expensive aircraft in history, the
B-2 *Spirit*, an all-composite flying wing, is reputed to be virtually
undetectable by radar. Its maximum cruise speed is 475 miles per
hour, or 185 miles per hour slower than the ancient B-52s.

More than twenty years ago, the strategic bombers of the USAF
abandoned their flashy B-58 *Hustlers*. Capable of speeds in excess
of Mach two and a pilot's delight compared with the ponderous
B-52 *Stratofortress*, the *Hustler* simply did not have the range-
payload capability demanded by then strategic bomber boss General Curtis LeMay. Even so, during its brief stay in the nation's
inventory of operational aircraft, in the skilled hands of Air Force
Major William R. Payne, a B-58 hustled from New York to Paris in
3.3 hours, or almost exactly one-tenth the time required by Slim
Lindbergh. That was in 1961. The record still stands. When I was
privileged to fly the *Hustler*, my mentor was Bill Payne. Courageous
man, he let me fly it chock to chock even though I had been absent
from the cockpit of high-performance aircraft for more than a
year. I learned firsthand that the four-engine delta-wing bomber
would indeed fly faster than Mach two at high altitude. More interestingly, it would ride through heavy, hot-day Texas turbulence
down low just above the treetops as steady as a rock at better than

650 miles per hour. In a similar environment, I had flown the B-52 down low at less than 300 miles per hour and it seemed that the four engine pods out on the wings were simultaneously flying in different directions. The cockpit caromed about like a loose-sprung pickup going flat out on a corduroy road. Just reading the instruments was difficult to impossible.

It should be noted that the B-52 wasn't conceived to fly close to the ground; and in the *Hustler*, I had a lot of help. Since the dawn of the supersonic era, Convair, the company that designed and built the *Hustler*, had maintained a talent for creating superior flight-control systems, starting with the delta-wing F-102 fighter. This result is in no small measure attributable to the unequivocal demands of two perfectionist Convair test pilots—Dick Johnson and Beryl Erickson. It was a deficiency in those skills that had earlier resulted in the tragic loss of Geoffrey de Havilland when he tried to fly too fast too low in the British *Swallow*, which, like the F-102, had no horizontal tail.

After proving that going faster than sound was no big deal more than fifty years ago, the military began insisting on Mach two and more. There the scientists had to do some extra work. Inlets for the early transonic fighters were fairly straightforward. As greater speeds were sought, the shock waves created at the inlets prevented the introduction of sufficient air to the engines, with an attendant reduction of thrust and increase in drag. Aerodynamicists determined that if the shock waves could be positioned by a movable inlet cone or ramp ahead of the inlet face so that they would be contained—that is, swallowed by the inlet—the captured energy of the shock wave would add to the overall efficiency of the propulsion system. At the same time it would greatly reduce the drag of that big umbrella of a shock wave stretching all the way to the ground. Without the added complexity of a shock wave positioning, variable area inlet, Mach two for aircraft with conventional air-breathing propulsion systems would have been very difficult and Mach three impossible. Of course, Mach three brought the further complication of dealing with the thermal thicket, where aluminum structures had to be abandoned. Still, twenty years after the first Mach one event had been recorded, the challenges of Mach three had been met. Operational SR-71s were routinely flying Mach three missions, although perhaps routinely is not exactly the right word. And that was thirty years ago.

The lessons learned from the B-70 and the SR-71 put an end to the fascination for ever-faster that had increasingly gripped the U.S. air forces since World War I. This fetish for faster was especially true of the fighter pilots during and right after World War II. Beginning in the midsixties, higher performance would increasingly become the domain of the missiles. More and more, all combat aircraft would be viewed as weapons carriers—air-to-ground and air-to-air missiles plus bombs. There are inert bombs, smart bombs, and precision-guided bombs. The last, with the addition of a little boost, looks very like an air-to-surface missile.

There remain a few fighters that can jettison all their external encumbrances—bombs, missiles, fuel tanks, ECM, sensor pods, and so on—and give a good account of themselves in any arena. It is mainly in the intercept role that maximum speed is of any consequence, but so is the amount of fuel required to attain that speed. Rat race in full afterburner for but a few minutes and your propulsion system may be sucking fumes before you get home. That is why the more recent the aircraft, the more the performance is being placed in the missile. Carried by the F-14 *Tomcat*, the Navy's *Phoenix* air-to-air weapon has a wholly independent target tracking and guidance system. It's a method called "fire and forget." Once launched, it's on its own and en route to the designated victim, which may be up to one hundred miles distant. The speed of the *Phoenix* can be as great as Mach three, and it can perform maneuvers in the course of its three-minute journey that would pull the wings off the *Tomcat*. And the *Phoenix* represents thirty-year-old technology.

Thus, the Mach meister crown so aggressively pursued by two feisty fighter pilots above the dun tones of the Mojave in the fall of 1947 may prove of marginal, if any, value to the fighter pilots of the twenty-first century. Instead of *ba-boom*ing their presence to those below, military pilots are increasingly seeking to tiptoe through the cirrus and avoid giving anyone, especially those with hostile designs, the slightest clue as to their whereabouts. Because the name of the game for the new combat aircraft is stealth, scientists have placed full-scale models in their anechoic chambers and bombarded them from every angle with all manner of radar signals and measured the resultant echoes. Then they go back and reshape the wings and fuselage and try again. Meanwhile, the aerodynamicists and propulsion designers tear out their hair. The drag has gone off the scale and there's no way for the engines to get enough air.

In the end, the performance is all screwed up and the stability and control characteristics are so weird that only the computer can fly the thing. The end product is like a B-2, which is indeed very close to being invisible to any radar we know of today. Its stability and control are wholly computer generated. So what if it costs twice as much as any previous big bomber and its maximum speed is only 0.70 Mach number? In fact, that lower speed is something that greatly pleases the stealth scientists. Really!? But of course. If it went very much faster, say 0.90 Mach number, the stagnation points on the airframe—the nose, the wing's leading edge —would get enough warmer than the surrounding air that infrared scanners would detect that change in temperature. Everyone has infrared detectors these days, even the deerslayers. The 20 to 30 degree temperature difference will illuminate your aircraft on a scanner like the eyes of a stag caught in a Jeep's headlights.

Recently we have learned that the B-2 must be kept under shelter when not flying, and when in the air it must avoid the rain, lest its stealth warpaint be washed away. We must all be grateful that Welch and Yeager taught us how to fly faster than sound, even in the rain.

So if the military doesn't care much about supersonic anymore, how about the commercial market? Potentially it's huge; politically it's dead. The reason is the sonic boom. The *Concorde* is not allowed to fly at supersonic speeds over land. In fact, it's not allowed to get close. Some early flights skirted the coast of Maine while still supersonic. Although the swift jetliner paralleled the shoreline ten miles or more out to sea, the inhabitants in the region complained about the intrusive sonic boom and the route had to be adjusted to follow a track farther to the east.

Occasionally the space shuttle lands at Edwards Air Force Base. It comes out of orbit smashing into the atmosphere at Mach twenty or so over Los Angeles and rattles the city's skyscrapers almost as sharply as a seven on the Richter scale. Since it doesn't happen more often than once or twice a year, there is no sustained protest. Let that happen eight or ten times a day on a regular basis, and commercial supersonic travel is a dead duck. And if a commercial supersonic transport cannot travel over land at supersonic speed, its commercial viability is zero. Just ask the *Concorde*'s sponsors. But even absent the *ba-boom*, the *Concorde* burns more than five times as much fuel per passenger mile than does a subsonic jet transport of comparable gross weight, such as the Boeing 777. To make supersonic a commercial success, the scientists must find a better way.

A manned aircraft flew supersonically for the first time more than fifty years ago. Since then many military aircraft have been produced that are capable of exceeding the speed of sound. The United States has built several dozen SR-71 reconnaissance aircraft that have customarily flown Mach three-plus (they are now retired), and one intrepid research pilot actually tiptoed up to

Mach 6.7 in an X-15 research rocket and came back to inform anyone who cared that, for atmospheric flight, he wasn't particularly
interested in pushing his heat-crinkled rocket ship any faster.
Slowly, the military strategists seem to be coming full circle.
Wonderful advance in aeronautical technology that it may be, a
supersonic capability is becoming superseded as an essential performance feature of future military aircraft. Whatever supersonic
or hypersonic zap as may be needed can be found in advanced missiles, both air-launched and surface-launched.

Have the scientists given up on more advanced supersonic
aircraft? For the military, the matter certainly seems to have been
put on hold. The most advanced fighters being introduced today
have a maximum speed of Mach 1.7 to 1.8, but that's without any
impedimenta attached to their wings. The older aircraft they replace are good for Mach 2.5. New bombers are decidedly subsonic,
even slower than their subsonic predecessors. It may be that the
application the military would find most operationally useful is a
supersonic logistics support aircraft, provided that investment and
operational costs could be substantially reduced below present
estimates. The idea of a truly fast rapid deployment force certainly
has great force projection appeal. However, recollecting that some
three-quarters of the troops sent to the Middle East in the Gulf
War rode on commercial jet transports, the military airlift pro-
viders will no doubt await commercial developments for this
capability.

Although NASA continues to insist that their spending on High
Speed Civil Transport (HSCT) research—$1.76 billion since 1992—
demonstrates their strong support for a viable SST, the resulting
configurations look for all the world like an overgrown *Concorde*,
better known as the twenty-year-old Russian Tupolev 144, reflecting the technology of the early 1960s. NASA's insistence that what
goes supersonic must make shock waves flies in the face of supersonic inlet design. Had shock-swallowing inlets not been invented

in the mid-1950s, routine Mach-two flight would not have been achieved, yet NASA devotes no research effort whatsoever to shock-swallowing wings. This in an era when quantum physicists are demonstrating that Einstein's immutable edict perhaps should read "maybe $E = mc^2$ sometimes." But is anyone working on a faster-than-light spacecraft to transit the universe in nanoseconds or less? There is serious doubt that it would bear much resemblance to the current space shuttle.

From the Drawing Board

Not long ago, the head of Boeing Aircraft publicly declared that his company is not a research enterprise. Rather, he said, it is a production company. That might raise a question: Why, then, is NASA writing multimillion-dollar contracts with Boeing to do research on future supersonic transports? Governments, especially the one in Washington, do have a penchant for spreading large bundles of lucre in unproductive places. The U.S. taxpayer should not therefore be surprised to learn that the past several decades of similarly misdirected research are unlikely to chart a clear course for investors who truly believe there is an SST in our future. One thing is certain: They're not going to throw their shareholders' money at another *ba-boom*ing *Concorde*.

Patience, frustrated travelers, the free-enterprise system may yet fulfill your dream of Los Angeles-to-Paris in four hours. There is the X-prize. This is an award of ten million dollars sponsored by the citizens of St. Louis and other public-spirited patriots. This largesse is to be presented to the creators of the first vehicle to take off without benefit of mother ship or other disposable boost device and, with three souls on board, ascend to an altitude of 100 kilometers, or roughly 62 miles. Not only is a safe return to Mother Earth a contest stipulation, but in addition the feat must be repeated within two weeks without incident, just to prove it wasn't wholly a fluke.

Already there are at least twelve entrants in the contest for the X-prize, including the redoubtable Burt Rutan, creator of *Voyager*, the first manned aircraft to circle the globe unrefueled. Almost certainly the entrants must be able to attain supersonic speed, and strong attention must be given to minimizing drag. What better way to do that than to eliminate drag-producing shock waves? How exciting it would be now, more than fifty years after the first *ba-boom* emanated from a manned aircraft, to have the private enterprise community create a boomless Mach-buster and open the doors for profitable commercialization of a supersonic transport. The X-prize sponsors are from the same St. Louis that spawned a group of businessmen to finance *The Spirit of St. Louis* to go after the Orteig Prize of $25,000, sending Lindbergh to Paris in 1927. Hindsight by the engineers as they dream over their drawing boards half a century after anointing our first Mach-buster is one thing. Hindsight from the power politics of the Pentagon just two months after those first *ba-booms* is another story.

From the Pentagon to the Executive Suite

As was his wont, Dutch Kindelberger, founder and president of North American Aviation, was making the rounds at the Pentagon. It was three days before Christmas of 1947 and he wanted to spread a little cheer and incidentally to let the leaders of the new U.S. Air Force know that North American Aviation was still turning out the best fighters in the world—best by more than just a little bit. Major Ken Chilstrom, head of the fighter desk at Wright Field, had just completed the first Air Force evaluation of the brand new XP-86 *Sabre*, and his eleven flights in the swept-wing beauty had gone well. The canny Kindelberger had already picked up a commitment from the Air Force for an initial production order of 225 *Sabres*.

Of course, it was only a handshake agreement, but in the Kindelberger-Atwood era that was as good as gold. It always had been and would be so again. The goal of that leadership team was to build the best and lowest-cost military aircraft in the world and to produce them faster than any of the competition. At the end of each year the accountants would sort it all out. If more than a reasonable profit showed up on the books, and this invariably was the result of more efficient manufacturing methods being devised in the company's plants, those funds were returned to the government. In the high-pressure war years of 1941 through 1944, nearly $200 million in such funds identified by internal company audits were voluntarily returned to the government. In a 1996 frame of reference, that would be $2 billion. Handshake deals with North American had proved a bonanza for the U.S. taxpayer. Even so, considering the postwar budget problems, the deal for the initial production run of *Sabres* was a real coup.

Dutch had one more stop—Air Force Secretary Stu Symington —then he could head back home. Alex Burton was at his side. Alex had been a test pilot for the company, but his true talent was in communications. People instinctively liked him. Dutch had sent him back to Washington to head up North American's office in the nation's capital. It was an inspired choice. As the two turned into the secretary's anteroom, Alex checked his watch, noting they were a minute early. Stu Symington was waiting, and he was clearly distraught. His greeting to Dutch was cool. As he ushered the North American leader into his office, he cut off Alex as he started to follow.

"Excuse us, Alex, we need a few minutes alone." He closed the door behind him.

"What's up, Stu?"

Without a word Symington handed Kindelberger a copy of *Aviation Week* dated December 22, 1947, opened to the page headlined: "Bell XS-1 Makes Supersonic Flight."

Dutch chuckled. "That's kind of old hat around Muroc, Stu. I understand that young Yeager is a real star. Congratulations. Larry Bell must be bustin' his britches."

"That's not the point, and you damn well know it. Already I've got a call from Joe Swing." He paused. "You know Swing, don't you?"

Kindelberger shook his head. "Can't place him."

"Two-star, Army paratrooper, classmate and good friend of Ike's. Fought a helluva war. Based in the Bay area now but spends a lot of time at Muroc. I hear he likes it at Pancho's."

Dutch shrugged. "So what did General Swing want, Stu?"

"He's already read this *Aviation Week* and he's really brassed off. Not because the information is highly classified, mind you."

Kindelberger hastily scanned the highlighted article from the magazine Symington had handed him. It was clear that the secretary was more than a little upset. Trying to sound soothing, Dutch scanned the magazine, where a typo caught his eye. "Was he mad because they misspelled Yeager's name?"

"No, damn it. He wants to know why everyone's cheering for Yeager. Says the folks at Muroc know your guy did it first in that new fighter—the P-84."

"P-86."

"Good Lord, Dutch, I called you on that three months ago. You told me it wouldn't happen, you'd keep a rein on your guy."

"Look, Stu, this guy Welch is a free spirit. He's also damn good. He got airborne at Pearl Harbor and knocked down four, maybe six, Japs. Then went to the South Pacific and got a bunch more. Now he's testing a new fighter, and I'm here to tell you that, like the *Mustang*, it's going to be by far the best in the skies—anywhere. I don't know if he went supersonic before your boy Yeager and I don't give a happy damn. But I can tell you this for sure—and it's a closely held secret—we had that aircraft, the XP-86, with Welch in the cockpit, clocked by the NASA guys at Muroc on their fancy new radar theodolite, the same one used for the XS-1 flights. It went as fast as Mach 1.04 and made a big boom. That was in mid-November. We asked for the coverage because Welch was getting funny jumps in his airspeed indicator on some earlier flights, and there was some talk of big booms heard on the base. But the first flight that could be considered in any way 'official' would be the one in mid-November."

Symington was stunned. Half to himself he mumbled, "Then Joe Swing was right."

"Why don't you let us help you, Stu. You're the first secretary of a brand new Air Force. What do you need more—a really hot new fighter, the first that can go supersonic, or a one-of-a-kind little rocket ship that has to be carried up by its mother, has less than three minutes of fuel, and doesn't even have a gun?"

"You couldn't understand, Dutch, you're not from Missouri."

On the table behind Symington's desk was a large picture of the secretary greeting a beaming, ramrod stiff Harry Truman as the president descended from his airplane at Lambert Field in St. Louis.

"I promised the president—and Larry Bell was standing right beside him—that no one was going to get out in front of the Bell XS-1 in the supersonic sweepstakes. Larry was really shook up several months ago when Bill Craigie told him the new North American fighter was nipping at his heels. Bell charged right into Harry's office and raised hell. Harry's good at giving it but not at taking it. He dumped the problem on me and that's when I called you. Jeez, I hadn't been in the job a week."

Dutch leaned back in his deep leather chair. With his hands clasped behind his head, he contemplated the ceiling. Hell, he thought, let Larry Bell and the Air Force have all the laurels. The actual sequence of events was hazy enough in any case. He sure didn't want to do anything to jeopardize the F-86 production order.

Putting on his most beguiling, tooth-filled smile, Dutch leaned toward the secretary. "Look, Stu, there's no solid proof of those early supersonic events in the XP-86. It's all cocktail talk and flight line rumor. Forget it. There'll be no discussion of these matters by anyone in North American. You have my word on it. The first true record of our fighter going supersonic is in the hands of Walt Williams, and that was on November 13th, more than a month after the XS-1 did its thing. You win all the way around. Larry Bell and his Air Force captain have their record, and the Air Force has its first supersonic fighter—it's a great Christmas present for the Air Force and the U.S. taxpayer."

Symington almost swallowed it completely, but he quickly recovered and drew on his well-tested Missouri mule-trading instincts, which taught never to accept the first offer.

"Not good enough, Dutch. That puts your demonstration of supersonic capability less than thirty days after Bell's. People will want to know why, if it's so easy for a conventional fighter, did we go to all the hassle and expense of doing the XS-1 in the first place. It would be clear to everyone that none of the XS-1 technology contributed to the success of the XP-86."

"And they'd be correct."

"Damn it, Dutch, we're not dealing with technological nuances; this is politics, and Bell must have his day in the sun."

"He sure didn't earn any medals in the war. Welch got stuck in Bell's P-39s flying out of Port Moresby. Sure, he got a few victories in that turkey, but when the wing from a nearby field started getting P-38s, George had a series of engine failures and bailed out over water to accelerate the transition to a decent fighter."

"You're not hearing me. I need some good press on this. It's a big American event. Hell, the Brits lost one of their top test pilots supposedly 'giving it a go.' We're in a continuous budget struggle with the other services. The taxpayers like to think they're getting their money's worth. We need to get the most mileage possible out of these advances. If the XS-1 and the P-86 stories come out almost simultaneously, we lose a lot of potential. Besides, Bell will feel shortchanged—and Harry won't like it. As a unique, well-isolated happening, the Bell XS-1 piercing the sound barrier is worth at least a Collier with a White House presentation plus maybe a Medal of Honor for Yeager. I don't want any me-toos from North American lousing up that act."

Symington was stumbling all over himself. He needed help. Dutch kept reminding himself—OK, OK, the trophies and records and laurels all go to the Air Force and to the president's favorite company. All North American wants is the privilege of continuing to produce the world's best fighters.

"I've got it, Stu. Milk the XS-1 story for all it's worth. Take six months. You'll not hear a peep out of North American about the Mach-busting capabilities of our F-86 before next June. But you are going to have to handle your Air Force troops. They'll be flying our airplane and I can't control what they have to say about it. Still, the performance will remain classified, and we'll do our best to steer clear of *Aviation Week* reporters."

"It's a deal." The Air Force secretary seemed relieved. He knew that Kindelberger would prefer contracts to accolades. By June he would need another positive report, and North American would bring it to him with a careful release of their F-86 story.

"And mind you," the Dutchman added, "There's nothing I can do about Joe Swing."

"My problem. I've a feeling the general is about to embark on an urgent, distant, and highly classified mission."

The two shook hands and exchanged warm Christmas greetings. Symington held on for an additional instant. Looking Kindelberger in the eye, he queried, "Did Welch really beat Yeager through the big wall?"

The Dutchman broke into his irrepressible grin, winked conspiratorily, and whispered, "You can be damn well sure you'll never hear such a story from North American. Once again, Merry Christmas." Chuckling, he strode out into the anteroom, where some curious staffers by their expectant expressions revealed they hadn't the foggiest idea what the meeting had been about. With no intention of helping them out, Dutch grabbed Alex Burton's arm, waved another season's salutation, and hastened out the door. With a little luck he could still make his flight to Los Angeles.

As they left, ever alert for bits of intelligence, Alex overheard the secretary speaking to his exec, an Air Force colonel. "For the Army representative to the Paper Clip Commission meeting in Lima, let's try to get General Swing assigned."

Dutch kept his promise to the Air Force secretary. Although according to his personal flight log Welch himself made at least two dozen "High-Mach" dive flights to supersonic speed between mid-October 1947 and the following April, the source of persistent *ba-booms* mysteriously echoing about the Antelope Valley remained undisclosed. Most of the flights were made in the number one *Sabre* prototype; number two started flying in March 1948. In addition, other engineering test pilots at North American were also becoming Mach-busters, and it seems virtually certain that some of the Air Force pilots at Muroc had a shot at it after Major Ken Chilstrom completed his Phase II flights in early December 1947 while under direct orders not to exceed 0.9 Mach number. It's hard to believe that Chuck Yeager didn't have an early crack at the Air Force's top fighter. He was overheard expressing discontent that "the Limey" was flying the airplane and at supersonic speed after "Bee" Beamont took the number two XP-86 supersonic in May 1948.

Thus, the total number of *ba-booms* laid on the floor of the Mojave in that winter and early spring by those imcomparable *Sabres* may well have equaled half a hundred. Even so, despite the ecstatic reaction of some of Pancho's ladies and the growing irritation of the Mojave's mink farmers, the secret of North American's insouciant slide into the realm of the supersonic was undetected, or at least unreported, by the press. Bob Hotz of *Aviation Week* took a bureaucratic drubbing from pious security sentries for breaking the story of Yeager's Mach one-plus flight of October 14 in the December 22, 1947, issue of the magazine.

In the peace treaty wrought between Hotz and Symington following the breaking of the X-1 story, Bob agreed to inform Stu of any similarly dramatic as-yet-untold Air Force events. So it was that when Beamont broadcast in the clear the details of his supersonic caper in the *Sabre* on May 21, 1948, Bob kept his promise and informed the secretary of his magazine's intent to run the story. When Symington's staff confirmed the truth of that account, Hotz had his news break validated. With some help from Dutch and careful perusal of George Welch's flight log, the date of April 26 became the "official" date for the first excursion past Mach one by the *Sabre*. It corresponded with the date on which Welch had made one of his many "high Mach dives." It also happened to be conveniently a bit more than sixth months after Yeager's historic flight, as agreed upon by Dutch and Air Force Secretary Symington. In addition, it was conveniently ahead of Bee's flight (we couldn't let the Brits steal our thunder) but protected Herb Hoover's claim to be the first civilian pilot to fly faster than sound, an event he had finally achieved in the X-1 on March 10, more than six weeks ahead of the date for Welch and his *Sabre* that was blessed by the politicos. Ironically, that "official" flight was made in the number two XP-86 prototype, the number one aircraft being laid up for instrumentation attendant upon the structural demonstration.

Having earlier completed the spin demonstration on the number two *Sabre*, Welch's satisfactory, expeditious, and uneventful completion of the demanding structural program and acceptance of the collected data by the Air Force before the end of September signaled the release for delivery to the operating forces of the first F-86A. This would occur almost exactly one year after the *Sabre's* first flight. In today's world of high-speed computers and super-tech management methods, this first-flight-to-delivery cycle for a twenty-first-century fighter might be expected to be completed within a decade—give or take a year or so.

North American Aviation was a bastion of competence and integrity with a management clearly focused on delivering superior products at the lowest possible cost to the taxpayer. As noted earlier, Dutch proudly returned to the U.S. Treasury the equivalent of $2 billion in today's currency for savings effected by his company in the war years. It was a period when other companies were going back to the government for more money to cover their cost overruns. In the same mode, Dutch was more than happy to give his best customer political cover for salving the egos of the bureaucrats and the brass while anointing a new icon among their own who would endure to enchant the kids and grown-ups alike at endless successions of air shows and other carnivals for more than half a century. For Dutch and his people at North American that was a meaningless price for the privilege of continuing to design and build the world's finest fighters.

The durability of that dedication to excellence was demonstrated more than a dozen years later. I had joined North American in mid-1954, in those halcyon days when Mach one was behind us, Mach two well in hand, and Mach three on the drawing board. At the outset, I was flying more than forty development flights a month as an engineering test pilot. Five years later, I was just wrapping up the F-100 zero launch program proving that, with a big enough solid rocket booster, a fully loaded *Super Sabre* could be blasted into flight off a trailer, eliminating the need for a runway. The company had just won in rapid succession development contracts for the X-15 rocket research aircraft, the F-108 Mach-three interceptor, and the B-70 Mach-three strategic bomber. It was a fantastic display of North American's credibility with its customers. For the engineers, these were heady times.

For the engineering test pilots, there would be a lot of waiting around. Instead of forty test flights per month, the average had dropped to eight. The X-15 was clearly destined to prove its cutting-edge technology advancements in the hands of NASA and military research pilots after perfunctory demonstrations of its functional acceptability by Scotty Crossfield, who had left NASA for North American hoping to do a lot more than that—and, in fact, he did press a bit beyond the limits set by the customer. The F-108 never got past the mock-up stage, while the first flight of the B-70 was a long way off—five years, as it turned out. I was backup pilot to Al White on the B-70 and was getting some flights in the B-52 to learn about flying big, heavy, jet aircraft and the mind-set of the Strategic Air Command.

Thus, in the fall of 1959, when Dr. Herbert F. York, recently appointed the first Director of Defense Research and Engineering under the Defense Reorganization Act of 1958, went to industry for recruits to staff his new domain, I had already determined I was ready to try something different. When Stormy asked me if I'd be interested, I readily assented to a two-year leave of absence from the company to help get the new agency under way. It should be noted that I had been in place at the Pentagon no more than six months when it became painfully clear that I could not in any conscience perform my duties in a truly impartial fashion under the assumption that I would be returning to North American. Consequently, I wrote Lee Atwood to inform him of this circumstance and to let him know I would not be looking for employment from North American upon leaving the Pentagon. I sent a copy to Herb York.

I had not foreseen the ascendancy of the big central government people with the election of Kennedy. This, of course, included the Pentagon takeover by McNamara and his Whiz Kids. A major shift occurred in the decision-making process, away from the people closest to the challenges of our national defense and to the highly sophisticated flimflam of cost-effectiveness studies and complex but meaningless computer-based management systems. This meant that the defense companies had to counter with their own brand of gobbledygook just to keep up. North American kept doing business the old way, maintaining a Washington office of but a handful of people, while their competitors staffed their facilities in the nation's capital with scores of hotshot big spenders, and that strategy was paying off.

After watching this imbalance evolve for a number of months, I took the opportunity, during a visit to North American for another purpose, to corner Ray Rice alone in his office. Ray Rice was then head of the aircraft division in Los Angeles. I sought to explain to him the rapidly changing nature of how the game was being played back in Washington, and the danger to the company of not devoting more resources there to staying out front.

I'll never forget his reaction. Ray Rice was a big man, broad shouldered and erect. He had penetrating ice-blue eyes that were magnified by the heavy lenses of his glasses. His voice reflected a certain sadness along with an inner determination not to surrender the strength of character and professional integrity that had helped mold the company he so proudly led. Without blinking or averting his gaze for an instant, he said, "Blackie, what's the matter with just building good airplanes?"

There may have been others at North American who sought to play the perfidious game introduced by the Kennedyites so they could use the huge defense budget to underwrite their political power, but not with the approval of Ray Rice. He personified the cast of characters who earlier on had produced those unchallenged champions—the *Mustang* and the *Sabre*.

From the Launch Pad

The occasion was a special meeting of the Society of Experimental Test Pilots for the purpose of debating rocket scientist Wernher von Braun on the potential merits of test pilot contributions to future space ventures. It was a dinner meeting held at the Miramar

Hotel in Santa Monica on the evening of August 5, 1959. As president of the society that year, I was point man for the attack on some of von Braun's recently published views concerning the utility of having a human pilot in the loop for out-of-this-world explorations to the moon and beyond.

Before turning to the events of that meeting, it is important to note that von Braun was a seasoned pilot—not just someone who had handled the controls under the supervision of a professional, but one who had completed the Luftwaffe flight-training course in 1938. He was frequently provided a high-performance, single-engine aircraft that he flew for making his many official visits out of Peenemünde. Much earlier, in 1931, at the age of nineteen, he had taken up gliding. At that time it was the only kind of flying that Germans were permitted under the terms of the Versailles Treaty. German youth and German aircraft designers of the twenties and thirties took to the world of unpowered flight with a style and enthusiasm that harked back to the first truly successful glider pilot, their creative countryman Otto Lillienthal, who was killed in a glider crash in 1898 after more than two thousand flights. Even today, the finest sailplanes available are designed and built in Germany.

Von Braun, however, was focused on travel beyond the earth, not just above it. A certifiable space nut and a highly intelligent one, he knew that space travel meant rocket power. Involved in the development of a rocket installation for the Junkers *Junior*, a light, single-engine aircraft, von Braun was hoping to be the test pilot for its first flight. His colleagues vetoed that idea on the grounds that his technical skills were too important to risk in such a vulnerable task. In any case, the project was canceled for one with better prospects, a larger rocket in a Heinkel 112.

Initially, the rocket installation on the He 112 was operated remotely from a blockhouse, and fortunately so, for there were a number of fires and explosions during these tests. However, when the test pilot chosen by the Luftwaffe to fly this early rocket research craft visited to witness engine tests, von Braun thought it would hardly be a confidence builder if the engine were to be demonstrated with the operators protected in a blockhouse. Consequently, von Braun climbed into the cockpit and, with the prospective test pilot standing close by, ran the prototype rocket engine up to full power. There were no fires or explosions, but it sure made a lot of noise. Later, over drinks that evening, von Braun confided to this soon-to-be rocketeer that it was the first time the engine had been operated from the cockpit.

Engine ground tests for rocket-powered aircraft would continue to prove hazardous, even twenty-five years later. Scotty Crossfield can speak to that. He got blown halfway across the engine test ramp at Edwards in the X-15 cockpit when the rocket ship exploded during an engine test run. Only the alertness and courage of North American flight-test supervisor Art Semone saved Scotty from incineration in the ensuing fire. That was in 1960.

Although denied the hot seat in those early experimental rocket flights of the late 1930s, von Braun still remained very close to any flight-test activity that had an impact on his space-bent ambitions. For example, questions about the stability of his rockets as they accelerated through Mach one could not be answered in the wind tunnels. Data could be gathered from Mach 0 to 0.85 and from 1.2 to 5.0, but not for the region in between. Aerodynamicists calculated that a heavy iron model dropped from a Heinkel 111 at 23,000 feet would go supersonic at about 3,500 feet on its way to the Baltic Sea. It was von Braun who dove a relatively high-performance, two-place aircraft (at perhaps Mach 0.5 in a top-speed dive) to chase these models as they went swooshing past him at Mach one-plus, permitting a colleague in the rear seat to obtain close-in camera coverage of the models while supersonic and to mark the splashdown for boat-based observers so that the models could be recovered.

Like Yeager, von Braun proved to be an outstanding chase pi-lot. Like Yeager, the German found that going through Mach one was no big deal, although the drag rise at sonic speed did initially limit the performance of the A-3/A-5 (the V-2's predecessors) to Mach 0.95. All this was being demonstrated in the fall of 1939 both by the drop tests and from the launch pads at Peenemünde. Later, the A-4s (V-2s) would slide past Mach one most uneventfully, rather like a slippery scuppernong grape popping free of its skin, and press on to peak at speeds as high as Mach five.

Unlike Yeager, von Braun came from wealthy landed gentry and had received a doctorate in physics at the age of twenty-two. Absent the wars (hot and cold), he would most probably have be-come a champion soaring pilot and distinguished professor emeri-tus of rocket science at an eminent German university. Yeager, by contrast, came from sturdy American stock that sprang out of the "hollers" of West Virginia. He managed a diploma from Hamlin High School, got his Air Corps wings as an enlisted pilot, helped deliver the finishing blows to the Luftwaffe, and emerged, at age twenty-two, a distinguished fighter pilot and double ace. Were it not for World War II, he might well have been found running an auto re-pair shop in Hamlin and having lunch at the Bobcat Restaurant.

In preparation for the August 1959 evening with von Braun, I had done some homework. I learned from the first page of his book *The Mars Project* that he identified test pilots as an essential ele-ment of the talent mix for successful space ventures. I had also used the acceleration profile he'd predicted in his book for an early orbital flight to program the centrifuge at the University of South-ern California. Just a year earlier, as witnessed by Marvin Miles, the highly respected aviation editor for the *Los Angeles Times*, I had ridden that centrifuge as it duplicated the orbital injection acceleration loads, as well as those estimated to accompany atmo-spheric re-entry. It was the first time a test pilot had been sub-jected to these stresses. Pictures at peak loads were somewhat dramatic, with the skin of the face drawn back taut and eyes narrowed to slits. Yet the ability to function throughout the runs proved to be virtually unimpaired.

Marvin made a big deal out of it. More than nine months had passed since Sputnik, and the United States still had precious little to celebrate. The story with pictures was handed over to the wire services. It was a slow news day. Not only was my dramatically stressed countenance on the front page of the LA *Times* but it also appeared with a headline story in virtually every major newspaper around the globe. I would learn that von Braun was aware of these experiments, as well as of a technical paper I had given earlier that spring at an aerospace symposium in Vancouver. The paper was entitled "Flight Testing in the Space Age," and in it I had again used his space-bound acceleration profiles, with appropriate credits, of course.

The guest speaker showed up right on schedule. A big man with a commanding presence but without the slightest trace of the prima donna, he seemed to feel particularly at home with pilots, especially test pilots. More than fifty from that tight fraternity were on hand, including Al White of B-70 fame, Bill Magruder, who would later lead the U.S. SST program from NASA, Scott Crossfield, who had recently had his most interesting first glide flight in the X-15, Lockheed's "Fish" Salmon, Douglas's Bob Rahn, as well as other luminaries from the aerospace world such as Harrison Storms, who had just won the X-15, F-108, and B-70 programs in rapid succession for North American. Later, Stormy would work closely with von Braun while leading the company's *Apollo* moon venture.

Wernher, the rocketeer, gave a dramatic discussion on the challenges of a voyage to Mars. He had studied the program in great depth and clearly identified the need for further research to yield improved propellants, more efficient structures, and lighter, more reliable computers. In his view it could all be preprogrammed before launch, even the landing on the red planet and the return of the space voyagers. There was no mention of contributions from a human pilot. Was he just baiting us?

When he had concluded, I asked what role he envisioned for the pilots on the mission. He responded: "We will anesthetize the pilots before launch, and after the autopilot has landed the spaceship safely, we will give them a wake-up injection so they can go out and explore the Mars landscape."

The ensuing uproar was greeted with a satisfied smile. He knew his audience, but he was only half kidding. Crossfield made his oft-quoted comment about the difficulty of economically replacing such a highly sensitive, infinitely variable bit of protoplasmic servomechanism that can be produced by wholly unskilled labor. Others recounted failures of the fledgling automation of that era, when electronics still meant vacuum tubes. Most test pilots had had experiences that were less than assuring, some fatal.

I recalled the Low-altitude Automatic Bombing System (LABS) on the F-100D. The maneuver was entered at treetop level and maximum speed. On pressing the bomb release button on top of the control stick, the autopilot was scheduled to pull the *Super Sabre* into a four-g half loop, releasing the bomb as the aircraft approached the vertical, then roll out just beyond the top of the loop in a course-reversal dive to escape the bomb blast. Too often, at the top of the half loop the autopilot seemed to become confused and would pull the nose of the inverted aircraft through too sharply, into a snap roll and incipient spin at low altitude. Cautious pilots, the ones with some instinct for survival, would disengage the autopilot after bomb release and fly the rest of the maneuver by hand. And there was the automatic landing system being developed by North American's Autonetics Division. Installed in an F-102 *Delta Dagger*, it made excellent hands-off landings, but after a takeoff to go around and watch the servos do it again, the mechanisms moved the flight controls to the full nose up position and then failed. Talk about a busy cockpit. After I'd finally wrestled the machine safely back onto the runway, I sought out the test engineer. He had assured me that such an event simply could not occur and had hastily disappeared, mumbling something about emergency leave.

Alas, not all such auto-device failures had survivable results. Lockheed test pilot Joe Ozier was a victim of such a failure. He had been an enthusiastic supporter of the test pilots' society and had served as a director and first secretary. The Society of Experimental Test Pilots (SETP) was barely a year old when Joe was returning his F-104 *Starfighter* to Palmdale after an apparently uneventful flight, unaware that he was flying with one wingtip tank full, the other empty. The early lateral trim system on the F-104 left the pilot's control stick centered, even though all roll control in one direction had been used up just to hold the wings level, as would be the case as the aircraft slowed for landing with asymmetrical tip tank loading. As Joe decelerated in his approach to the runway, he was unable to hold the heavy wing up and tragically rolled into the ground.

Von Braun could offer only a wry smile and note: "See how fast we are learning." As the stimulating if inconclusive meeting ended, I invited von Braun to join me in the bar for a drink. He readily accepted.

We took a table in the Miramar's cocktail lounge. To the waitress the big Prussian intoned, "A large draft beer." She turned for my order, but von Braun took her elbow in his left hand and, with his right thumb and forefinger about two inches apart, added, "and a bourbon." Holy cow! This guy outweighs me by at least eighty pounds and he's acting as though we're back in a prewar dueling club. I ordered a beer, hoping he wouldn't be offended if I didn't try to keep up.

I'd just completed a program of sixteen severely suborbital rocket launches in an F-100, and he wanted to know all about it. NASA was getting ready to launch some *Mercury* capsules and eventually would let a man ride along. My booster burnout altitude was about 500 feet, while the *Mercury* suborbital shots would be more like 100 nautical miles. Still, even before the *Apollo* fire and the *Challenger* tragedy, the NASA crew was a cautious lot. Before they finally got John Glenn into orbit, they would put up three apes, Sam, Ms. Sam, and Ham, on suborbital shots, and one, Enos, for two full circuits of the earth. Von Braun was helping to rationalize the program that was soon to get started.

First I told him about the two programs that had preceded the F-100 rocket launches—the F-84G in 1952–1953 and the Russians' copycat MiG-19 program in 1957. In both of these cases, an operational aircraft with empty cockpit was first launched to check things out. The aircraft were of course destroyed as they crashed shortly after booster burnout. For the F-100 we figured we were smart enough, or the pilot was gullible enough, to put a man in from the start, although some steel and concrete dummies were launched beforehand to test the booster and the launcher. The first piloted try was just fine. Unfortunately, on the second shot the booster hung up and couldn't be shook free of the *Super Sabre*. I had to bail out. So much for saving aircraft.

Still, Wernher wanted to hear about these details, about the centrifuge and the Navy cat shots and the simulator—all part of the training regimen. But he wasn't interested only because of the *Mercury* program. Every dedicated space scientist knows that an economically viable space program will come a lot closer to political survival with recoverable boosters. Why should the biggest piece of gear on the launchpad be unceremoniously dumped into the Atlantic Ocean? If it had wings and flight controls, perhaps it could be flown back to a runway and landed undamaged for repeated use.

In the early 1990s an American company, Orbital Sciences Corporation, started doing just that. They use a Lockheed L-1011 *Tristar* airliner from which satellites are rocketed into low earth orbit, starting from 40,000 feet and 0.8 Mach number instead of

motionless at sea level. It works. After all, the X-1 and its successor programs paved the way for such off-the-shelf recoverable
boosters. It may prove to be their most significant contribution.
Struggling through the first seven miles of the earth's atmosphere
and accelerating through the first 500 miles per hour of velocity
eats up a lot of energy in a regime where rockets are least efficient.

Von Braun took me back in time to the winter of 1944–1945,
when two V-2 rockets were given wings to extend the missiles'
range. One failed shortly after takeoff for causes unrelated to the
winged configuration. The other went well until re-entry, when
speed in excess of Mach three was encountered. The resultant heat
was more than the wings could withstand. On the drawing board
was a more sophisticated version with a pressurized cockpit, tri-
cycle landing gear, and flight controls more closely resembling
those for conventional aircraft. The war ended before it could be
constructed. Since it was not a project approved by the generals—
indeed, it was relegated to a very special file—von Braun laugh-
ingly called it his method for following Hess to England.

He told of his own early concerns for the physiological effects of space travel. In 1931, while studying at the Institute of
Technology at Zurich, he and an American medical student there
decided to explore the results of high accelerations on mammalian
anatomy. Unable to construct a centrifuge large enough for hu-
mans, they settled for laboratory mice. The device was crude but
capable of putting the mice under very high g's—too high. Indeed,
Wernher was ejected from his immaculate Swiss boardinghouse
room when his landlady discovered a ring of mouse blood on the
pristine walls.

The German scientist then shared a story of how he had continued these anatomical studies in the course of the A-4 launches.
Two mice were picked from a nearby medical laboratory near
Peenemünde to be given rides in the nose cone of one of the big
rockets. They would be the first creatures on earth to experience

supersonic flight and to go out of the atmosphere. One of the mice was excited about it all and felt proud to be part of this great experiment. But the other was less enthralled.

"At the end," said the less happy rodent, "we're going to crash into the earth at very high speed and die."

"Perhaps that's true," replied the proud pioneer, "but I can't help thinking it beats working in the cancer ward."

As von Braun inhaled his third shot of bourbon and sipped the beer chaser with a repressed smile, I asked, "But what of the dreaded sonic wall?" He shrugged, noting that by the early 1940s the Germans had a great deal of wind tunnel data out to Mach four-plus, along with information about the transonic regime gathered from the high-altitude drop tests of heavy models. "For the transonic," he said, "we learned that the wings should be swept; beyond that, keep them thin." To close the subject he added, "Look, we flew more than thirty-five hundred rockets much larger and more than twice the weight of your X-1. All of them went supersonic, most beyond Mach four, and with aerodynamic controls. Once understood and explained by the likes of von Karman, supersonic was no barrier, but superheating, as we went to Mach three and beyond, that was a problem. It still is. The trick is to get out of the atmosphere as quickly as possible."

This animated discussion had gone on for some time. It was past midnight and a busy day lay ahead. I tendered a profusion of thanks on behalf of the SETP and bid von Braun a hasty farewell, certain that our paths would cross again. They almost did, but much later.

After the triumph of the moon landings in 1969 came a fading of public interest in the space program. In 1972, von Braun left NASA for the aerospace industry. With the shift, a less pressured pace became possible. The space meister returned to his first love—soaring. He carefully sought an operation where he could socialize and soar unencumbered by his fame. He joined a firm I had left several years before. His offices were in Germantown and Hagerstown, thirty to fifty minutes north of the nation's capital. I had recently taken up soaring and become unalterably hooked. It's flying in its purest form, the way the hawks and eagles do it, and yes, the gulls and pelicans, the condor and the albatross.

Prior to the soaring, with three preteens, two sons and a daughter, we had flown as a family in small propeller planes to many corners of our continent—to the Virgin Islands, to Labrador and Newfoundland, including St. Pierre et Miquelon, followed the Mississippi from its delta where it emptied into the Gulf of Mexico up to St. Louis before the arch was built (and after), maneuvered the twists down in the Grand Canyon before such flights were against the rules, sensed the pulsing heat of Death Valley, tracking just a few feet above its surface, saw Big Sur country and watched the fog roll in beneath the Golden Gate Bridge, endured the turbulence above the High Sierras and threaded the magnificence of the Rockies to land at our highest airport, at Leadville, snapped pictures from a unique perspective of the great leaders whose faces are preserved in stone on Mount Rushmore, visited with friends on the shore of Lake Michigan, and stopped in at Montreal during Expo.

Most of the flying was done in a Piper *Twin Comanche*. At a top cruise speed of 192 miles per hour it was hardly supersonic, but it proved a super platform from which to observe and learn about our nation and its neighbors. The two boys alternated as copilot while Donna kept peace in the rear seat. Susan, our youngest, was not yet up to handling the controls. Indeed, the sons were not yet tall enough to see ahead over the instrument shroud. They quickly learned to perform as very good wing levelers, first by twisting their heads from side to side to check the position of the wingtips relative to the horizon. Later, they discovered the gyro horizon on the instrument panel. In a sense, they became instrument pilots before learning to fly contact. But once I discovered soaring, I became convinced it would be the best way to introduce our two sons to aviation independence. Besides, as a glider pilot, solo flight is permitted at the age of fourteen. For powered aircraft, the minimum age for solo is sixteen.

Unpowered soaring flight provides a confidence in one's ability to make good decisions and to put the aircraft very precisely onto a selected landing spot, whether it be the home airport, a farmer's cornfield, or the ninth fairway. After all, the termination of each glider flight is a deadstick landing. Moving even more distant from the world of the supersonic, I traded the *Twin Comanche* for a Bellanca *Citabria*, a single-engine aerobatic trainer and quite adequate glider tow plane. It provided the additional benefit of teaching aspiring aviators to be quite comfortable in spins, rolls, loops, inverted flight, and other unusual circumstances not normally undertaken in the long-wing sailplanes.

Soaring also teaches a lot about weather—how it can assist a pilot in many ways and how it can threaten his very survival. I used to avoid flying under clear-weather cumulus clouds because of the often severe turbulence to be found there. Now a line of such clouds going in the general direction of my route provides a welcome boost in my cruise speed and often a significant reduction in fuel consumption. Flying the mountain wave can be truly exhilarating, but get sucked up into the roll cloud on the lee side of the ridge and you and your craft may be spit out in pieces. Remembering all those challenges and the rewards of the exhilaration they can offer must have drawn von Braun back into the sailplane cockpit for his unfortunately early but well-managed final glide.

Our family was flying with a glider club located on the Frederick Municipal Airport in Maryland, about forty miles north of Washington. The vice president for marketing of von Braun's firm paid a call. He was an old friend. I explained how the club operated and offered to give him a ride. No time for that, he said—

besides, he was just checking for a colleague. After a few questions, he drove away. I did not know the purpose of the visit, but had I known I would not have argued with his assessment. We were too big an operation and too close to the Washington scene.

With the help of Senator Glenn Beall of Maryland, Wernher was introduced to Bill Holbrook, a world-class soaring pilot who was manager of flight operations for the Kelly-Springfield Corporation's executive aircraft based at Cumberland, Maryland. They were located a couple of ridges west of Frederick and light years distant in terms of the worldly gloss of Washington. There was a small cadre of soaring pilots who flew their sailplanes out of the Cumberland airport—an easy group to whom "Mr. Brown" and his family were welcome additions, especially when it became apparent that Mr. Brown was an able, helpful, and dedicated member of the brotherhood. One day, when a few of the members, including von Braun, were having lunch at a restaurant near the airport, one of the more sophisticated members of the group pulled the waitress aside and asked, "Do you know who that big fellow at the table is?"

The waitress shrugged and shook her head.

"Why, that's Wernher von Braun."

"Is he somebody important?"

Clearly, the old space meister's privacy was in good hands. He put in some great hours along those Appalachian ridges, soaring with the small group that kept their gliders at the field and the occasional visitor, and, perhaps more memorably, with the many hawks that find their homes there. Unfortunately, in 1977, while still a youthful and vigorous sixty-four, cancer brought a swift and untimely end for the illustrious Prussian before he could put some final records in the books.

When I reflect on that one evening we shared nearly forty years ago, it is quite clear that von Braun was far more prescient than the macho test pilots. In 1988, Fred Singer, chief scientist at the Department of Transportation, was exploring the concept he called HUF (Hypersonic Unmanned Freighter), an Orient Express for packages. By doing away with the human pilots, a great deal of weight and expense could be saved, but one doesn't need to fly at hypersonic speeds to accomplish that. Just think—no windows, flight instruments, cockpits, heating, cooling, adjustable pilot seats, control yokes, rudder pedals, audio speaker systems, and none of those fancy displays and instruments. Air package pioneer Fred Smith of FedEx should love it, but he may encounter some problems with his pilots' union.

In 1989 I visited the Soviet space research facilities at Tsagi with a small group of U.S. engineers and scientists. There we were shown their *Buran*, which looked very much like NASA's space shuttle. Like the space shuttle, the *Buran* had been sent into orbit and returned to earth in a manner just like the American version, but with a difference. *Buran* had no people on board and, better than the HUF, it had exceeded Mach 25. Videos of a very smooth, fully automated landing at the Russian space center were shown. This highly successful venture nearly ten years ago featuring a remotely managed trip into orbit and return was wholly dependent upon Russian avionics equipment that technologically was at least ten years behind that of the United States in terms of size, weight, sophistication, and reliability. Still, the flight went from blast-off to touchdown without a hitch . . . and without the accompanying presence of a living, breathing pilot.

With these clear examples of the world's zooming technological expertise, surely we can dramatically reduce, if not halt altogether, the terrible drumbeat of airline fatalities that are increasingly attributable to pilot error. Too often these tragedies are accompanied by the failure of system operators to provide the cockpits with technologies that have been available for years—advanced devices that would almost certainly have averted a number of the disasters.

More than a decade ago, a high-level commission determined that advanced design and a greater level of automation made a two-man crew quite adequate for even the largest of airliners, many of which had been designed for a crew of three. It was not because pilot error had ceased to be a concern. Indeed, one of the more visionary members of that commission suggested that in the not-so-distant future it might prove feasible to think of a flight crew consisting of only one pilot plus a big dog. The pilot's sole job would be to feed the dog. The dog's job would be to bite the hand of the pilot if he reached for any of the cockpit controls.

Sorry, Wernher, I never got a chance to acknowledge the wisdom in your foresight. Even so, I expect that our airline pilot son will be long retired before the first passengers are carried in fully automated airliners. For the freight haulers, it could happen more quickly. Going supersonic from the launchpad was even less significant a challenge than it is for today's fighter planes, but it remains an elusive goal for any commercially viable civil aircraft. The *ba-boom* over the Atlantic from space shuttle launches or *Concorde* operations are tolerated, but a method for swallowing those shock waves and recovering their energy must be devised before worldwide supersonic commercial operations become routine.

From the Mythmakers

"Recomposed after the jolt (lighting the rockets), Chuck turned his attention toward the Mach meter. It was getting closer and closer to Mach one. The heavy, horrifying buffet began. It felt as if giant sledgehammers were pounding the aircraft all around him in wildly rapid succession. It gave him the sensation that the plane was being twirled and twisted until nothing would be left of it."—Nancy Levinson, "Chuck Yeager—The Man Who Broke the Sound Barrier" (1953).

"Airplane control and stability were completely normal as 1.0 Mach was attained and passed. . . . If the Mach meter hadn't been in the cockpit of the plane, you'd never have noticed the smashing of that barrier they used to call 'the brick wall in the sky.' "—William R. Lundgren, *Across the High Frontier: The Story of a Test Pilot—Major Charles E. Yeager* (1955).

"Each time he flew, Yeager approached a little nearer to the speed of sound. Eventually he reached a speed of Mach 0.94, and felt the aircraft bucking under the hammer blows of shock waves that would have smashed anything else in the air at that time. But he had complete confidence in the X-1's structure, and finally, on October 14, 1947, he opened up the four-chamber rocket engine to full power for an all-out attempt to reach supersonic speed. Fighting to keep control, he watched the needle on the Mach meter swing past Mach 0.94 on to 0.96, 0.98 . . . suddenly, instead of getting worse, the hammering stopped. Yeager had become the first man to fly into the calmer conditions that lie beyond the 'sound barrier.' In doing so, he had proved the barrier does not really exist.

"By 1956, Britain's delta-wing Fairey Delta 2 research aircraft, powered by an ordinary jet engine, was able to demonstrate that a properly designed aeroplane can approach and pass the speed of sound with no more noticeable effect than a flicker of needles on the cockpit instruments as it does so."—Tre Tryckare, *The Lore of Flight* (1960).

"At 40,000 feet, we were still climbing at a speed of .92 Mach. Leveling off at 42,000 feet, I had 30 percent of my fuel, so I turned on rocket chamber three and immediately reached .96 Mach. I noticed that the faster I got, the smoother the ride.

"Suddenly the Mach needle began to fluctuate. It went up to .965 Mach—then tipped right off the scale. I thought I was seeing things! We were flying supersonic! And it was as smooth as a baby's bottom: Grandma could be sitting up there sipping lemonade. I kept the speed off the scale for about twenty seconds, then raised the nose to slow down.

"I was thunderstruck. After all the anxiety, breaking the sound barrier turned out to be a perfectly paved speedway. . . . And that was it. I sat there feeling kind of numb, but elated. After all the anticipation to achieve this moment, it really was a letdown. It took a damn instrument meter to tell me what I had done. There should have been a bump on the road, something to let you know you had just punched a nice clean hole through that sonic barrier."—General Chuck Yeager and Leo Janos, *Yeager* (1985).

Since the reality of the first manned supersonic flights as portrayed by Yeager's "Shucks, twarn't nuthin' " and Welch's enigmatic shrug, the popular literature and other accounts insisted on reporting as factual their wholly fictional though nonetheless spine-chilling reports of Yeager's sonic adventures. Many found their origins in tales of encounters with compressibility occurring during vertical dives from maximum altitude by World War II propeller-driven fighters, even though the maximum speed achieved without serious structural damage was 0.86 Mach by Fred Borsodi in an F-51 *Mustang*. That flight was sufficiently exciting and loosened enough rivets that *Mustangs* were subsequently limited to a maximum Mach number of 0.80. A British *Spitfire* did reach 0.90 in a full-power vertical dive just before it shed its propeller and most of the engine cowl. Because of the security wraps on much of the reporting of early X-1 and XP-86 flight tests, literary license tended to become truth. A little creative writing couldn't hurt the cause, and some of the pilots could use an income supplement. In any case, there was a full platter of wild rides awaiting before the truly incredible high-speed digital computers proved capable of predicting unerringly the results of any projected flight.

No other distortion of the truth had quite the impact of the British film *Breaking the Sound Barrier*. This dramatically effective production, fatally flawed by unadulterated technological nonsense, so captured the imagination of the poorly informed moviegoer that for years the average man on the street in the United States was convinced the British had done it first. To this day, marginally astute aeronautical enthusiasts believe that Geoffrey de Havilland lost his life attempting to take the DH.108 *Swallow* beyond Mach one. Actually, he was tuning up for an attempt to break the existing absolute speed record and knew he would encounter some seriously unstable conditions down low at 0.87 Mach number. In that era, the rules covering international speed records required that they be flown at an altitude above the ground of 1,100 feet or less. The data recovered from the crash remains indicated that the *Swallow* was flying at a speed of 0.875 Mach number when the forecast pitch instability was encountered and the aircraft came unglued. There was no intention on that flight of seeking the supersonic laurels.

Ironically, another *Swallow*, one of the three built, but this one with an improved pitch control system, would indeed a year and a half later set a new world speed record of 605.23 miles per hour, and five months after that it would be the first British-built aircraft to fly faster than sound. Both of these events found the illustrious de Havilland test pilot John Derry at the controls, although his finesse of the sound barrier was hardly the piece of cake encountered by Welch and Yeager some eleven months earlier. From his start in a dive from 45,000 feet until his recovery at 23,000 feet, Derry endured a series of wild, out-of-control pitching oscillations. The dry, understated panache of Derry's account of his near-death experience served only to embellish the inspired hyperbole of the David Lean film.

Epilogue

The impulse to tell this story originated over forty years ago in late October 1954. George Welch had been killed on Columbus Day demonstrating in the F-100A the upper right-hand corner—the point on the aircraft's performance envelope where pushing too hard can mean real trouble. If no one's been there before, just hitting the design point can be pretty dicey. It was intended to be a 7.3 g's, supposedly symmetrical pull-up at 1.55 Mach number. Unfortunately, as the nose rose to generate lift of more than seven times the weight of the *Super Sabre*, the air, which had been passing over the top of the wing quite smoothly, suddenly became disturbed and burbly, wholly blanking out the vertical fin and destroying its ability to keep the aircraft on a stable heading. The rudder mounted on the back of the fin, which the pilot can control from the cockpit with his rudder pedals to correct heading anomalies, was similarly denied the smooth flow of air required to perform that function. A small disturbance in yaw and the aircraft suddenly wanted to swap ends.

The data from the flight-test recorder later showed that Welch, short and slight of build as he was, in his near panic-driven effort to keep the *Super Sabre* straight, exerted a force of 360 pounds on the rudder—try that in the weight room during your next session at the local body shop. The nose structure, not designed to fly sideways at those speeds, broke and folded back, with the canopy bow crushing Welch's chest before separating from the rest of the fuselage. By some miraculous instinct for survival or as a consequence of the structural failure, the ejection seat was fired and the parachute deployed, but at such high speed that several panels of the 'chute were torn out, making the rate of descent quite high.

The pilot of a B-47 transiting the area at an altitude of 25,000 feet observed the *Super Sabre*'s steep dive commencing above him at about 45,000 feet, streaking beneath the swept-wing bomber, and then suddenly disintegrating at a height of perhaps 20,000 feet. He reported seeing two parachutes, noting that two people had apparently ejected from the fighter.

He was half right. The F-100 carried a drag 'chute in its tail to help decelerate the aircraft after landing. That parachute also broke loose and blossomed as the aircraft came unglued. Thus, there were two chutes, but only one designed for crew survival, and it was lowering the crumpled test pilot much too swiftly to the floor of the Mojave Desert.

Bob Baker and J. O. Roberts, test pilot colleagues at North American, flew swiftly to Welch's side from the Palmdale flight-test facility in a company *Navion*, landing on a one-track dirt road in the desert. When they reached the fatally injured pioneer of supersonic flight, there was still a pulse. But in a matter of a few minutes, he was gone. When the *Super Sabre* had broken up, it signaled his passing with one last unequivocally supersonic boom that presaged his demise with a characteristic double crack of an intensity that surely cowed the coyotes and evoked rattles from the sidewinders for many miles around the crash site. Since October 1947, the sonic *ba-boom* had been Wheaties's trademark.

It was also a very loud and clear wake-up call for North American. Over the complaints of Pete Everest and Chuck Yeager that there were serious stability and control problems with the F-100, Welch had said the two Air Force test pilots were too picky and took his case to the tactical units scheduled to receive the new airplane. They flew it and loved it, mainly for the big jump in performance it gave them. They wanted the *Super Sabre*; and, on the basis of their stamp of approval, deliveries to the operational squadrons started. And there followed losses, too many losses. Over a very short period of time, one Air Force F-100 pilot was killed and four others bailed out after getting into unrecoverable spins.

Going into his last flight, George knew he had a problem—at least the evidence points in that direction. He spent the night before that final test at Manhattan Beach, not at his home in Brentwood's Sullivan Canyon. Were there too many tensions at home? He had returned from a recent trip to Washington to report having met this great new "daisy" at the ritual after-work cocktail hour gathering of North American test pilots at Patmar's. On occasion, this new daisy would join the test pilots. More often than not we would still be wearing our flight suits. She was a large, well-constructed blonde. Her broad, high-cheekboned and blue-eyed countenance, her clear-skinned good looks revealed her Slavic background. In his diffident way, Welch seemed enamored of the girl and took pleasure in showing her off. As an airline stewardess, she felt herself to be a part of his aviation world.

Later, at a small wake held in her Manhattan Beach apartment, she would confide that on his last night, George had sought a mothering solace that might relax the nerves grown taut in contemplation of the morrow's moment of truth. A warm comforting embrace and finally sleep, nothing more, then to slide silently off to his date with destiny in the early morning hours. There had certainly been moments of greater emotion earlier in their brief encounter. A couple of months later she disappeared, returning after a week or so to report that she had aborted a very small fetus. "It"—this infant who had sprung to life within her as she and George were carelessly caught up in the eroticism of a late summer evening, heightened always by the knowledge that each new dawn meant he would once again resume his other life, on the dangerous edge of new discovery—"It was a little boy," she said with an ineffable sadness.

I had been with North American but four months when Welch was killed. On our first meeting, I was shocked to find him wearing his hair in long, blond ringlets. This was more than a decade before such hair styles for men would become commonplace. He still wore a grey company badge that read Senior Engineering Test Pilot, even though he had been with the company for ten years and top test pilot for at least seven. The rest of us wore the same grey badges that announced simply Engineering Test Pilot. A month or so later, George was made chief engineering test pilot and switched from the grey badge of the specialist to the white badge of a supervisor. It was a meaningless switch. George simply was not the management type. As his commanding officer at the time of Pearl Harbor had characterized him—magnificent in the air, worthless on the ground.

On a number of occasions, sitting next to him at Patmar's as he sipped his martini, I felt I could have been contemplating the countenance of a man twice his thirty-six years. The brow was creased, the crow's feet at the corners of his eyes were deep. More unusual were the radial lines around his mouth, as if some jackleg quack had performed a clumsy face-lift.

This seemingly accelerated aging process had also been observed by George's Australian wife, Jan: "It was as though in a year or less, he had suddenly become a very old man, and I felt helpless to arrest the process." She was not alone. On the day of the fatal crash, old Pearl Harbor squadron mate and good friend Ken Taylor, then an Air Force colonel at the Pentagon, was en route to Los Angeles at the behest of Dutch Kindelberger to discuss with George the possibility of his taking a nonflying job with the company.

It should be noted that being an engineering test pilot at North American Aviation involved a lot more than testing aircraft and writing flight reports. Visiting Air Force pilots wanted to meet and talk with the test pilots. Often this was done over dinner in the evening. These evenings often stretched out late, and with ample lubrication. Then there were the frequent trips to Wright Patterson Air Force Base in Dayton and to the Pentagon to brief the top brass and civil hierarchy about development progress. Operational bases were visited not only in the United States but also in the Far East and around the NATO countries. These latter trips often included flight demonstrations in which the observing military pilots expected hotshot test pilots to put the *Sabres* and the *Super Sabres* through their paces, not up high where they belonged but down on the deck where the Air Force watchers could have a good look—up close and personal. And all of this before the advent of jet transports. More often than not the all-night "red eye" flights were taken, leaving Los Angeles around 9:00 P.M. and arriving in Washington or Dayton at eight or nine the next morning. The overseas trips were even more exhausting.

North American's medical director was also a flight surgeon. "Doc" Lloyd took a special interest in the test pilots. Welch complained about the rigors of the trips, especially the problems he had adjusting his body clock to the local time and the consequent inability to get to sleep at local sleeping hours. At first, Doc gave George some sleeping pills. Then there was the complaint that he couldn't stay awake for the briefings, so Doc provided some wake-up pills—"uppers" and "downers" are what some might call these medications today. Those who traveled with him sometimes thought that Welch had become addicted to these drugs.

Then there were the financial pressures. In fashionable Brentwood, Jan moved with a fast set that included Liz Whitney, whose ranch was near the Welch canyon home. George made good money, Jan's family was certainly well-to-do, and Jan was anything but a big spender. As in Australia, she dressed simply and preferred the beach to the party scene. Still, the cash demands were large and could be distracting. One way for George to increase his income was to complete the demonstration on the F-100 with its now apparent faults and collect his bonus, which was $10,000, a not inconsiderable sum in 1954. Then he could identify the shortcomings and collect again on demonstrating the aircraft modified to correct the problems.

The Air Force, especially Everest and Yeager at Edwards, already were saying that the F-100's handling qualities were unacceptable. The challenge was to survive the first round, and George was becoming more and more aware that this just might test his skills too far, push his luck over the brink. But did he have the clanks? His face said yes—although fourteen years of full-throttle living complicated by a history of malaria might have etched a similar result. His newfound friend at Manhattan Beach would have said yes. We will never really know the truth.

The search for other truths continues. Very soon after the disintegration of Welch's *Super Sabre* over the Mojave, I joined a North American peacemaking mission to Edwards Air Force Base. There were some afternoon meetings to discuss methods for salvaging the F-100 as a frontline Air Force fighter and close out the flight-test demonstration of a workable configuration. Everest and Yeager were there, and Yeager, about to depart for command of an F-86 fighter squadron in Germany, sought to tighten his toehold on the ziggurat of test-flying supremacy by sounding off on some eccentricities of fighter behavior out at the margins, trying to relate his experience in the ultrathin air of the stratosphere where rockets play to the serious business of supersonic down where the air is dense and hard and unforgiving. But no one took any great offense; after all, he was the customer's golden boy and North American could ill afford to ignite his hostility. A few drinks and a congenial dinner were marked by attentive listening to oft-told tales of miraculous deeds against enemies of wars now past and new advances into the mysterious world of always greater performance. Then the North American contingent piled onto the trusty DC-2 that ferried people and critical parts between the LA plant and the desert test sites and flew back to the civilized or, more appropriately, heavily populated regions of southern California.

Next morning, I caught the early-morning shuttle flight from Los Angeles. As I disembarked from the DC-2 at the company's Palmdale flight-test operations, I noted that Bud Poage was in the dispatcher's shack by the corner of the hangar. One of Welch's closest friends, Bud had been devastated by his death. He had not gone with us to Edwards. I ducked into the shack to say hello.

"Hi, Blackie, how'd it go at Edwards yesterday?"

"OK, I think. Of course, Yeager had to spout off about how we ought to run our flight-test programs. . . . But, what the hell, I suppose we have to listen. After all, he was the first guy to go supersonic."

I can't remember ever seeing Bud so upset. His eyes were afire. Still, he looked around to make sure we were alone. Then, quite precisely, he spoke: "That's just not so. Wheaties boomed the daylights out of Edwards several days before Yeager made his 'historic' flight. We just don't talk about it. Not then. Not now."

Bud turned his face away as it contorted in an agony of pent-up loss, helpless frustration, and barely bridled anger. Welch had been Bud Poage's best friend. Bud believed passionately that the supersonic laurels bestowed on Yeager really belonged to Welch, and he was intensely frustrated by his inability to set the story straight. As noted earlier, Bud had been a fighter pilot in World War II and gave a good account of himself. After the war, he joined North American as a liaison pilot. Early on he struck up a friendship with George Welch. It would seem they were total opposites—Welch the seemingly unflappable risk-taker, Poage the quiet ultra-conservative who played it safe. They both had girl-friends at Pancho's Happy Bottom Riding Club in the Mojave. George talked of marriage to Millie while his wife was about to deliver their first child. Bud married Mona and there was never anyone else for him, even though most of the other test pilots' wives would have nothing to do with her—she was one of Pancho's girls, wasn't she?

Welch liked having Bud around. They shared a taste for dry martinis and, though he professed to have neither the training nor inclination for the work, at George's urging Bud became an engineering test pilot. He had at least one harrowing escape when he and Dan Darnell parachuted from a flaming, disintegrating AJ-1 *Savage*. He neither liked nor fully understood the growing complexities of experimental flying, and soon after his friend's demise he switched to the role of company transport pilot, flying people and material between LA and the Mojave. In 1965, barely forty-five years old, he died of a coronary.

It was earlier in 1954 that I had first met Bud Poage. In the spring of that year, he was back East at the Naval Air Test Center at Patuxent River, Maryland, to do a demonstration of the T-28 trainer for the Navy. Having been recalled to active duty for the Korean fracas, I was winding up a two-year stint as a Marine pilot at the Test Center and looking for a job. Over dinner on several occasions, Bud encouraged me to seek employment with North American as an engineering test pilot. By June I had been taken on board, and, unlike Bud, was thoroughly enjoying the challenge.

On that late October morning in the dispatch shack at Palmdale, I could offer little solace for his grief. With my clasp of his shoulders I tried to let him understand I shared his sorrow. But I really didn't and couldn't. I had arrived too recently, had yet to pay my dues. The true meaning of his outburst would not be fully revealed for many years. It was one of those memory bits that will stay with me forever. But with the Air Force still North American's best customer, there was no useful purpose in shattering one of the wild blue yonder's most treasured icons. Years later, many other corroborating bits of evidence came my way. Ten years ago I started to probe into the matter with some degree of focus. As other witnesses came forward, the truth is tantalizingly close to being unequivocal.

There was the strange call from newly anointed Air Force Secretary Stu Symington imploring Dutch Kindelberger to restrain the company's new fighter from going supersonic. The impetus for that out-of-character call clearly came from hangar talk at Muroc and some off-base banter around the bar and in the bedrooms of Pancho's renowned establishment.

It is interesting that in Pancho's biography, after examining in that lady's colorful prose the devotion that tied her to Yeager, she is quoted as having said:

> Chuck was the first pilot to crack the sound barrier and don't let anyone try to tell you any different. There are all kinds of stories about yahoos diving F-86s to supersonic speed but that's a lot of bullshit. Chuck did it first and he *piloted* the airplane to make his record. Any bitch dog or monkey can be sent around the world in a capsule and can push buttons on a signal—Pavlov proved that a long time ago. Chuck did his flight using his own brain and pilot know-how. Most of these news people don't know a hero from a drugged monkey.*

The famed female air racer and proprietress of the Happy Bottom Riding Club may have had some trouble sorting out George Welch and John Glenn and the chimp named Ham, or separating a swept-wing *Sabre* from a *Mercury* spacecraft, but it is for sure relevant that she was painfully cognizant of the bar talk at her hacienda, where it was authoritatively whispered that Welch had "done it first." He was the only yahoo who had flown the F-86 (née XP-86) prior to Yeager's October 14 caper. In the words of an

---

*Grover Ted Tate, *The Lady Who Tamed Pegasus* (1984).

earlier, perhaps more enduring scribe, "The lady doth protest too much, methinks." But give the lady credit. Even in those long-gone days, she had a good take on the media crowd.

And there was a lot more going on at Happy Bottom than drinking and bragging with pickled pilots slamming full gallop into closed corral gates at midnight. There were the young, lovely, lonely, down-on-their-luck ladies Pancho took under her wing. Some found a long-sought chance for lifelong pairing; some even took it; and for some, it worked. Others found brief moments of starlike association and became the occasional princess, suspected it wasn't forever, but embraced the short-lived association with men they knew were different, special, and therefore capable of raising their sense of instantaneous passion so explosively. What lay beyond was not terribly important, at least not at the moment. In the fall of 1947, the memory of war was not that far distant, with all its poignant farewells, promises of forever, and failures to return—sometimes with a notice of regrets from the Secretary of War or a Dear Jill, or, more often, nothing.

In a sense, the often exhilarating immediacy of wartime living, the cram-a-life-into-a-weekend syndrome, had been transferred from the distant fighter strips on New Guinea and in England to the high desert of the Mojave. The challenge was no longer one of mortal combat. Rather, it was an unfolding of the mysteries allied with slicing through the sonic wall and of reaching for the airlessness of space, and returning to tell about it. Of those venturers, Kipling might well have asked, "What Dame of Chance brought them forth to joust at the dawn with death?"

Such was the aphrodisiacal lore told with a diffident shrug at Pancho's and at Patmar's and at other select watering holes from Hollywood to the beach communities of Los Angeles. So it was that George Welch, frequently constrained to overnight in the desert to meet an early-morning flight schedule, whiled away the evenings at Pancho's. Not given to garrulity, more often than not he sought the solo company of Millie Palmer, one of the lovelier specimens who had found temporary refuge at the Happy Bottom Riding Club. It was to Millie that George confided on an early autumn evening that she should be listening for his historic boom, and returned for a subsequent tête-à-tête to learn that she had indeed been nearly blasted out of her bed by the *ba-boom* of the sonic shock wave emanating from his supersonic *Sabrejet* early that morning. George swore Millie to secrecy, but the security environment at Pancho's was quite sievelike. The rumors spread to Pancho and caused the outburst in defense of Yeager noted earlier. It was but one of many.

Millie confided this historic sonic event to her first cousin, Staff Sergeant Clint Merrill, USAF, who was based at Travis Air Force Base, a military air transport service facility near San Francisco. He was a flight engineer on C-54 transport aircraft, the Air Force version of the Douglas DC-4. Sergeant Merrill was assigned to the run between Buffalo, the home of Bell Aircraft Company, creators of the X-1 rocket plane, and Muroc, in logistic support of the X-1's operations there.

Just before Christmas of 1947, the magazine *Aviation Week* broke the story that an X-1 piloted by Chuck Yeager had gone supersonic the previous October 14. The event was presumed to be highly classified. Without denying the story, the Air Force threatened to bring charges of publishing official secrets against the editor, Bob Wood. Around Muroc the story was old hat. So was the news that the X-1 was not number one in the supersonic hit parade. Clint Merrill remembers a flight he made from Muroc to Travis shortly after the public airing of the event. As flight engineer, he sat between and just behind the pilot and copilot on the flight deck. In the left seat was a U.S. Army two-star, a major general. The supersonic story was very much on the general's mind. As the C-54 droned above the San Joaquin Valley en route to San Francisco, Clint remembers the two-star remonstrating with some agitation,

"But why are they giving all these big slaps on the back to Yeager? Everyone knows that George Welch did it first."

Apparently everyone did not know that Welch did it first. Those who did were clearly informed, directly or indirectly, that it wasn't in their interest to make noises, any more than it bode well for Welch's future to talk of those early *ba-booms*. George really didn't give a damn. Everyone who meant anything to him—his family, close friends, and the very tight community that was the heart of experimental flying at the dry lake bed known as Muroc—knew the real order of things. What the papers and the bureaucrats and the medal givers wanted to characterize as truth, that really didn't matter. In like fashion he'd been recommended for the Medal of Honor at Pearl Harbor, but some of the intervening brass thought he should have waited for orders before intercepting the sneak attackers and substituted a lesser award.

As one moved up the hierarchy of North American Aviation, sensitivity to the customer's needs, both technical and philosophical, was more acutely tuned. This was in the forties and fifties, and for many, more than forty years later, the code of silence retains its hold. From the flight line to the executive suite, from engineering to public relations, from the shop floor to the contracts office, at the upper levels of the organization chart, whatever the Air Force wanted, the Air Force got, especially in the way of purely cosmetic issues that had no impact on the bottom line or on the quality of the product.

Thus, if the Air Force wanted to canonize a young captain as the very first Mach-buster, go for it—and let no remonstrance be heard from anyone at North American. This decision was made especially easy for a number of reasons. Yeager was, and remains, a person easy to like. Despite his rugged independence, from early on he had a clearly focused sense for making the most of opportunities that might enhance his hero image. However, the ultimate access to international renown occurred when author Tom Wolfe found Yeager more highly endowed with "the right stuff" than were the astronauts and ensconced him at the peak of the right stuff ziggurat. His book and the subsequent film, with Sam Shepard as Yeager (and Yeager as Pancho's bartender), moved the rocket pilot from a limited stage as aeronautics' star performer to the global arena as media superstar and the world's foremost battery salesman.

George Welch, on the other hand, was a loner. He didn't warm to people easily and didn't seem to care. Of his many associates in the Army Air Force and at North American, he had but a few real friends, and many liked him not at all. One of his fellow test pilots, who felt especially bruised by Welch's failure to recognize his peculiar talents (which actually lay more in the realm of stunt flying and boudoir stunts), had the poor taste to regale the wake held at Patmar's on the evening of Welch's fatal crash with shouts of "I'm glad he's dead! I'm glad he's dead!" much to the disgust of colleagues and strangers alike. Others held their peace but still found it difficult to feel real sorrow. The truth is that not many, if any, knew the real Welch, perhaps not even Wheaties himself.

Welch wasn't excited about keeping score. He was as diffident about his wartime victories as he was about his peacetime achievements. Squadron mates say he really splashed at least one and perhaps three additional enemy aircraft at Pearl Harbor. It is interesting that his officially confirmed victories came in bunches. Of the sixteen total aircraft credited to him, the record-keepers say he got four on two days, three on two days, and on one day he got two. It is noted in the squadron history that on the day he got only two, he also had a "probable." Is it possible there were days on which he may have nailed only one enemy aircraft but simply did not take the time to fill out the paperwork? Fellow fighter jocks, and historians who have researched the matter in some depth, say there are at least four or five more that should be added to his tally, pushing his total to twenty or more. And that despite being dragged back to the States soon after the war's first day for bond rallies, being laid up in Sydney with malaria, and then leaving the combat arena for good just as the quality of the competition in enemy cockpits was entering a rapid downhill slide.

George's war started with second-rate equipment against the cream of the enemy's pilot talent. He shot down his last four planes six months before Yeager got his first victory flying against a Luftwaffe wholly depleted but with enough moxie left to shoot him down on his eighth mission. By the time Yeager got back into the air, Welch had been home for a year and had already started to work for North American as an experimental test pilot.

In the private world of the fighter pilot, where aces let their hair down and their wingmen sometimes speak truth, Yeager was twitted for having stumbled into an undergraduate class of neophyte Nazi aviators of which he shot down three, while observing two crash into each other in their hurry to get back to home base. In his biography, Yeager relates how he closed in on the students— "I came in behind their tail-end Charlie and was about to begin hammering him, when he suddenly broke left and ran into his wingman. They both bailed out. It was almost comic, scoring two quick *victories* [really?] without firing a shot. But, apparently, the big shortage in Germany was not of airplanes, but of pilots" (emphasis and parenthetical comment added).

Since on the same flight Yeager went on to shoot down three more of the hapless students, he became an "official" ace. If he'd seen five others crack up in landing and spotted them first, presumably he could have been anointed a double ace on the same day. Could his ultrasharp eagle eyes have missed some of the action? Still, before the war fizzled out altogether and the feckless, untrained German youths were allowed to lay down their swords and shields, the West Virginia scourge shot down another five, including the first Me-262 jet, which he caught with its landing gear down on final approach to its home base.

Throughout his war, Chuck was flying the incomparable *Mustang*, without a doubt the top fighter aircraft of the war. But give the guy credit. There were a lot of Yanks thrashing around in the same skies, flying the same great *Mustang*, with many of the same opportunities, who went back to England, mission after mission—in fact, completed their tours—without the first coonskin to nail onto the barn door. Mind you, we're not comparing eagles to turkeys. These were two eagles—Welch and Yeager. Welch took off into the war on its very first day with enemy fighters strafing his airstrip. He was flying a second-rate fighter against the best trained and most experienced tactical airmen in the Pacific. Flying out of New Guinea, the circumstances and national priorities weren't much different. All the best still went to Europe. The P-39 wasn't much of an improvement over the P-40 he flew at Pearl Harbor, although he still used it to shoot down enemy aircraft. After ditching enough of the clumsy *Airacobras* because of "engine trouble," George finally got into a half-decent fighter and fashioned his last nine (or ten or eleven) victories while flying the fork-tailed devil, the P-38 *Lightning*. One can only fantasize what Welch might have achieved had he started the war with a *Mustang* as his mount and stayed in the fray until it ended . . . or what a score Yeager might have run up had he begun in 1940 with the Eagle Squadron.

Who would dream that two such uncontestably superior fighter pilots from the same side of the last great air war would square off little more than two years after the cessation of hostilities in an undeclared, indeed undeclarable, contest, the details of which wouldn't even be discussed? At the time, no one found it in his interest to discuss it, except perhaps George Welch. And George, in his own crazy fashion, found a method for opening and reopening the matter. With a vintage Welch shrug, an enigmatic smile, he made the sonic boom his special signature, a statement whose fullest meaning only a few could understand. Was it wholly ingenuous on the part of North American's public relations department that, as the new *ba-booming Sabre* became operational, a company-sponsored Mach-busters' Club was founded? For a number of years, the only route to membership was in the cockpit of a *Sabre*. When the two-seat *Sabre* started flying, a number of distinguished citizens who were not pilots could be initiated into the club. Since only two of the dual-seated *Sabres* were built, the Mach-busters' pin and certificate were highly cherished mementos among a carefully selected group of Air Force officials, aviation leaders, industry executives, the press, and, of course, *Sabre* pilots.

These flights in the *Sabre* two-seater also provided an opportunity for the company's demonstration pilot to note to his captive audience the effortless slide beyond the sonic wall as he put the *Sabre* into a shallow dive. The unspoken message clearly was: This supersonic stuff is no big deal for North American. We know how to design them so they'll just slip right through. With the thousands of *Sabres* to be found around the world, the membership in the Mach-busters' Club became quite large. Since only three X-1's were built, Bell Aircraft was at a disadvantage. Besides, no one even considered building a two-seat version of the little rocket ship.

Not only did Welch boom Muroc before it became Edwards in the early months of the first *Sabre*'s existence, including several booms recorded by Walt Williams's theodolites in November 1947, but he would also later use the boom as an introduction to the flying demonstrations he performed for *Sabre* squadrons around the United States and later in the Far East during the Korean War. As for the theodolites, these were the very same highly accurate, radar-assisted optical tracking instruments used to give "official" confirmation to Yeager's October climb through the sonic wall— for posterity, as it came to be recorded at least, a first.

The U.S. Air Force belatedly and officially admitted in June 1948 that the *Sabre* had indeed exceeded the speed of sound. It was indicated that this event had occurred on April 26. Shortly thereafter Roland "Bee" Beamont, intrepid British fighter ace and test pilot, was invited to have a go at "breaking the sound barrier," as the feat was characterized in the title of David Lean's forgettable film. It was an event that had proven tragically elusive for British pilots and a matter of considerable frustration for their aircraft designers. Yet, on May 21, when Bee took the number two XP-86 supersonic and became the first Brit to get there, it was such a nonevent that he couldn't believe he'd done it. But observers on the ground heard the *ba-boom*, and cockpit instruments confirmed that supersonic reality. Back home, the British boffins didn't want to validate the data, perhaps preferring that the honor be postponed until it could be won in a British aircraft.

As for our neighbors to the North, Al Lilly, then chief test pilot for Canadair, was the first Canadian to fly supersonic. He did it in a Canadair-built *Sabre* Mark I on August 10, 1950. Our other cousins "down under" also used their home-built *Sabres* to acquaint themselves initially and in depth with the world of supersonics. Indeed, fighter pilots from some thirty-seven nations received their supersonic indoctrination in the incomparable *Sabre*.

In 1953, when Chuck Yeager was grooming Jackie Cochran for an assault on the women's 100-kilometer, closed-course speed record, he incidentally escorted her in a dive through the great sonic wall, making her the first female to go supersonic. Quite naturally, they were both flying *Sabres*. A few weeks later, Jackie did set a new speed mark for women pilots, and she did it in a Canadian-built *Sabre*.

It was around that time, on May 25, 1953, to be precise, that Welch upped his boom habits a notch by taking North American's brand-new YF-100A supersonic in level flight on its very first outing, an event of but thirty-five minutes from liftoff to touchdown.

Captain Charles E. Yeager, who has flown faster than the speed of sound in the Bell X-1, waves from the cockpit of the world's speed record holder, the North American F-86 *Sabre* jet fighter, St. Louis Air Show, October 1948. *Courtesy of Archives II, College Park, Maryland*

Then, on the same day, to prove it was not a fluke, as has been the allegation of some concerning the first flight of the earlier, simpler *Sabre*, he blasted through into the supersonic regime on the *Super Sabre*'s second flight as well. But it took the first public showing of the prototype F-100 on October 19, 1953, to really grab people's imagination. There, Welch zeroed in on the small wood-frame operations shack at Palmdale Airport near the spot where the aviation press had assembled. In a shallow dive and with full afterburning power, he passed over the field below 1,000 feet and clearly supersonic. There was an earshattering *Ba-BOOM*; glass in the shack's windows shattered and the door frames splintered. Fortunately, no one was injured, but the flight plans for future demonstrations were dramatically altered. After landing at Palmdale and mingling with the press, Welch responded to the rather dramatic evidence of boom power with a puzzled smile, as though to say, "You mean I was really supersonic that time? Gol-lee."

As noted, Welch was not exactly well loved by many of the North American people. He was independent and a loner. He could play the prima donna, sometimes to the point of rudeness. He had an IQ that went nearly off the scale yet loved to play highly creative if wholly crazy pranks. Being anything but dumb, he kept open lines to top echelons of the company and sought never to endanger North American's interests. Although he would have been the last to admit it, many of the old hands believe that George had a direct line to Dutch Kindelberger. After all, Dutch had hired him at the suggestion of General Hap Arnold. Welch was smart enough to know that the guy at the top wanted to get news about his company's latest product direct from the person best equipped to deliver that information. There was no one in a better position to do that than his test pilot. And it could save the big boss a lot of reading.

This straight line to the top also explains the cautious way in which Welch communicated to the technical people the fact of his earliest supersonic caper. No one remembers that Dutch told anyone about Air Force Secretary Stu Symington's admonition not to take the XP-86 supersonic. Maybe that's because the only one Dutch told about that phone call, other than Lee Atwood, was Welch, and he told him as a heads-up, not as an order to hold a tight rein on his *Sabre.*

Ed Horkey was assistant chief technical engineer at North American in the fall of 1947. Included in his responsibilities was engineering flight test. A Cal Tech graduate, he had gone to work for North American right out of college. His strong technical background and natural leadership qualities moved him rapidly up the promotion ladder. He and Welch were about the same age, and they got along well. George had a very quick mind and could absorb a large quantity of technical material seemingly at a glance. He was especially interested in supersonic technology.

A *Mustang* had been used by NACA as a flying wind tunnel with a small wing section mounted at the point of maximum wing thickness. In a dive, air passing over that small model would reach supersonic speed, and forces on the model could be measured. Welch had seen film of that model in supersonic flow. In addition, when the sunlight was at just the right angle, he had noted shock waves on the wings of *Mustangs* he was testing in high-speed dives. And remember that Major Fred Borsodi, the Air Force test pilot flying out of Wright Field, had seen the same thing and managed to get film of these shock waves on the *Mustang*'s wing. These pictures were shared with North American. Welch and Horkey talked about this a lot. They were both convinced, for different reasons, that characterization of this phenomenon as a "sound barrier" or a "sonic wall" was pure hokum.

George's father's name was Schwartz. There was naturally a bit of pride in the German heritage, especially when Horkey's people started talking about captured German design data related to supersonic flight. And no discussion of German supersonic technology was complete without examining the rocket work at Peenemünde. It bears restating in this rehash that the V-2 missiles, huge for their time, were several times the weight of a *Sabre*, or an X-1 for that matter, and substantially larger. By the end of the war, more than thirty-five hundred of these V (for vengeance) weapons had been launched. For each the maximum speed attained was generally in excess of four times the speed of sound. And they hadn't self-destructed. They had aerodynamic controls and stabilizers that had functioned just fine at those impossibly high speeds.

Welch and Horkey and aerodynamicists such as Harrison Storms, Larry Greene, and Rose Lunn talked about swept wings and wings that were much thinner, and they conjectured not whether, but how high, must the *Sabre* go and how steeply must it dive to achieve supersonic flight. The V-2 had enough oomph to push it through to supersonic speed while climbing almost straight up. The *Sabre*, especially the early prototypes, didn't have anywhere near enough thrust for that, but get it to 35,000 feet and push it over pretty steep, you'll probably make it. Better yet, go to 40,000 and you won't need to get so steep. Take it to 45,000 and unless you pull the power back or deploy the speed brakes, you're going to lay a *ba-boom* on the folks under your nose on your way down. At least that was the way the performance folks working for Ed Horkey had it figured out.

In addition to Millie Palmer, there were others on the ground in the Mojave Desert that attested to Welch's supersonic capers as evidenced by the sonic booms. They included North American's ground crew working at Muroc. People such as Bob Cadick, who had followed his father to North American, and who, like his father, had joined the engineering flight-test department—Bob remembers the *ba-booms* very early in the opening days of the *Sabre*'s flight-test history. And Bud Poage remembered. There was no doubt in his mind about the order of things.

There were no secrets at Muroc. The security rules were strict, so there wasn't much shouting or chest thumping, but everyone knew about the X-1 and its purpose, and they knew George Welch was flying the XP-86 and just might beat Yeager to the mark. They also knew that if he did, it wouldn't be "official" because, after all, the new Air Force was still paying the bills, just as the old Army Air Corps had, and no matter how many booming protests Welch might lay on the dry lake bed, the X-1 was going to be first. So Bob Cadick and the other North American troops managed a conspiratorial wink or two and buried prideful grins in their beer as Pancho bought a round in celebration of Yeager's historic flight.

At the upper echelons of North American, the discipline was much tougher. Walt Spivak was chief project engineer. He was responsible for ensuring that engineering drawings were transformed into shop drawings that the production line could convert into real hardware. He was a taciturn but hard taskmaster. Walt Spivak and George Welch had quietly become close friends, at the professional level. Neither understood well what the other did, but they had developed an active reciprocal respect. George shared his concerns about design problems with Walt, and Walt explained the difficulties of giving George all the special features great fighter pilots would like to have in their new aircraft. George also confided in Walt. He felt safe in telling Walt that he had taken the XP-86 supersonic early in its flight tests, and he knew the secret would be secure there. How right he was. Even today, fifty years later, Walt will only obliquely admit that he knew about it. After all, a confidence is a confidence, no matter that Wheaties has been dead for over forty years. No careless blabbermouth is Walter Spivak. The pride of sharing and keeping a mutual trust is still a sign of personal integrity that he is not willing to abandon. The world could do with a few more from the same mold.

It would be a couple of months after the actual event before editor Bob Wood would break the X-1's Mach-busting story in the *Aviation Week* issue dated December 22, 1947. It would not be until six months later, with the magazine's issue of June 14, 1948, that the public would be told that the XP-86 had also gone supersonic. The date reported for that event was April 26, 1948, at least six months after we know for sure it really happened. It all fit in with Harry Truman's determination to give Bell and the newly created U.S. Air Force their day in the sun.

Two great fighter pilots had a joust in the clear skies over the Mojave Desert. For one, the only purpose of his craft was to demonstrate that a manned aircraft, however useless it might be for other tasks, can fly supersonically. For the other, the goal was to maintain his nation's military superiority in a dangerous world. That his craft incidentally proved to be capable of supersonic flight would have but a modest, albeit palpable, impact on its combat capabilities. It is carefully documented that Yeager first went supersonic in the X-1 on October 14, 1947, at about 10:30 A.M., having been dropped from an altitude of 20,000 feet by the B-29 mother ship at 10:26. We know for certain that Welch took the XP-86 supersonic, not once but twice, on November 13, 1947. The event was carefully measured by the same radar theodolite and operating crew that validated the X-1's supersonic event. But the XP-86 first flew on October 1, 1947, and had the opportunity to exceed the speed of sound on numerous occasions prior to the explicitly documented event in mid-November. On several occasions, Welch noted, and reported to North American engineer Ed Horkey, funny jumps in his airspeed indicator in the course of dives from high altitude. It was these reports that led to the confirmation flights of November 13. And note that it took more than a day or two to get scheduled on the radar theolodite range. Although the bureaucracies of that era were less cumbersome than those of today, the requests, the approvals, and the paperwork still had to go up and down the line before anything happened.

As for the unofficial event, Welch had the opportunity on his first flight. Gear extension problems on that first outing caused the next flight on October 9 to be made with the landing gear down and locked. By the time for the next two flights came around, the landing gear had been fixed, although the flight-test card still called for both flights to be made entirely with the gear down. These two flights took place on October 14. On the evening of the 13th, Welch had learned that Yeager was going for it on the 14th.

Thus, it is not inconceivable that, contrary to Air Force instructions, Wheaties sucked up the landing gear on the second of those flights—the first was aborted when the airspeed system was found to be inoperative—and laid a *ba-boom* or two on Muroc in salute to Yeager's official indoctrination into the supersonic club. Between October 14 and the officially documented supersonic flight of November 13, Welch had fifteen flights in the *Sabre*. The first of these that was advertised in the test plan as a "high Mach investigation" took place on November 3 and was almost certainly supersonic. It was also almost certainly scheduled as a consequence of Welch's earlier conversations with the test engineers about funny jumps in his airspeed instrument readings.

We are left with the possibility that Welch went supersonic as early as October 1 on his very first flight in the *Sabre*, just as he did on his first flight in the *Super Sabre* six years later. That would have been almost two weeks before Yeager. He most certainly flew faster than Mach one no later than November 3, or nearly three weeks after Yeager. In brief, their individual achievements of this aviation milestone are separated by no more than a figurative nanosecond in the overarching span of time connecting the course of human events.

The nature of their respective supersonic penetrations were also vastly different. Yeager had to be borne aloft by a mother ship, relied on rocket propulsion, went supersonic in a slight climb, and, with less than three minutes of fully powered flight at his command, had to make a dead-stick landing at the end of the flight. The Fédération Aéronautique Internationale (FAI), which certifies all aeronautical records, will not recognize any records that do not include a conventional takeoff and successful landing. Much later, on January 5, 1949, Yeager, very conscious of the FAI rules, did make his one-and-only attempt to take the X-1 supersonic from a ground takeoff. It was unsuccessful. Dick Frost, Bell engineer and flight-test supervisor at Muroc in charge of that attempt, restricted propellants to slightly more than one-half the normal load for an air launch. The X-1 landing gear was designed for landing after all propellants had been expended. By Frost's calculations, the loads he permitted were for an early morning takeoff, before the runway heated up. The fact that it was early January also helped. In any event, Chuck ran out of fuel at 23,000 feet at a speed of less than 0.95 Mach number. It was a meaningless event, in any case. *Sabres* had been laying booms along the Antelope Valley for more than a year without the aid of a mother ship.

More interestingly, this flight was for Yeager another close encounter with the Grim Reaper. In his excitement to get off as quickly as possible so as to limit the loss of supercooled propellant because of boil-off, Chuck forgot to hook up his oxygen mask. The X-1 cabin was pressurized by nitrogen from large high-pressure spherical tanks in the fuselage. Thus, as the flight progressed, the proportion of oxygen in the cabin air diminished. By the time of fuel burnout, there was precious little oxygen for life support left in the cockpit of the tiny research aircraft. Talk about your breathless moments! The fuel lasted not much more than a minute, and only a little bit longer was required after burnout to get the orange rocketship back on the dry lake at Muroc.

The X-1 was a one-of-a-kind aircraft built for research purposes only. Its accomplishments are a special tribute to the determination of NACA leaders such as John Stack of Langley to continue expansion of their aeronautical knowledge via research aircraft when for a period their research wind tunnels had been stymied by choking in the transonic range. The diverse team from NACA, Bell, and the U.S. Air Force was blessed with the special talents of engineering pilots such as Dick Frost of Bell and Jack Ridley of the Air Force, and the forceful on-site leadership of Walt Williams of NACA—not to mention the innate pilot skills hidden beneath the inimitable "aw, shucks" personality of Chuck Yeager.

Welch, on the other hand, made only conventional takeoffs and landings in his *Sabre*, relying on a single air-breathing jet engine for the entire flight. He took the XP-86 supersonic in a dive. There can be no doubt that the *Sabre* was the first aircraft anywhere in the world to take off conventionally on its own power, accelerate to supersonic flight, and make a fully powered approach and landing. The realization of this spectacular aviation first is a great tribute to the creativity and splendid teamwork of the North

American Aviation Company. Thousands of *Sabres* were built. Without a doubt they provided a clear margin of superiority to U.S. fighter pilots in the Korean War. Coming after the *Mustang*, unchallenged as the best fighter of World War II, the *Sabre*, master of MiG Alley, gave the company the equivalent of nearly two decades of continuous Superbowl championships in the realm of air combat, where almost-just-as-good is a death warrant. George Welch was a worthy member of that illustrious team.

So who really went supersonic first? We'll never know for certain, and does it matter all that much? After all, years earlier the German V-2s had already demonstrated thousands of times over that there really wasn't much to it. Had NASA been running the V-2 program, you may rest assured they would have had an ape in the nose cone for a more definitive report early in the test program. As for manned aircraft, whether it was Welch, then Yeager, or Yeager, then Welch, possibly even on the same day, we're not exactly sure. But we are sure that no one else was even close; unless, that is, one wishes to play by the FAI rules, which say that each contender must take off on his own power. In that case, it was unequivocally Welch. But one might also invoke the rule that speed records must be demonstrated in level flight. Applying both of these rules, the laurels belong to the late Rusty Roth, test pilot for Republic Aviation. Rusty took the XF-91 supersonic in level flight after a conventional takeoff and climb to 35,000 feet on December 9, 1952. His thrust came from a turbojet for primary power plus an auxiliary rocket.

If we're looking for the first Mach-buster in level flight on pure turbojet power, the credits again go to Welch for his flight to supersonic speed in level flight after a conventional takeoff and subsequent landing on May 25, 1953, in the first outing for the YF-100A. The Russians claimed earlier on-the-level supersonic flights in conventional air-breathing fighter prototypes in 1952, but they had to dive from considerable height to get over the drag rise hump in the high subsonic range to achieve a stabilized supersonic speed at constant altitude. Diving into a record run is also prohibited by the FAI.

If we're not interested in a speed record, but simply the event—the first man in a vehicle that exceeds the speed of sound—then we're back where we started: It was either Yeager or Welch, flip a coin. And despite some authoritative tomes to the contrary, there is no doubt that Welch was the first civilian pilot to go supersonic and Yeager the first military pilot to do so. But don't expect the moving fingers, having writ, to turn back and change a word of it. In grabbing for the brass ring of the supersonic merry-go-round, the media mythmakers usually have their way, or at least that's the way it has been for more than half a century. Still, rewriters of our history have been very busy of late changing the gloried, storied past and generally accepted perceptions thereof. How about adjusting myths and halos and indulging in a bit of iconoclasm concerning supersonic firsts? There is the added bit of satisfaction in knowing that what we pass down to the generations who follow is as close to the truth as we know how to make it. One might even call it an obligation.

I have sought to construct situations and conversations as I believe they actually occurred. To the extent possible, I have reviewed these chapters with those who were present or had a better day-to-day grasp of what actually took place, and I have made revisions in the interest of truth as appropriate. If any of the more creative sections of this account strain the credulity of those privileged to be closer than I to that wonderful duel in the sun, I repeat Walt Williams's mantra—"show me the data."

Alas, only a few of the old North American Aviation survivors of those halcyon days in the Mojave Desert during the fall of 1947 know for sure and really give a damn. The wonderful Ed Horkey, a most enthusiastic supporter of this adjustment in aviation history, went to his reward in July 1996. I was talking to him on the telephone just an hour before he died. His joyous enthusiasm had never seemed stronger. As for others who care, one might add the fighter pilots and all their comrades in arms who survived the Korean fracas, where the *Sabres* made the difference.

Now, more than half a century later, the irrelevance of it all is reflected in the military's indifference to the challenge of extending the supersonic capabilities of manned aircraft. Furthermore, those early *ba-booms* over the Mojave Desert may have marked the end of an era extending over a century and a half, wherein the measure of man's progress was the growth in the speed with which people and things could be moved from place to place over the globe. The timid reluctance of our scientific bureaucrats even to attempt to stifle those sonic booms condemns our commerce to accept being stranded for the foreseeable future on the high subsonic plateau first achieved by our commercial jetliners forty years ago.

For some perspective, reflect that the captain of the *Concorde*, that ancient supersonic veteran of more than two decades of scheduled Atlantic crossings at Mach two, apprises his passengers as the aging supersonic transport accelerates beyond Mach one, "Ladies and gentlemen, we have just exceeded the speed of sound, the biggest nonevent in aviation history."

Wheaties Welch must be smiling. Our leaders could use a touch of his insouciant courage.

Bibliography

Beamont, Roland. *Testing Early Jets*. Shrewsbury, UK: Airlife, 1990.

Braun, Wernher von. *The Mars Project*. Urbana, IL: University of Illinois Press, 1953.

Bridgeman, William, and Jacqueline Hazard. *The Lonely Sky*. New York: Henry Holt, 1955.

Gunston, Bill. *Faster than Sound*. Sparkford, Somerset, UK: Patrick Stephens, 1992.

Gurney, Gene. *Five Down and Glory*. New York: G. P. Putnam's Sons, 1972.

Hallion, Richard P. *Supersonic Flight*. New York: Macmillan, 1972.

———. *Test Pilots*. Garden City, NY: Doubleday, 1981.

———. *On the Frontier*. Washington, DC: NASA, 1984.

Hughes, Chris, and Walter Dranem. *North America F-86 Sabre Jet Day Fighters*. North Branch, MN: Specialty Press, 1996.

Karman, Theodore von. "Supersonic Aerodynamics—Principles and Applications." *Journal of the Aeronautical Sciences* 14, no. 7. Institute of Aeronautical Sciences, The Tenth Wright Brothers Lecture, New York, July 1947.

Levinson, Nancy. "Chuck Yeager—The Man Who Broke the Sound Barrier," Hamlin, West Virginia, 1953. Unpublished manuscript.

Lundgren, William R. *Across the High Frontier: The Story of a Test Pilot—Major Charles E. Yeager*. New York: Wm. Morrow, 1955.

Matthews, Henry. *DH.108*. Beirut, Lebanon: HPM Publications, 1996.

Morley, Richard A. "Fred Borsodi, Profile of a Test Pilot, Engineer, Pilot, Patriot." *Journal of the American Aviation Historical Society*, September 1996.

Neufeld, Michael J. *The Rocket and the Reich*. New York: Simon & Schuster, 1995.

North American Aviation Inc. *Aerodynamics Handbook, Rept No. NA-47-941D*. Los Angeles: North American Aviation, Oct. 1, 1947.

Norton, Donald J. *Larry, a Biography of Lawrence D. Bell*. Chicago: Nelson-Hall, 1981.

Peek, Chet. *The Taylorcraft Story*. Terre Haute, IN: Sunshine House, 1992.

Rotundo, Louis. *Into the Unknown*. Washington, DC: Smithsonian Institution Press, 1994.

Stanaway, John. *P-38 Lightning Aces of the Pacific and the CBI*. London: Reed Consumer Books, 1997.

Stuhlinger, Ernst, and Frederick I. Ordway III. *Wernher von Braun*. Malabar, FL: Krieger, 1996.

Tate, Grover Ted. *The Lady Who Tamed Pegasus*. Bend, OR: Maverick, 1984.

Tryckare, Tre. *The Lore of Flight*. Stockholm: Cagner, 1960.

U.S. Army Air Force. *Preliminary Pilot's Handbook for Model XP-86 Aircraft*. September 19, 1947.

Wagner, Ray. *The North American Sabre*. Garden City, NY: Doubleday, 1963.

Wegener, Peter P. *The Peenemünde Wind Tunnels*. New Haven, CT: Yale University Press, 1996.

Welch, George S. Flight Log, October 4, 1940–October 12, 1954. Unpublished personal papers.

Wolfe, Tom. *The Right Stuff*. New York: Farrar, Straus, & Giroux, 1979.

Yeager, Chuck, and Leo Janos. *Yeager*. New York: Bantam Books, 1985.

Young, James, Chuck Yeager, et al. *The Quest for Mach One*. New York: Penguin Putnam, 1997.

Index